Other Books by John van der Zee

Fiction:
THE PLUM EXPLOSION
BLOOD BROTHERHOOD
STATELINE

Nonfiction:
LIFE IN THE PEACE ZONE:
AN AMERICAN COMPANY TOWN
(with Hugh Wilkerson)
CANYON: THE STORY OF THE LAST RUSTIC
COMMUNITY IN METROPOLITAN AMERICA
THE GREATEST MEN'S PARTY ON EARTH:
INSIDE THE BOHEMIAN GROVE
THE IMAGINED CITY: SAN FRANCISCO IN THE
MINDS OF ITS WRITERS
(with Boyd Jacobson)

BOUND OVER

Indentured Servitude and American Conscience

by

JOHN VAN DER ZEE

Foreword by
JOHN PATRICK DIGGINS

SIMON AND SCHUSTER
New York

Copyright ©1985 by John van der Zee
Introduction Copyright © 1985 by John P. Diggins
Published by Simon and Schuster
A Division of Simon & Schuster, Inc.
Simon & Schuster Building
Rockefeller Center
1230 Avenue of the Americas
New York, New York 10020

SIMON AND SCHUSTER and colophon are registered trademarks of
Simon & Schuster, Inc.
Designed by Irving Perkins Associates
Manufactured in the United States of America

1   3   5   7   9   10   8   6   4   2

Library of Congress Cataloging in Publication Data

Van der Zee, John.
Bound over.

Bibliography: p.
Includes index.
1. Indentured servants—United States—History.
2. United States—History—Revolution, 1775–1783—Causes.
3. United States—History—Revolution, 1775–1783—
Social aspects.   I. Title.
HD4875.U5V36   1985   305.5'6   85-2243
ISBN 0-671-54118-8

In memory of
HERMAN VAN DER ZEE
and
VERNON HUNT:

each his own man;
both, men for others.

CONTENTS

Foreword by John Patrick Diggins 9
Preface 21
Introduction 29

Part I: TOUCHED

1. JAMES MADISON   37
2. ALEXANDER HAMILTON   43
3. THOMAS JEFFERSON   49
4. SAMUEL ADAMS   55
5. BENJAMIN FRANKLIN   60

Part II: BOUND

6. JOHN LAWSON   69
7. JOHN HAMMOND   82
8. MARY MORRILL   92
9. GEORGE ALSOP   100
10. THOMAS HELLIER   109
11. JENNEY VOSS   121

12. ROBERT COLLINS   128
13. DAVID EVANS   135
14. WILLIAM MORALEY   146
15. SALLY DAWSON AND SALLY BRANT   160
16. HENRY JUSTICE   170

Part III: SEIZED
17. HENRY PITMAN   181
18. JAMES ANNESLEY   194
19. PETER WILLIAMSON   209

Part IV: STIRRED
20. DANIEL DULANY   231
21. ALEXANDER STEWART   241
22. GOTTLIEB MITTELBERGER   249
23. ALEXANDER TURNBULL AND CARLO FORNI   261

Part V: RELEASED
24. MATTHEW THORNTON   273
25. JOHN HARROWER   281
26. JOHN LAMB   295
27. MATTHEW LYON: 1   305
28. CHARLES THOMSON: 1   310
29. JOHN SULLIVAN: 1   317
30. CHARLES THOMSON: 2   325
31. JOHN SULLIVAN: 2   331
32. MATTHEW LYON: 2   338

Part VI: TRANSFORMED
33. DANIEL KENT   347
34. ANDREW JOHNSON   355

Bibliography 365
Index 375

FOREWORD
SOCIAL REALITY
AND
NARRATIVE HISTORY

PRESIDENT FRANKLIN D. Roosevelt once began an address to the Daughters of the American Revolution with the greeting "Fellow immigrants." It was an appropriate reminder of the common heritage of all Americans except the native American Indians, the only group with genuine ancestral claims upon the American past. Yet the Indians gradually lost out to the successive waves of immigrants from almost all nations of the Western world—and today the Eastern world as well. This unprecedented historical development is not without the cunning of irony. For the majority of immigrants who came to America in the seventeenth and eighteenth centuries were forced to do what most native Indians would never deign to do: labor with their hands, work the materials of earth not as hunters and warriors but as farmers and artisans who believed that nature or God beckoned man to transform the environment and thus produce value by the improvements made from sweat and toil. But why did the earliest settlers believe in hard work and opportunity, the very values that today seem to be eroding in the face of a culture that admires the pleasures of consumption and the life of leisure?

Historians have long speculated on the forces that have shaped the American character. Some look to the environment and its abundance of land and resources. Others cite a Protestant religious heritage and the creative tension between piety and prosperity. Still others have investigated English political ideas and the values of dissent, natural rights, and individual liberty. Perry Miller, the great historian of the colonial period, suggests that the two political acts that brought forth the birth of the Republic, the Revolution and the Constitution, were far from decisive in forging the American character and value system. As to the precise "moment" when America came into being, Miller believes historians

> might have pushed that moment of conscious decision further back than the Constitutional Convention. Settlers came to the colonies for a number of reasons that were, so to speak, in the situation rather than in their minds, yet none came without making an anterior decision in his mind. They may have been forced by famine, economic distress, a lust for gold or land, by religious persecutions, but somewhere in their lives there had to be the specific moment when they said to themselves or to each other, "Let's get out, let's go to America." The only exception to this rule is, of course, the Negroes; they came not because they wanted to but because they were captured and brought by force. Maybe that is why they, of all our varied people, seem to be the only sort that can do things by instinct. Maybe that is why Willie Mays is the greatest of contemporary outfielders.

What exactly was on the minds of English, Irish, Scottish, German, and other immigrants when they said, "Let's get out, let's go to America"? Thanks to John van der Zee's *Bound Over*, we know now the reasons that prompted many Europeans to come to America and the conditions in which they arrived. Somewhere between one-half and two-thirds of all the colonists came to the New World as "voluntary slaves," indentured servants, apprentices, tenants, bond servants, and the like, all agreeing to the status of a redemptioner in one form or another, a person who, lacking the means, accepts free transportation as the price of four to seven years of unrelenting servitude to an unknown master.

Herodotus insisted that the chief aim of history is to "preserve from decay the remembrance of what men have done." It may also be necessary to recover from oblivion the remembrance of what history has done to man, and how man, especially the eighteenth-century American, struggled to liberate himself from oppression and exploitation to become the master of his own fate, a free, autonomous individual who would never again consent to any authority that does not originate in his own conscious will. The idea that America was "born free," that its people naturally enjoyed "equality of condition" and did not, as Tocqueville argued in *Democracy in America,* have to struggle to wrest power and liberty from Old World class domination is one of those conventional wisdoms that will have to be reconsidered in light of the evidence and insight that we now have in *Bound Over.*

As a novelist, van der Zee is perhaps as interested in the rich texture of human drama as he is in the political and historical significance of his work. He did not, it should be pointed out, begin his book as a professional scholar steeped in the crosscurrents of colonial historiography. His curiosity about indentured servitude had its origins in contemporary America, specifically the plight of Asiatic immigrants in California and Latin immigrants in Florida, both groups having been recently brought to this country under various conditions of contractual servitude. He soon discovered that what had seemed a present aberration had actually been a prevalent feature of colonial life. Other historians have taken note of the phenomenon, and in *American Slavery, American Freedom,* Edmund S. Morgan has demonstrated the connection of indentured servitude to the importation of African slaves in seventeenth-century Virginia. Van der Zee is the first writer to attempt to relate indentured servitude to the

American Revolution itself as its "forgotten social undercurrent."

The American Revolution remains today as controversial as it was in the halls of Parliament in the 1770s. Many years ago the Revolution was viewed as a result of the mismanagement of the British imperial system, an empire that, it was said in the eighteenth century, had been founded in a fit of absentmindedness, with the result that America benefited from a policy of "salutary neglect." The imperial school of thought no longer dominates the attention of contemporary historians. Yet there still is no consensus about interpreting the Revolution. Although no contemporary scholar would deny that the colonists had a right to rebel, differences arise over the nature of the grievances and the reasons used to protest them. At the risk of oversimplifying, one might describe the two major schools of thought as the political and the social interpretation, one emphasizing the role of ideological convictions, the other the importance of economic tensions.

To some extent the contemporary political interpretation arose from a problem that previous historians had left unresolved: Insofar as America actually benefited from the British imperial system, the Revolution cannot be directly attributed to the colonists' discontent with their status within that system. Several historians have addressed this issue by showing how the British method of political representation and economic regulation frustrated the colonists no matter how slight the material consequences. But it was Bernard Bailyn's seminal *The Ideological Origins of the American Revolution* that demonstrated why colonial attitudes became inflamed to the point of an irrepressible break with the Mother Country. After examining the pamphlet literature of the Revolution, Bailyn discovered that the colonists were using the very Whig, Republican ideology that the Crown's opposition had used in Parliament, and thus colonial leaders saw every move made by England as a deliberate "conspiracy" against American liberty in an effort to reimpose monarchical tyranny, the nemesis of republicanism. To resist British rule was the duty of the American and the clearest sign that America could be a "Republic of virtue."

In *Bound Over* one finds evidence of Whig, Republican ideology among colonial leaders who had experienced indentured servitude—suspicion of power, distrust of wealth and the corruptions of luxury, and a fear that America would relapse into Old World bondage. Indeed it might be said that Americans who had endured the arbitrary power of a farming or merchant master had even more reason to believe that every assertion of British authority brought America closer to a return to indentured servitude, a system of power relations that colonists had once accepted as a necessity but now came to be seen as a curse from the past. As van der Zee makes clear, memories of servitude weighed heavily on the minds of leaders like Tom Paine, Ben Franklin, Joseph Galloway, and Alexander Hamilton. But it remains to be considered whether those who had once felt the tyranny of servitude would emerge as classical republicans dedicated to civic duty or economic liberals aspiring to individual opportunity. From Machiavelli to Montesquieu the great dream of classical political philosophy was the citizens' acceptance of the authority of the political state. In America's political culture, however, an opposite tendency seems to have emerged, perhaps best expressed by Whitman: "Resist much, obey little." In any event, van der Zee shows how the experience of indentured servitude made many Americans not only suspicious of British rule but keenly aware of man's tendency to exploit fellow man, an attitude deeply felt in the debates over the Constitution and continuing into the Civil War itself. What Lincoln learned from the Bible his successor, President Andrew Johnson, an ex–indentured servant, learned from personal experience.

Bound Over has as much relevance to the social interpretation of the Revolution as the political. The historians who subscribe to the second intepretation, mostly younger and influenced by the causes of the 1960s generation, generally focus on social groupings and especially the aggregates of socio-economic classes rather than individuals or elites. They have attempted to approach history "from the bottom up," and, unlike the political historians, they tend to see more evidence of class and class conflict. One of the leading works of this genre is Gary B. Nash's *The Urban Crucible,* which studies eighteenth-century New York, Philadelphia, and Boston in an attempt to show the connection between poverty, popular unrest, and the American Revolution. Nash and many of the "new social historians" have been influenced by the British scholar E. P. Thompson and his thesis of "the moral economy." Briefly, the thesis holds that the behavior of eighteenth-century urban crowds was animated by collective attitudes toward social justice, attitudes that built upon liberal ideas of natural rights and even religious convictions regarding personal responsibility and the moral bonds of community. Inspired by Thompson, many American social historians have attempted to discover in colonial society evidence of popular discontent leading to collective protest and perhaps even to class consciousness itself.

The new social historians will need to consider the ideas, suggestions and insights found in *Bound Over*. Where they focus on social groups, van der Zee focuses on individuals; and where they look to the affective bonds of sentiment that make the individual an integral part of a given community, van der Zee suggests that the very meaning of bonding had an unpleasant connotation in eighteenth-century America, at least to those who experienced it as enshacklement and submission. Nevertheless, it cannot be denied that the many characters who appear in *Bound Over* struggled from the bottom up and were keenly aware of poverty, oppression, and powerlessness. What, then, did such experiences have to do with their own attitudes toward liberty and property, attitudes deeply felt long before colonists had read Locke and Montesquieu? In his *Two Treatises on Government*, Locke claimed that in the beginning "the whole world was America," implying that in the New World men related to each other as equals as they formed the social contract and laid the basis for popular government. Van der Zee shows, however, that the contract on which indentured servitude was negotiated was "a game in which one side held all the cards." Did the colonist lose faith in the liberal idea of the social contract or did he embrace it all the more, believing in equality as a natural condition of man whose rights remain inviolate precisely because they had once been violated? The doctrine of inalienable rights enunciated in the Declaration of Independence drove home the point that man cannot alienate that which nature has endowed him with as the very definition of his being. Indentured servitude violated that doctrine, and with it the American conscience.

Bound Over partakes of a Melvillian sensibility in which author van der Zee identifies with the same elements specified in the great classic *Moby Dick:* "mariners, renegades, castaways." The book is truly a "people's history," to borrow Page Smith's expression. But we soon discover there is no singular entity "the people" but instead myriad different personalities who endured a common experience with different values and perspectives that must be captured through their own words and their own eyes. In the text we meet the kidnapped victim Robert Collins and the tormented murderer Thomas Hellier. We also come to know Carlo Forni, perhaps the first labor organizer in American history; John Lamb, Washington's military officer; Matthew Lyon, the Irish runaway and romantic who, having freed himself from servitude, would never again submit to alien authority, as fellow Irishman Edmund Burke tried to warn Parliament; and the incredible Jenney Voss, "the London jilt" whose exploits with the Sadler gang make her and her cohorts the eighteenth-century Bonnie and Clyde. In *Bound Over,* history comes alive in the form of individual biographies reconstructed by a writer who wants us to share his inner sympathy with his subjects. Van der Zee's peculiar historical style—which intertwines, in the spirit of John Dos Passos's *U.S.A.,* "Voices" offering chorus of convictions together with collective portraits of discrete characters—raises the issue of narrative history, an issue that is currently being debated by scholars in literature and philosophy as well as history.

For centuries, from the time of classical antiquity, it was assumed that to know something was to tell its story. For historians like Herodotus and Thucydides, who wrote as orators, history was a form of rhetoric meant to convey certain moral and political truths. This didactic tradition continued in the works of modern English writers like Edward Gibbon and Thomas Carlyle; and in nineteenth-century America prominent writers like George Bancroft, Francis Parkman, and Henry Adams sustained the practice of history as narrative art.

In recent times, however, narrative history has fallen out of favor. One reason, however valid, is that it became identified with patriotism, the odes to national heroes whose deeds school children were to learn by heart. For certain writers, narrative history also came to be seen as little more than the study of elites, whereas true reality lies pulsating in the lives of the inarticulate masses. As scholars of American slavery and the working class are aware, the challenge of writing about those who have been left out of standard historical records is enormous. Among the many virtues of van der Zee's research and writing is the discovery that history can be narrated from the lower depths. It was said of Trotsky that in his historical writings the proletariat found "its pen." Those Americans whose ancestors endured the ordeal of indentured servitude may owe the same compliment to the author of *Bound Over*.

A second criticism of narrative history, more technical than political, had to do with the problem of causation that had been taken up by philosophers and literary artists at the beginning of the century. "Old-fashioned" narrative history had postulated a singular, linear series of events, each of which was in turn the effect of the previous event and the antecedent cause of the next. In this respect the narrative constituted an act of authority, since it was assumed that the story of events provided the causal chain of connections leading to historical understanding. It was for this reason that many creative writers, sensing that exact understanding of experience had eluded them, revolted against orthodox narration, whether in history or prose fiction. "History," declared James Joyce, "is a nightmare from which I am trying to awake." As a novelist, van der Zee is too sensitive to the problem of sequential explanation to succumb to the fallacies of older narrative history. Indeed *Bound Over's* style is discursive and cyclical rather than linear and progressive, one that is, as we shall see, perfectly consistent with the eighteenth-century mode of literary discourse.

The third challenge to narrative history, one that is itself presently being challenged, came from the rise of "scientific history," once a nineteenth-century positivist dream that aimed to discover the "laws" of society. Today this method has been given impetus by the advent of computer technology, with its great promise of establishing the statistical foundations of historical knowledge. The analytical approach distinguishes itself from narrative history in its attempt to measure and quantify the data of human experience and to eliminate as much as possible the subjectivity of the historian himself. Scientific history, today called "cliometrics," has made important inroads in economic and political history, where the rates of industrial growth and indices of voting behavior can be run through a computer. Eminent scholars like Lawrence Stone and J. H. Hexter have voiced reservations about the unfulfilled promises of quantitative history. But ultimately what scientific methodology cannot deal with is the emotional dimension of history, what the French call *mentalité* and *sensibilité, the "vie effective et ses manifestations,"* as Georges Lefebvre put it when he called upon historians to begin studying the qualities of human feeling that relate to love, death, joy, sorrow, ambition, failure, pity, guilt, compassion—"the emotional complex that corresponds to the event which happened to and was felt by the single individual." *Bound Over* succeeds in this challenging task of not only recovering what people did but what they felt as their consciousness experienced the pull of conflicting emotions. It also should be mentioned that van der Zee's method of drawing upon the autobiographical records of his subjects proved highly appropriate and perhaps inevitable. For as the philosophers R. G. Collingwood and Wilhelm Dilthey observed, autobiography opens the main door to the human world because it enables us not only to know the actions of historical figures but to understand their meaning. In this respect *Bound Over* approaches history not simply from the bottom up but from the inside out.

The interior quality of *Bound Over* brings us to one of the most controversial issues in the writing of history—the role of intuition and imagination, the area where meaning and value can be elucidated by retrospective reflection and interpretation. Van der Zee does not view society as something divorced from the activity of consciousness. On the contrary, he attempts to generalize about the nature of America's social structure as it was experienced by the historical figures themselves. But since what they experienced may not have been fully articulated, or only hinted

at by a gesture or murmur, van der Zee engages in what Collingwood called "interpolation," legitimate speculation about the
emotions the colonists must have felt as the historian tries to "re-
enact" in his own mind their hopes and fears. As with the novelist, van der Zee meditates on his characters' complex motives,
and he never misses an opportunity to provide vivid detail and to
re-create dramatic scenes, perhaps realizing, with Oliver Wendell
Holmes, Jr., that "most people reason dramatically, not quanti-
tatively." But van der Zee uses the imaginative process not simply to afford the reader pleasure but to enable us to grasp many
of the harsh truths of American history. "Imagine it, the way it
was, the way it must have been," he advises, and then proceeds
to describe the enormous amount of grueling work involved in
clearing the land in the pre-industrial era, work that property
owners foisted upon indentured servants as though they were the
wretched of the earth. Rather than using the imagination to escape reality, van der Zee compels us to confront it and to understand the meaning of suffering and struggle.

The form and structure of *Bound Over* warrants a concluding
comment. The narrative style is episodic and indeed at times
almost picaresque in its treatment of colorful figures and their
incredible adventures. Here, too, *Bound Over* enjoys a certain
verisimilitude, for it often partakes of the literary form that Daniel Defoe and other eighteenth-century novelists used to depict a
society of dropouts and castoffs who survived by their own wits.
But van der Zee is not necessarily depicting his characters as
free, self-sufficient individuals, a charge often leveled at the
eighteenth-century "bourgeois" novelist. Instead the people of
Bound Over are almost always constrained by the suspecting
presence of others, not to mention the economic power of their
masters. Yet van der Zee's use of eighteenth-century story types
and plot structures is in keeping with a great literary tradition
wherein the form of narration—romance, tragedy, comedy—offered much of the meaning of the discourse. As Hayden White
has pointed out, narration provides the best means of representing the nature of historical reality because historical events are
the products of human actions whose meanings require the tap-
estry of narrative reconstruction. In this respect to know Amer-

ica is to tell its history, whether it be the story of servitude or the struggle toward freedom.

John van der Zee is a novelist who works in the business world and writes non-fiction when dealing with the plight of the working class. After *Bound Over* is read, he will need no further introduction to the historical profession. The book itself suggests what happens to American history when a new talent approaches an old subject.

JOHN PATRICK DIGGINS
Paris, 1984

PREFACE

IN HIS essay "Looking Back on the Spanish War," George Orwell lamented the fact that of all the human beings who lived in slavery in the ancient world the names of only two have come down to us: Epictetus, the Stoic philosopher, and Spartacus, leader of the slave revolt.

This book is an attempt to recall, before they too are lost to us, the names and lives of America's age of servitude. It is, at best, a beginning. From such an enormous enterprise, so sweeping a social transformation, the great bulk of information remains to be extracted. It is from among the yet undiscovered diaries, from court records, and from reminiscences filed perhaps under other categories—still to be examined by students and scholars with the necessary time, grants, and academic affiliations—that the story of our national time of bondage will be completed.

Accepting these limits in putting together this book, counting on the available few to represent the still-silent many, I have tried to remain faithful to the individuals themselves: their lives, their experiences, and as much as possible their words. Though

21

this may have resulted in a certain repetitiousness in subject matter and an untidy chronology, it is hoped that human individuality will produce a compensating variety, while at the same time illuminating a few discovered, rather than imposed, conclusions.

This book would not exist without two prior works of serious scholarship, Abbott E. Smith's *Colonists in Bondage,* and Richard B. Morris's *Government and Labor in Early America.* Together these books served as both awakener and guide, documenting the extent and influence of the practice of servitude, its importance to the personal and political life of colonial America, and suggesting where to look for the individual stories which are the novelist's absorbing concern. I would recommend them to anyone interested in the subject, as well as Edmund Morgan's *American Slavery, American Freedom* and Cheesman A. Herrick's *White Servitude in Pennsylvania.*

Again and again, while doing research for this book, I was the beneficiary of gratuitous acts of kindness and thoughtfulness on the part of individuals to whom I was a stranger and who represented institutions with which I had no prior connection. They became to me the essence of professionalism and disinterested scholarship. Among them are: the staff and students of Doe Library at the University of California at Berkeley; John Fralish and Sally Weikel of the Pennsylvania State Library at Harrisburg; Mary Ann Hines of the Library Company of Philadelphia; Mrs. Frances Fugate of the Virginia Historical Society; the staff of the British Library; Amy Hardin of the Historical Society of Pennsylvania; Joanne Zellner of the Library of Congress; Beth Carroll of the American Philosophical Society; Edouard A. Stackpole, director of the Peter Foulger Museum in Nantucket, Massachusetts; Kathy Dyer of Enid, Oklahoma; and David Fraser, librarian of the Historical Society of Pennsylvania.

For services above and beyond the call of scholarship, I would like to thank James Gilreath, American history specialist of the Library of Congress; Walter C. Johnson, formerly associate director of the Rosenbach Museum and Library in Philadelphia; Idris Evans of San Francisco and his brother-in-law Elvyn Jenkins of the University College of Wales at Aberystwyth; and

William Halsey of the classics department of the University of California at Berkeley.

For permission to quote and paraphrase existing work, I am indebted to Sharon V. Salinger of the University of California at Riverside, whose study on women indentured servants I would recommend to anyone seriously interested in the subject; to the William L. Clements Library at the University of Michigan for permission to quote from the memoirs of William Moraley; and to the Historical Society of Pennsylvania, for permission to use the letters of Daniel Kent.

I am once again indebted to family and friends for the sustaining advice, information, and encouragement required to complete this book, in particular John P. Diggins of the University of California at Irvine; Robert Asahina, my editor at Simon and Schuster; Jim Anderson of Washington, D.C.; Ron Lambers and Noel Brown of the University of San Diego; Charles Savio, attorney-at-law of San Antonio, Florida; Katy van der Zee, my friend and traveling companion; Peter van der Zee, my friend and fellow researcher; and especially Diane van der Zee, whose faith in this work never wavered, even when my own did.

To all these, old friends, new friends, and paper-acquaintances, I owe debts I cannot repay. I can only assure the people named that I have tried to use their advice, support, and information honorably, and that I will do my best to pass on to others their consideration, thoughtfulness, professionalism, and generosity.

JOHN VAN DER ZEE

BOUND OVER

*Sir, they [the Americans] are a race of con-
victs, and ought to be thankful for anything
we allow them short of hanging.*

—SAMUEL JOHNSON
Boswell's Life, 1775

INTRODUCTION

ON NOVEMBER 30, 1774, the brig *London Packet* docked at Philadelphia. Its chief cargo, not unusual for the time, was 122 indentured servants, British and continental men and women who would be bound into servitude for an average of four years in exchange for passage. Probably some had agreed to a certain term in England; others would have to bargain with agents, masters, or shipowners here. A certain number may have been transported for criminal offenses; a few may have been kidnapped or shanghaied by unscrupulous labor contractors. All of these were common practices in the American servant trade.

Except for the important distinctions that their existence as individuals was acknowledged by law, and that after their term of servitude they were to be granted the full rights of freemen and women, the status of these people was essentially the same as that of slaves. They, the work they did, and the clothes on their backs belonged entirely to their masters. They could be hired out, sold, or auctioned, even if this meant separating them from their families. They could be beaten, whipped, or branded.

If they ran away they could be punished by an extension, often a multiplication, of their term of servitude; in some colonies, runaways were hanged, a process too wasteful to apply to slaves, who retained, after all, the value of capital.

The resemblance to enslavement began at least at embarkation, where both voluntary and involuntary emigrants were herded on board "white guineamen" and crammed below decks in unsanitary conditions with insufficient provisions.

On the *London Packet,* this had meant nine weeks of confinement in a stifling hold, and an outbreak of "putrid fever" that had swept through the entire ship. Five bodies had been thrown overboard en route, and no more than five people among the complement of indentured, cabin passengers, and crew had escaped infestation.

Among the diseased cabin passengers was a marginally free man, a failed schoolmaster, staymaker, and preacher, who had barely been able to scrape together the price of his passage. In this atmosphere of incarceration, disease, and forfeited human rights, he made his passage to the New World, an appendage of a practice developed for the population of it.

Such a passage was a fearful demonstration of the fragility of human freedom, as well as the fierce price of slipping back into servitude. The experience was to mark the man, just as the disease festering among the indentured below deck marked him now, leaving him so weakened that he had to be carried off the ship, disembarking only after the rest of the passengers and crew had left.

Thus Tom Paine arrived in America.

One year later, still in a fever, but one transformed and focused now by the fighting at Lexington and Concord, Paine wrote this of his adopted country: "This beautiful country which you saw is America. The sickly state you beheld her in has been coming on her for these ten years past . . . The pestilential atmosphere represents that ministerial corruption which surrounds and exercises its dominion over her, and which nothing but a storm can purify."

Paine was among the least literary of writers. He read few

books, relying instead on newspapers, talk, and his own observations and experience. It was his weakness and his strength,
compelling him to adopt the vernacular directness of his new
land, and incorporating into his writing the secular passion of the
Methodist preacher and the yarn-spinning of the colonial drum-
mer. He took his material hot from life, and he was marked
forever by what he saw.

"It is the nature of compassion to associate with misfortune,"
Paine wrote in *The Rights of Man*. "In taking up this subject, I
seek no recompense—I fear no consequence."

In perhaps his single most influential piece of writing, the first
installment of *The American Crisis,* written in 1776, at one of the
lowest hours of the American Revolution, speaking to frightened
and isolated colonists, whose General Washington had yet to win
a battle and whose armies were in retreat, Paine rallied Americans with imagery he knew would be familiar to them, in the
famous article that begins, "These are the times that try men's
souls. . . . Britain, with an army to enforce her tyranny has decided that she has a right (*not only* to TAX) but 'to BIND *us in*
ALL CASES WHATSOEVER,' and if being *bound in that manner* is not slavery, then there is no such thing as slavery upon
earth."

The capitals and italics are Paine's own.

Washington, moved by this article, ordered it to be read aloud
to his brigades. He too—plantation owner, slaveholder, aristocrat—had been associated with indentured servitude.

Washington was *named* after an indentured servant. George
Eskridge, the legal guardian of George Washington's mother and
for many years a member of the Virginia House of Burgesses,
had been kidnapped as a boy in Wales and sold in Virginia,
where, after serving out his term, he angrily tore up his hearth-
stone bed with a mattock.

According to Jonathan Boucher, the Maryland rector who tutored Washington's stepson, Washington himself owed what ru-
dimentary education he'd received to a convict servant named
Hobby, who tutored him in reading, writing, and keeping accounts.

As a Virginia planter and early colonial industrialist, Washington had bought and used indentured labor; but he insisted on redemptioners, people who accepted bondage in exchange for passage, rather than transported criminals or people spirited away by kidnappers. And he specified that families not be separated.

As a British officer in the French and Indian War, Washington had urged upon the colonial authorities the enlistment of servants in the Virginia volunteers, warning that if such provision were not made, servants would run off and enlist in the regular army anyway. He himself recruited numbers of indentured servants for his regiment.

In a country desperately short of skilled labor, with work to be done in almost every direction one looked, these were not inexpensive principles. In 1784, Washington issued a request to purchase the terms of skilled joiners or bricklayers which, beyond his personal reservations about criminality and the sundering of families, displays the desperate ecumenism of the short-handed manager: "I would not confine you to Palatines [Germans]; if they are good workmen, they may be from Asia, Africa or Europe; they may be Mahometans, Jews or Christians of any sect, or they may be Atheists."

From Washington the landed aristocrat to Paine the newly arrived indigent immigrant, there were few colonial Americans untouched by the practice of indentured servitude. It was the state of destitution most immediate to everyone, the wall-less prison and poorhouse, the condition that could reclaim you no matter how far or how fast you fled it, as much a New World product as corn or the potato. It haunted the colonial imagination, found voice in the works of Defoe and Smollett, Goldsmith and Richardson, and, later, Stevenson and Scott. It gave to words like "liberty," "freedom," and "tyranny" a physical reality that people were willing to suffer and die for. It is the forgotten social undercurrent of the American Revolution, the desperate sucking tide that made the unthinkable challenge to the most powerful naval and military force on earth a worthwhile risk, and prompted the guarantees of individual rights written into the government that evolved afterwards. We are, in fact, as Americans, the descendants of bound people, tied now by that binding in ways we have forgotten, which it would serve us well to remember.

From 1609 until well after the founding of the Republic, half of all the colonists who came to America arrived under some form of involuntary labor. To them fell the largest share of the hardest work in an unfamiliar country. They cleared the land, drained the swamps, built the roads, first plowed the unbroken ground. They cooked and cleaned and nursed and midwived. They worked, and died, in greater numbers than anyone else. Theirs were the hands and backs that worked the transformation from wilderness to settled prosperity, a change so sweeping that its signs have vanished, so that the completed colonies seem somehow to have sprung fully into being direct from their charters. In the process, these men and women, drifters and convicts, rogues and whores and the chronically poor, reluctant, coerced, unpaid, overworked, overwhelmingly ignorant and unskilled, vanished themselves, transformed into what we have come to think of as the American people.

In her landmark examination of the nature of revolutions, *On Revolution,* Hannah Arendt tells us that the reason for the success of the American Revolution in making its gains permanent in the Constitution, and its failure to usher in a new world order, spring from the Revolution's being a political and not a social upheaval. The predicament of poverty, in the form of misery and want, was absent in America, yet present everywhere else in the world. The Revolution concerned not the order of society but the form of government. So its gains, instead of being overwhelmed by the needs of people in want, as was later the case in France and in Russia, were allowed to become seated.

This argument leaves a fundamental condition of the American Revolution unexplained. If the ordinary men and women of America were not driven by want, then what were their unifying grievances against the British? What was the feeling that prompted people who were admittedly better off than their counterparts elsewhere to risk their lives against the world's most formidable military power? What was it that made the words of men who had read the Enlightenment thinkers resound among people who had never heard of Locke or Rousseau? What compelled people who were living better than their own ancestors had to march and fight, freeze and bear wounds for seven years against the nation whose rule had uplifted and protected them?

Tocqueville, in his classic *Democracy in America,* maintains that in the New World, without the constraints of feudalism or an *ancien régime,* Americans were born free and equal and did not have to struggle for their rights, as did the people of Europe, thus eliminating the rise of a reactionary right or a radical left. Yet, if Americans truly felt born "free," if they really were secure in their sense of political liberty, what explains their feeling those liberties so threatened by England? Why were the acts of the colonial authorities and of Parliament so often linked by colonial speakers and pamphleteers—Samuel Adams, John Adams, James Otis, Thomas Jefferson, John Dickinson, Stephen Hopkins, Joseph Galloway—with slavery and tyranny?

There was only one British practice which could, and did, actually subject colonial men and women to tyranny and enshacklement. The experience of servitude was both widespread and intensely personal. The practice was present, at least at the settlement stages, in every colony; the most prosperous colonies, Virginia and Pennsylvania, were economically founded on it. Moreover, the uprooting and transplanting of people to the New World—usually occurring in youth, in some cases in childhood, involving the separation from parents, brothers, sisters, and home—produced, as we shall see, over and over again, the kind of emotional trauma that individuals never entirely escape, and whose effects resounded through the decades. No other colonial experience was so common and at the same time so profound.

Thus people with dissimilar and sometimes conflicting interests could be united into a common opposition that focused and directed their deepest energies and frustrations against a single target: the Old World hierarchy extended to the New, the transporting authority under which they had been brought over, which continued to rule them with the potentially arbitrary power of a servant's master, and which, in order to be truly autonomous individuals, they would have to discard.

PART ONE
TOUCHED

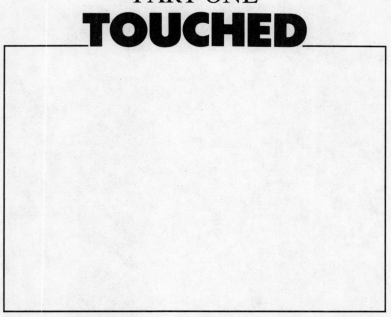

1

JAMES MADISON

In 1653, a man named John Maddison was granted six hundred acres of Virginia land "in the County of Gloser, on the north side of the Mattapony River." Whether Maddison, a ship's carpenter, had originally come to America as a servant is something lost in the fogs of the Atlantic passage, but work for skilled labor of this kind was not short in England at the time, and skilled freemen were not generally inclined to emigrate. Whatever John Maddison's New World origins, he understood the machinery of the indentured servitude intimately, for he applied it with great shrewdness to the building of a family fortune.

The largest and the most expansionist of the American colonies (its boundaries at one time included the present states of Kentucky, North Carolina, West Virginia, and Tennessee, as well as what later became the Northwest Territory), Virginia offered a bounty of fifty acres of land to each new settler, freeman, redemptionist, or indentured servant. By the time of Maddison's grant, this had become an organized racket. At depots established in the poorer sections of London, people were kidnapped or "spirited"—inveigled away while drunk, and kept prisoner for a month or more—until they could be shipped off to the colonies by the conspiring master of a vessel. The land grant would be entrusted in their name to the landowner who paid for their passage, with the understanding that title would pass to the servant when his term of service was up. Maddison grasped the opportunity in the fact that few servants, indentured or redemptionists, ever actually settled on their own property.

Of five thousand servants who entered the colony of Maryland between 1670 and 1680, fewer than 1,300 proved their rights to their fifty-acre "freedom dues." Of these, almost nine hundred sold their rights immediately and claimed no land for themselves. Only 241 took warrants for land, while 139 proved their rights but took no warrant. In all, less than 4 percent of the people who entered the colony as servants finished out their time and settled as freemen.

What had become of the others? Probably a quarter of them had died. The work on the plantations of Maryland and Virginia was arduous, especially for people chronically malnourished and new to the heat and diseases of the Southern climate. Others had run off to the Western wilderness or Eastern ports or cities, it being considerably more difficult to spot a runaway white servant than a fleeing black slave. Some—more than stayed at any rate —having served out their time, collected payment for their earned land and sailed back to England—an indication of just how desirable life in America seemed to the average Englishman, even those who'd been to the New World. Others squandered their money and drifted on, becoming hired hands or slipping back into servitude, remaining in the estate in which they had come. Their descendants linger on into the present day as the "poor whites" of the South or the gaunt survivors of Appalachia.

It was John Maddison's gift to spot the opportunity in a problem, and to profit from the mistakes of others, which is preferable to profiting from one's own. He realized that for the price of an individual's passage—six pounds—he secured a "headright" which in the form of unallotted land could be combined into an estate which would multiply in value. By this means, with an occasional extra fee to an English merchant or "spirit" who pro-

vided inveigled or kidnapped extra candidates for indenture,
Maddison began to play Monopoly with the wooded uplands,
fertile valleys, and the swamps of colonial Virginia.

Buying and selling distant lands, but holding on to those which
adjoined his property, the alert ship's carpenter extended his
domain, converting the headrights of immigrant colonists into
valuable real estate. There was in England during these years a
general desire to see people emigrate, not out of any zeal for
empire but as an outgrowth of fear of overpopulation. High taxes
and the enclosure laws had driven agricultural workers and village dwellers off the land and into the cities, where they gathered
and loitered, a threat to order and the comfort of the propertied
classes.

In addition, the political turnabouts of these years, the rise of
Cromwell, the Restoration, the wars between England and Scotland, the periodic purging of religious dissenters—Quakers,
Catholics, Presbyterians—provided a steady stream of people
who for one reason or another were considered officially undesirable.

Then there were the convicts. Britain, in the beginning stages
of becoming the first industrial nation, with masses of dislocated
people and an increasing frequency of crime, had no prison system. There were jails, like Newgate in London, but no systematic
incarceration for punishment between release and death, which
was the payment prescribed for over three hundred different offenses. Banishment, in the form of transportation to the colonies,
seemed both a practical and humane idea, a riddance of a domestic problem with at least the first halting impulses toward rehabilitation.

Not that the criminals were to be coddled. During the voyage
it was customary to keep felons below decks and in chains; a
man would be confined in a hole not more than sixteen feet long
with fifty other men, chained to a board with a padlocked collar
about his neck. In London and the provincial towns, the herding
of convicts onto ships bound for America became a periodic civic
diversion, rather like an execution. Local people gathered to yell
at and exchange gibes with the castoff convicts and occasionally
to throw mud and stones at them. Like most indignities, these

could be cushioned by money or influence, and there were instances of privileged felons with the required clout riding to the
docks in carriages and accepting transportation in the comfort of
a private cabin.

From these and other sources—Irish rebels, Scottish prisoners
of war—John Maddison acquired the headrights that made his
acreage grow. In 1657, he acquired eight hundred acres; in 1662,
three hundred more; in 1664, two hundred. By his death in 1683,
he was the colonial equivalent of a landed English gentleman, a
man who essentially *did* nothing but instead *was* something, with
a full complement of servants and Negro slaves to do whatever
needed doing for him.

By 1751, when John Maddison's great-great-grandson was
born, the family, whose name had been simplified to "Madison,"
had become part of Virginia's ruling gentry, an aristocracy as
lavishly landed as that of the England the Maddisons had long
ago left. James Madison, Sr., great-grandson of the ship's carpenter, had built an estate, Montpelier, carved from the acquired
lands, where his son Jemy was raised in a rare new kind of
isolated colonial splendor.

The eldest of ten children, James Madison was bookish and
withdrawn. Frail, tutored at home, surrounded by slaves and
indentured servants who rendered physical labor of any kind
unnecessary, influenced by both the Enlightenment and the frontier, he represented one of the earliest and best of a new breed,
the American intellectual. Following his graduation from the College of New Jersey (Princeton), Madison remained another year
studying Hebrew, then returned to Montpelier in a state of profound depression. He did not "expect a long or healthy life" and
therefore refused to prepare for a profession or work for the
acquisition of worldly goods.

For three years, the young Madison remained at home, con-
templating the Enlightenment ideas he'd been exposed to at
school and applying them to the microcosm of plantation life at
home. To a reflective young man at an age when he was expected
to begin making his way in the world, the source of his own
family's position must have been of concern to him. It was a
drama whose recurring pattern of indenture and freedom gained,
or freedom frustrated, was acted out before his eyes.

He saw the most arduous of rural work—land clearing—assigned to the people least prepared for it: the underfed urban poor, further weakened by nine to twelve weeks' confinement at sea. He saw exposure, long hours, and disease considered part of the year's "seasoning" a good servant required, even though in colonies with extreme climates, like Barbados, as many as four-fifths of a shipment of servants died in the first year. He observed the desperation of servants who ran away, and viewed with sympathy the disproportionate penalties they paid: up to a month added servitude for every day absent, whippings and fetterings, additional terms of servitude for fornication and "bastardy." He saw the entrapments that could be used to keep a servant from ever gaining his or her freedom or claiming land.

We know he saw these things, because he later tried to ameliorate them. When in 1792 a Madison servant named Billey ran away and was recaptured, James Madison, ignoring the customary penalties of flogging and multiplication of term, gave Billey his freedom, subject to a seven-year indenture. A man should not be punished, Madison said, for trying to obtain the liberty he had heard members of Congress orating about.

There were, of course, the Negro slaves; but slavery, though evil, was an ancient evil, as old as agriculture and therefore perhaps incorrectable. Indenture and redemption had begun as institutions in the New World and were therefore part of British rule, abuses like the Stamp Act or the quartering of British troops in private homes, an imposition that could be challenged and changed. Young Madison, isolated in rural Virginia yet cultured and in touch with the intellectual currents of his time, realized that America represented something exceptional in the world, and that some of the things that made her exceptional were wrong. He read, he observed, he thought, he stirred. He applied himself to the task of changing them.

From 1776 until his retirement from the presidency in 1817, Madison served almost continuously in public life, where it was his declared intention "to provide a decent and independent subsistence for myself" and "to depend as little as possible upon the labor of slaves." From the House of Delegates of Virginia to the Continental Congress, from the Constitutional Convention to the House of Representatives, to the office of secretary of state

and the presidency, he maintained this unique compounding of
extremes: the intellectual frontiersman, the Federalist who advocated checks on the power of government and the assurance
of individual rights, the practical politician who maintained that
practicality included matters of conscience.

At the Constitutional Convention of 1787, Madison, in perhaps
his finest hour, as always the intellectual leader, as usual the
master parliamentarian, guided into law the guarantees against
the abuses of power that have given the American system of
government its enduring adaptability.

Madison abhorred tyranny, whether exercised by one man
over others, or by a majority over an individual. "Wherever the
real power in a Government lies," he said to Jefferson, "there is
the danger of oppression." From his own "experience and inves-
tigation" he had sensed within man the potential for exploitation.
Give all power to the few, he maintained with John Adams, and
they will oppress the many; give all power to the many, and they
will oppress the few. Since it was in each man's nature to pursue
unchecked his own interest, the way to insure liberty, both public
and private, was to check interest with interest. Through the
complex, intricate structure of mixed representation and
countered authority that Madison led into law, multiplicity of
interests was used to justify and energize a system of endless
bargaining, capable of containing man at his most selfish and his
most altruistic. It was an expanded federal republic whose incorporated capacity for change was its greatest assurance of the
preservation of its fundamental principles.

Born to wealth and personal liberty, Madison sought to improve upon his legacy. He helped bequeath to us, as part of the
endless bargain, the human rights advocated by Locke and Rousseau and Paine, whose exercise in Britain had led to arrest, persecution, and banishment—and indirectly to John Maddison's
family's enrichment. The people of the new Republic would
make whatever they would be of themselves. There would be no
transportation of Americans.

2

ALEXANDER HAMILTON

JAMES MADISON shared an uneasy friendship with another prodigy and strong nationalist who also appears to have been touched by servitude, though to a much different end.

In the West Indies, where Alexander Hamilton was born in 1757, servitude took on both a fainter character and a stronger intensity than in the mainland colonies. Because of the limited amounts of land, freedom dues of acreage were replaced by lump-sum payments in cash or commodities, or even annual wages. Early on, the islands were largely given over to the growing of sugar, plantation labor ideally done by black slaves, who were less expensive to maintain than white servants and who could be easily replaced when tropical heat and disease claimed workers' lives in quantity.

By the middle of the seventeenth century, the cultivated islands of the Indies were a plantation economy with few white freeholds. This became a source of alarm to the colonial authorities, especially during the French wars of the 1670s and 1680s, when it was feared that in the event of a French-aided Negro uprising the proportion of white men would not be enough to maintain the militia. The planters, merchants, and colonial authorities complained that not enough servants were being sent to them and suggested means for increasing the traffic.

In 1667, the government of the island of Barbados requested "that we may have a free trade and a supply from the Kingdom of Scotland of Scotch servants with whom being supplyed in good numbers (as experience heretofore had been had) will render both Commodity and Security to the planters."

In 1672, Jamaica passed a law requiring each planter to keep one Christian servant for every ten Negroes on his plantation; similar acts were soon passed in Antigua and St. Christopher. Things grew so desperate that the islands even paid contractors for servants, however and wherever they managed to find them.

Though the supply of white servants in the Indies seldom equaled the demand, it was their physical presence that was required rather than their labor. The strange situation arose in which the most insistent demands for servants came from the island colonies which had least economic use for them.

It was into this society of unnecessary necessity that James Hamilton, an exile from an aristocratic Scottish family, stepped sometime in the 1740s. Entirely cut off from his wealthy family, without position or useful skills or luck, Hamilton existed in a state of genteel aspiration and financial penury that was to haunt his son's entire life, and influence the founding of the Republic.

It is not known why James Hamilton left Britain. As his father's fourth son, there was little possibility of his inheriting the family estate, but there also seems to have been no interest in providing him with the kind of situation usually considered suitable for gentlemen: in the church, the military, government, or even an arranged marriage. By choice or by chance he seems to have settled in a place where he could cash in a claim of minimal heredity: a Scottish lineage and a white skin.

Whether James Hamilton arrived in the West Indies as an indentured servant or redemptioner is not recorded. Given his circumstances and the place in which he chose or was forced to live, it seems he could have been little else. He was neither planter nor merchant, overseer nor government official, about the only categories of work reserved in the islands for free white men. It was common practice in the West Indies of these years for clerical work to be done by indentured servants. And once in the Indies, Hamilton certainly lived more like a servant than the son of a landed Scot: drifting from job to job, serving mostly as a clerk, living out of wedlock with a woman publicly charged with "whoring," and fathering two illegitimate sons.

When the Hamilton "family" split up, it was the mother of the two boys who left him, moving to the island where her ex-husband lived, and reappropriating his name. When she died, James Hamilton was unable or unwilling to assume responsibility for the two still-young boys.

Alexander Hamilton's illegitimacy disqualified him from what little of an estate his mother left. On the island of St. Croix, where she died, he was legally classified as "an obscene child."

On his own at the age of eleven, Hamilton found work in a countinghouse, where by the age of fourteen his advancement had outstripped his father's entire career. When the owner of the business was forced by illness into an extended stay in New York, Hamilton managed the entire enterprise, dispatching ships, making trades, concluding deals. What had inhibited his father, he realized, did not bind him.

Yet then and throughout his life Hamilton was haunted by his father's loss of station, his lack of achievement in life. It was in the Indies that the character of the later Hamilton—defender of privilege, fearful and distrustful of everyday people, the statesman who sought to remind his adopted countrymen that "jealousy is the usual concomitant of love, and that the noble enthusiasm of liberty is apt to be infected with a spirit of narrow and illiberal distrust"—took root.

When it was decided that the gifted Alexander should be sent to study in New York, it was not his father but the local merchants who paid his way. In the physical and psychological space of Revolutionary America, Hamilton spread his wings and soared: King's College graduate at sixteen, political pamphleteer at seventeen, army officer at eighteen, aide to Washington, the commander-in-chief, at nineteen.

Adopted into Washington's retinue, his "family," Hamilton

felt ever afterward a son's mixture of dependence on and resentment toward his benefactor.

As his American career advanced, Hamilton continued to identify with his father, still wandering impoverished in the Indies. A society in flux, without a hierarchy, offered unlimited opportunity to a young man with brains and ambition. Yet at the same time was there no way to secure one's position? A land that tossed you up so quickly could just as quickly dash you down. Being a gentleman was not enough when even a gentleman could conceivably become a bondservant.

Hamilton feared the mob. Having married into money, he supported the interests of money, while professing a gent's distaste for moneygrubbing and mismanaging his own finances. Bankrupt twice, he died in debt. Yet his vision of a moneyed industrial America proved to be the true one.

Like eyewitnesses to an accident who, filtering an experience through different personalities, arrive at widely differing versions of the same events, Hamilton's vision of America was not Madison's. Yet both agreed on the means for that vision: a strong central government. And in *The Federalist* papers they set themselves to bringing it about.

"I consider Napoleon, Fox and Hamilton the three greatest men of our epoch," said Talleyrand, "and I do not hesitate to award first place to Hamilton."

Yet in America he was not trusted. He was adored by his followers and respected by his enemies, but something always kept him from the popular prize of elective office. People seemed to sense the proconsul in him. The desperate fear of losing all that by desperation he had achieved. He founded the American Treasury, and maintained it in keeping with his own peculiar principles, allowing the rich to take certain advantages, while claiming none for himself: the scrupulousness of the impoverished gent, above mere moneygrubbing.

He contacted his father, still poor in the West Indies, and invited him to come to America. His father never came. You can never grow too old or too prominent not to be injured by those close to you in youth.

No matter how far or how fast Hamilton fled his lowly origins,

he couldn't escape them. In the lively, influential, often scurrilous political gossip of the times, in the pamphlets signed with
sonorous, classically resonant pen names, in the gazettes tenta-
tively testing the muscles of mass communications against the
limits of libel, and in the correspondence of an age that savored
the well-turned phrase, both his birth and his precocity were
flung at him as insults. "A bastard bratt of a Scotch pedlar" was
how John Adams characterized him. "A second Bonaparte,"
suggested Adams's wife, Abigail.

There was always something different about him. He was the
one strong nationalist without conflicting loyalty to a state. Other
men were Virginians by birth, Pennsylvanians, Massachusetts
men or New Yorkers. Hamilton, unclaimed by any state, had no
strong reason to press for any state's identity against the federal
government's. He was an American or he was nothing, and even
in this he felt alienated from his adoptive country. "Every day,"
Hamilton ruefully concluded, "proves to me more and more that
this American world was not made for me."

Madison and Hamilton, both exposed in youth to situations of
indentured servitude, drew drastically different conclusions
about society and man. They had stood together in favor of a
strong constitution. They had both contributed to *The Federalist*
papers. In the Continental Congress and at the Annapolis Convention they had collaborated on matters of finance; but when
the time came for Hamilton's greatest coup, the one that would
combine public and monetary achievement, the federal assumption of state debts and the chartering of a Bank of the United
States, Madison, influenced by his fellow Virginian Thomas Jefferson, began to depart from, then oppose, the Hamiltonian vision of America.

Madison believed that institutions were flawed and in need of
correction; Hamilton felt that men were flawed and in need of
restraint. At the crucial moment, in what he claimed was a matter
of conscience, Madison, floor leader in Congress, withdrew his
support.

Hamilton's spectacular career had peaked.

The stresses of thwarted ambition widened the cracks in his
character into fissures that seethed with the emotions of his boy-

hood. He took up with the wife of another man, who blackmailed him, after which Hamilton published a startling admission of the affair. He attacked political opponents with a vehemence that turned cabinet and party rivals into sworn personal enemies. Impeached as secretary of the treasury, he resigned, though he was cleared of the charges against him. His son, defending his father's good name and political position, was killed in a duel, upon which Hamilton's daughter went mad. The secure order he had sought since his days in the turbulent Indies was receding from him. He had entered a fall which in its extremes threatened to eclipse his father's.

Madison, burdened by the idea of servitude, had helped write into law the means of eliminating the conditions that produced it; Hamilton, threatened by servitude, attempted to insure the station of those who had risen beyond it. Hamilton's death, in a duel at the hand of Aaron Burr, seems a throwback to both class-conscious ideas of honor and personal anarchy. There is a certain loss of faith in the power of government, a last desperate grasping at position, a headstrong loss of restraint producing an extravagant wastefulness of life. The gesture amounted to more than the act: a life flung away as Hamilton's father's life had been flung away, against a man who, though he was someone Hamilton hated, was not even his true rival, but his counterpart, whose view of America has opposed Hamilton's down to the present day.

3

THOMAS JEFFERSON

HAMILTON'S GREAT antagonist would seem, of all Revolutionary figures, to have advanced the furthest toward a new colonial aristocracy. Scientist, architect, writer, philosopher, inventor, planter, Thomas Jefferson was a fourth-generation Virginian who owned three plantations, dozens of slaves, and assembled one of America's first great private libraries. Yet he was considered by many a dangerously radical figure, a "Jacobin" admirer of the extremes of the French Revolution and supporter of the most controversial writings of Paine; a deist who posted in his study the portraits of his holy trinity: Bacon, Newton, and John Locke. Anguished over the issue of slavery, he appears to have had a long affair with a mulatto woman, Sally Hemings, and to have conceived with her as many as five children.

Jefferson was the great-great-grandson of a Welshman who emigrated during the seventeenth century. A man who enjoyed the comforts of his estate, Jefferson once attempted to trace a family coat of arms only to come up empty, and later wrote with contempt of men who assumed the right to tyrannize others because of the accident of a gentle birth. As a Welshman, Jefferson's immigrant ancestor would have been part of an often-reviled minority in Britain, a people in a permanent resentment toward the fact of English rule.

In his authoritative study of colonial servitude, *Colonists in Bondage,* Abbott E. Smith tells us that during the seventeenth century the only way for a poor man to emigrate to America was under some form of indenture. Without lands or title, a member of an oppressed minority in Britain, with a history that appears to be unrecorded elsewhere, it seems reasonable to assume that Jefferson's ancestors arrived in America under bond to somebody else.

They would have been part of a large and interesting company. Daniel Defoe, a journalist and political pamphleteer as well as a novelist, wrote about indentured servants and set part of *Moll Flanders* in the Virginia of Jefferson's forefathers' time.

"They were of two sorts," a woman, later revealed to be Moll's ex-jailbird mother, describes the Virginia settlers, "first such as were brought over by masters of ships to be sold as servants. 'Such as we call them, my dear,' says she, 'but they are more properly called slaves.' Or secondly such as are transported from Newgate and other prisons, after having been found guilty of felony and other crimes punishable with death."

In Virginia, Defoe's woman suggests, "many a Newgate-bird becomes a great man, and we have several justices of the peace, officers of the trained bands and magistrates . . . that have been burnt in the hand."

Just how extensive the transportation of convicts from Britain to the colonies was may be gauged from the fact that it wasn't until after the American Revolution that the British began shipping felons to Australia. It is estimated that between 1730 and 1770 at least 70 percent of those convicted at the Old Bailey were shipped to America. According to Smith, another estimate, counting only felony convictions, determined that fewer than 8 percent of Old Bailey prisoners were executed, "and the remainder, with very few exceptions, transported."

This dumping of Old World problems in the New, which increased as the colonial era wore on, produced great fear and resentment in the colonies. Benjamin Franklin suggested that the colonists in exchange should export rattlesnakes to the British Isles, and both Maryland and Virginia passed ordinances against the practice, which were later overridden by Parliament.

Transportation also helped condition British attitudes toward the American colonists, reinforcing prejudices and personal bias when the time of colonial protest began, and Americans were widely characterized in Britain as "convicts" and "knaves."

Colonial opinion was scarcely more hospitable toward the importation of thousands of thieves and murderers. "There can be no doubt," says Smith, "that the convicts vastly increased the amount of lawlessness and crime in those colonies where they lived. We read in the newspapers of brutal murders . . . of robbery and arson attributed to them."

The great majority of convicted servants were sent to Virginia and Maryland, where they were put to work on tobacco plantations, whose owners were often drunken, brutal, and sadistic. The nature of the servants' origin seemed to justify firm treatment by whoever decided to impose it, and owners up to and including the governor of Virginia and the members of his council were known for beating, whipping, and branding convict servants. Humane treatment, it was pointed out, would only encourage further convict dumping on the part of the Mother Country. There was also a general feeling that owners could skimp on "freedom dues" for convicted servants, which led to an attempt to legally classify convicts as a separate and lesser category of labor, something between redemptioners and slaves.

The convicts, in response to this harsh treatment, usually ran away when they could, returning to England if possible, even at the risk of hanging, before their terms were out. According to Sir John Fielding, who wrote an account of the transportation of criminals in 1773, he heard several convict servants declare that they would rather be hanged than transported a second time.

In addition to the penalties imposed for crimes committed abroad, the individual colonies passed laws establishing servitude as a legal punishment for debt. The temptation this offered to the unscrupulous or financially desperate planter to take advantage of people who were economically and legally bound to him, who could be exhausted and broken though not owned, would have been extremely difficult to resist.

Poor, unlettered, unorganized, the indentured servants had small hope of calling upon what legal recourse was available to them. The courts generally favored the masters, who had the added advantage of being able to penalize their workers without resorting to the legal process at all. Whipping was a prescribed punishment for infractions as minor as failure to obey an order properly and promptly, while for a servant to set hands on his master was an act of treason, punishable by death. In South Carolina at one time the penalty for apprehended runaways was a year of added servitude for every week of absence.

A system of punishment this severe, applicable to the great bulk of men and women arriving in America, makes the Revolutionary leaders' charges of British enslavement more than the simple hypocrisy suggested by Horace Walpole and Samuel Johnson.

"How is it," asked Dr. Johnson, "that the loudest yelps for liberty come from the drivers of slaves?"

In fact, free American colonists were among the most individually independent people in the world. And the "tyranny" of George III could hardly be described as harsh by the standards of the time. Yet the claims of enshacklement and enslavement were used as a rallying cry by men as diverse as the modest and temperate Washington and the oratorical firebrand Patrick Henry, who said to the Virginia House of Burgesses: "Is life so dear or peace so sweet as to be purchased at the price of chains and slavery? Forbid it, Almighty God! I know not what course others may take, but as for me, give me liberty or give me death!"

Such words were chosen not merely for rhetorical flourish but for the simple and powerful imagery they conjured up among people who lived among servitude, who had in many cases risen out of it and who could still be threatened by the prospect of slipping back.

In his earliest political writing, *A Summary View of the Rights of British America*, Thomas Jefferson stated the grievances

against the Crown in terms an indentured servant could have
applied almost verbatim to his own condition: "You do not listen
to us. You are cheating us. You are unfair. You take back what
you have given us. You punish the innocent. You play favorites."

Unlike Madison, Jefferson continued to live amid and off the
work of slaves. His estate at Monticello, where he withdrew in
relief after each period of public service, was dependent on
forced labor. Throughout his life he was stretched on the rack
between moral repugnance of slavery and practical dependence
on it. As President, he forbade the importation of slaves, yet,
perhaps fearing exposure, he failed to free his own slave mistress
or their children. He outraged the South by opposing slavery in
the Louisiana Purchase territory, and awarded his daughters gifts
of slaves as wedding presents.

Yet at his best, in the writing of the Virginia Constitution and
of the Declaration of Independence, Jefferson was a marvel of
consistency, articulating principles to which his career was dedicated, in language which seems to have fixed them for all time.
Freed of the ancient and personal constraints of race, he seems
to have enunciated, as if he were one of them, the most pressing
desires of bound white men and women: the rights of the individual citizen against totalitarian control, the importance of broad-
based suffrage, the development of the West in the hands of
independent farmers, abolition of primogeniture, civilian control
over the military.

It was to these people that Jefferson's statement in the Declaration of Independence that government "shall not take from the
mouth of labor the bread it has earned" had its most immediate
and poignant meaning. This was well understood by Jefferson's
Federalist opposition, who predicted in 1796 that were Jefferson
elected President "the refuse of Europe who have fled from the
pillory and the gallows and are here stirring up revolution" would
"rush from their lurking places, whet their daggers and plunge
them into the hearts of all those who love order, peace and religion."

In fact, Jefferson's was among the most tranquil and least di-
visive of American presidencies. The territory of the nation dou-

bled; war was avoided despite provocations from England and France; and the Bill of Rights, eroded by the Alien and Sedition Acts, was restored. In the first widely popular American presidency, Jefferson had shown how the philosophical could be wedded to the practical.

In 1796, the Comte de Volney, a French republican and friend of Jefferson's since the days of the French Revolution, noted after a visit to Monticello his surprise at seeing there slave children "as white as myself." Some of these, it has been assumed, were the offspring of Jefferson and Sally Hemings, but others were probably the children of indentured servants or the offspring of servants and slaves.

Allowing for the droit de seigneur exercised by white masters over black slave women, surely this alone doesn't account for the thousands of mulatto children born, especially in the South, throughout this era. It was white and black workers, living and working under the same conditions, occasionally even joining forces politically, as in Barbados, who had the greatest need and opportunity for liaisons.

Descended almost certainly from bound immigrants, an employer of indentured labor, a father, like many of them, of mulatto children, Thomas Jefferson articulated the desires of the bonded and marginally freed people who were to become the American working class. He brought the visionary into the present and put his ideals, as much as possible, into practice. He put his trust, despite discouraging evidence to the contrary, in the good sense of ordinary people, with whom he seemed to have an instinctive rapport. His faith rewarded him with a career unique in its combination of popularity and lasting achievement. And a life which seems satisfyingly free of regret.

4

SAMUEL ADAMS

ALMOST EVERYTHING that Thomas Jefferson was, Samuel Adams was not. A Bostonian with the city man's unashamed practical incompetence, poor, austere, parochial, zealous in behalf of independence even at the price of violence, puritanical and manipulative, he was the forerunner of the American city political boss. Sam Adams's great gift was for agitation, and more than any other man he was the irritant who kept relations between Britain and the colonies chafed.

The son of a prosperous brewer, Adams was educated at Harvard, trained for the law, then took over the family brewing business, which eventually slid into default, thanks to Adams's preoccupation with Massachusetts politics. Since shortly after his graduation, Sam Adams had been involved in an economic and political struggle between farmers and town artisans on the one hand, and the Boston mercantile aristocracy on the other. The ''sound money'' aristocrats insisted on accepting only silver in payment of debt, which they then exported to their creditors in England, leaving the Massachusetts colony short of hard currency, and further depreciating the value of the existing paper money. The merchants were popularly considered the Tories of their generation, and among the debtors even a French invasion was pictured as preferable to "remaining as the Slaves and Vassals of these mercantile overlords."

Adams enunciated the feelings and fears of the financially embattled with particular directness and poignance, because he was among them. In addition to owing Crown and creditors for the default of the family brewery, he had, as tax collector for the city of Boston, been so haphazard in his performance that his carelessness had become a local scandal, heightened by his misappropriation of public funds for his own purposes. Only his impressive ability to mobilize gangs of angry men on the streets of Boston seems to have saved Adams from prosecution.

Although his most immediate concerns may have been financial, Adams's grievances widened out to include authority at large: the mercantile aristocracy, the governor of the colony, Parliament. He viewed the gentry and the merchants as sinister degenerates, undermining the original Puritan fiber of Massachusetts Bay with a taste for luxury and materialism. Poor himself, he seems to have lived much of his life in a dudgeon, resentful and frustrated, hungering for confrontation, irreconcilable in the most peaceful of times, unbuyable by the rich, exulting in every sign of conflict as the signal for an irreparable breach. You get the feeling that what Sam Adams really would have preferred for America was a state of impassioned austerity somewhat on the order of Mao's China.

"I doubt," said Thomas Hutchinson, the Tory governor who was Adams's one-man Gang of Four, "whether there is a greater incendiary in the King's dominions."

The source of Sam Adams's power was his command of an organization of disaffected men, much like himself, called the Sons of Liberty. Made up of men who ranged from workingmen and small businessmen to gangs of trained street thugs, the Sons were men without land, men in danger of debt, newly escaped from the shadow of servitude, in danger of subsiding into it.

Indentured servitude had existed in Massachusetts since the

first days of the colony. As early as 1633, the colony of Massa-chusetts Bay had made servitude a legal penalty for crimes as small as the theft of corn or fish, while by the 1680s the courts were empowered to order terms of from six months to seven years as payment in the judgment of debt. To the yeomanry and town laborers threatened by penalties such as these, in a colony where wealth and power seemed to be concentrated increasingly in the hands of a few merchants who demanded payment in scarce hard currency, terms like "slave" and "vassal" hardly seemed overstatement.

Adams, a skillful propagandist, was able—through pamphlets, letters, newspapers, and speeches—to make this threat seem both sustained and immediate.

He yearned for the colonies to declare independence and make war, and he put his feelings in terms clearly understandable to the threatened. The only alternative to declaring independence, he said, was for Americans to become "Slaves to Scotchmen."

And the people responded. "Would you believe it," wrote an English army officer, "that this immense continent from New England to Georgia, is moved and directed by one man?"

On March 5, 1770, a regiment of British soldiers, goaded be-yond endurance by a Boston "rabble of saucy boys, negroes and mulattos, Irish teagues and outlandish jack tars," opened fire on the crowd of civilians, killing or mortally wounding five men. The British troops had been subjected to a crescendo of insult from gibes and snowballs to posted threats and brickbats, in a city where the beating up of redcoats had escalated into something of a local pastime. John Adams claimed that the members of the mob were merely the instruments of designing men; other ob-servers, among them British Prime Minister Lord North, sensed a familiar hand in the design: "Sam Adams' Regiments," he called the band of men.

The following day, Adams eulogized the fallen men in a fiery speech at Faneuil Hall. He demanded the immediate withdrawal of British troops from Boston. The dead, some of whom had participated in as many as twenty previous riots, were exalted as martyrs, and the incident ennobled as the Boston Massacre. It became a local tradition, commemorated ceremonially each year; a minor local provocation was transformed into the Slaughter of the Innocents.

Occupying the extremist position of the Whig movement, Adams rejoiced in scolding the less zealous for ideological impurity. He organized boycotts of British goods, fomented street demonstrations, and, through affiliate Sons groups in other cities, made people throughout the colonies look to Boston for leadership in the assertion of colonial rights against the British.

The colonists' opinion of the Mother Country was by no means consistent. Colonial attitudes fluctuated greatly, especially during the latter part of the British period. When the British were necessary, as during the French and Indian War when British troops secured the frontier against incursions, or profitable, as during the same period they enriched colonial merchants with the cost of their provisions, they were popular. It was only as life grew more secure and less lucrative that the redcoats became "lobsterbacks," an offense and an imposition.

Sam Adams's masterpiece of agitation came in 1773. The British had imposed a modest tax upon imported items, among them paper and tea, provoking yet another colonial boycott. To break the boycott, some cheap tea, undercut so that its price would be attractive even with the payment of the tax, was shipped to Boston. Realizing that the boycott would probably crumble, Adams disguised certain of his "Mohawks" as slaves and Indians and dispatched them to seize the cargo and dump it into Boston Harbor in what became known as the Boston Tea Party, "the boldest stroke," conceded Governor Hutchinson, "yet struck in America."

Sam Adams was an oppositionist, a man happiest when engaged in provocation. He excoriated "mercantile avarice," and put his faith in the farmers and workmen whose firm patriotism "must finally save this Country" from "the horrors of slavery" and "degenerate Britons."

He formalized sedition in the Committees of Correspondence, and through them and the Sons made himself the watchdog of New England liberty. The steps to power were in place; with the outbreak of the Revolution, he quickly climbed them. He sought to pack and prearrange the Continental Congress as he had Boston's town meetings.

Yet Adams's opposition required a visible, authoritarian foe; with independence declared and a Congress in session, he faced the dilemma of the aging provocateur who, his aims largely achieved, turns his rancor against his allies rather than part with it. He quarreled noisily with other members of the Congress, accused Hancock, the president, of extravagance, denounced the betrayal of libertarian ideals, called men "papists"; but his cries no longer reverberated among the people. They were no longer frightened by his ghosts. They stopped listening. He became an anachronism, a cranky dissenter from an earlier America, the man who stands against whoever is in charge.

With the winning of the war, the political effectiveness of the least conciliatory man in America had ended. As the Adams family became socially eminent and politically powerful, Sam Adams rose to a modest affluence: He acquired a carriage and a team. The old Roman, the man who had longed for an American Sparta, had had his fires banked. He had bought in, sold out, "matured."

Yet were it not for Sam Adams's sustained rage, his abrasive insistence on separation and independence, his ideological calling to account of compromise, it is doubtful if the hour would ever have struck for full colonial independence. Some more temperate, reasonable course—dominion status, a trade union, some gradual shift of power perhaps from the Island to the Continent—would have evolved. Men would have been more reasonable, less headstrong, calmer, less impulsive. Tolerant. Safe.

In his use of the imagery of tyranny and enslavement, combined with his mobilization of disaffected men sprung from or threatened with servitude, Sam Adams gave men the courage of their grievances. In the looming common shadow of an unyielding authority, he frightened men into bravery. He honed the cutting edge on the Continental cause, grinding out grievances on the spinning, gritty stone of economic desperation. He forced men to live up to their own words, and made gentle people firm in the assertion of their rights. He made the silent continent roar.

5

BENJAMIN FRANKLIN

IN 1722, a certain Boston printer who had published in his newspaper opinions offensive to members of the Massachusetts Assembly found himself censured and imprisoned for a month. The operation of the paper fell by default in 1723 to the printer's apprentice, who was also his brother, the seventeen-year-old Benjamin Franklin.

Franklin had been indentured to his brother to learn the printer's trade at the age of twelve. Under the terms of his contract, written in the form of an original and copy on the same sheet of paper, then torn in such a way that the two edges—"indentures" —matched, the younger Franklin was to serve as an apprentice until the age of twenty-one. He would have been allowed journeyman's wages only during the final year.

It was a situation Benjamin initially resisted, deeply resented, and eventually fled.

"Though a brother," he recalled years later in his *Autobiography,* "he considered himself my master." The prerogatives of this master included bursts of temper and beatings.

"I fancy," Franklin concluded, "this harsh treatment of me might be a means of impressing me with that aversion to arbitrary power that has stuck to me through my whole life."

Apprenticeship of this kind, the recruitment of a young servant for unpaid labor in exchange for room, board, and the acquisition of an independent skill, was a practice dating back to the medieval guilds. It was traditionally used as a method of trade education, as well as a source of relief for poor children, orphans, and the illegitimate.

By the time of the American colonial period, the original apprenticeship system was breaking down under the pressure of laissez-faire economics; and long terms of servitude like Franklin's were used chiefly as a source of cheap labor.

Nevertheless, because of the shortage of skilled workmen of all kinds in the colonies, men who had acquired a skilled trade were presented with opportunities for advancement denied "navvies" in Britain. Skilled workmen could and did establish independent businesses, acquire land, and enjoy the trust of community office. Yet few workmen of any kind were to experience a rise as spectacular as Franklin's.

Already precociously practical, Franklin sensed in his brother's imprisonment a chance to end his own. In order to continue publication of his suspended newspaper, Franklin's brother, on the advice of friends, agreed that it should be printed in the future under the name of Benjamin Franklin, in order to avoid further censure by the Assembly. The apprentice would front for the master, who could not be held fully accountable for the statements published by his underling.

In return, the young Franklin's indenture was to be returned to him with a full discharge on the back, while Franklin was to sign new indentures for the remainder of the term, which were to be kept private.

"At length," Franklin later recalled, "a fresh difference arising between my brother and me, I took upon me to assert my freedom, presuming that he would not venture to produce the new indentures."

Instead the older Franklin so resented this assertion of independence that he blackballed his brother among the other printing masters of Boston. It was yet another show of the arbitrary power that Franklin so despised, and it drove him from the city. Unable to find work, the young Franklin headed for the only other colonial cities which offered opportunities in the printing trade: New York, where he worked for a brief time, and Philadelphia.

On his arrival in Philadelphia, Franklin, who had walked and rowed a boat much of the distance from New York and had been caught in a rainstorm, was mistaken for a runaway indentured servant and "in danger of being taken up on that suspicion." It was, Franklin admitted, an unlikely beginning for the career that was to follow.

Diligent, shrewd, modest in asserting his talents, amenable to compromise, bent on both personal and social improvement, Franklin developed a range of competence remarkable even in an uncommonly versatile era. Founder of the *Pennsylvania Gazette* and the Philadelphia Library, organizer of the local fire department and police patrol, originator of the plan for the University of Pennsylvania, member of the Assembly, inventor of the Franklin stove, experimenter with natural sources of electricity, he was the quintessential American, yet at the same time the first colonial man who was truly a citizen of the world.

Fluent in French, Italian, and Spanish, he served as minister to France and lived some seven years in Britain, where he was elected a member of the Royal Society and contemplated settling permanently. Yet Franklin considered himself "a tree whose roots are most at home in American soil."

There were always reminders of the fact that he had initially risen and prospered in America as he could have nowhere else. From this, there were obligations that were owed, abuses that required correction.

In Philadelphia he had worked at a print shop with an indentured servant who had studied at Oxford. Curious to see London, the young man had run off to the city with his allowance, spent it all, and was wandering the streets hungry when he was offered a handbill by a crimp recruiting labor for the American colonies. He had signed the indentures and come over, without a word to friends or family of what had become of him. "He was lively, witty, good-natured and a pleasant companion," Franklin observed, "but idle, thoughtless and imprudent to the last degree."

If a man who had started at Oxford could so topple, then so could a self-educated ex-printer's apprentice. Such wild fluctuations in fortune—determined not by birth but by diligence, exertion, individual ability, and the strangely amorphous circumstances of this new continent—existed in America as nowhere else; and the future of the country, Franklin realized, depended to a great degree on the personal character of Americans and the quality of their response to a new land's challenge. He saw it as his responsibility to exemplify and shape that character. The sense of personal and social responsibility, the consuming interest in improvement, the eagerness to learn, to diversify, to adapt, the admonitions to the young published under the name "Poor Richard," all spring from this impulse, the sense that America's peculiarities would be the country's making, or her undoing.

Franklin opposed America's becoming a dumping ground for the unwanted and incompetent. When subscriptions were undertaken for an orphan asylum in the newly settled colony of Georgia, Franklin refused to contribute. The colony was being settled not with "hardy industrious husbandmen, accustomed to labor," but with "families of broken shop-keepers and other insolvent debtors, many of indolent and idle habits, taken out of the jails who, being set down in the woods, unqualified for clearing land and unable to endure the hardships of a new settlement, perished in numbers, leaving many helpless children unprovided for." Better, maintained Franklin, that the Orphan House be built in Philadelphia, and the Georgia orphans transported there to be raised.

In 1774, Franklin was in London as agent for the colonies of Massachusetts, Pennsylvania, and New York, as well as master of the American colonies' postal system, which he had converted from chronic loss into a profit-making operation. As the best-known American in England, the friend of some of the best minds in the Empire, while at the same time spokesman for the colonies' repeated grievances, Franklin was caught in the crossfire between Mother Country and unruly stepchild.

In January of 1774, Franklin was summoned, as agent of Massachusetts, to appear before the King's Privy Council. Some years before, Franklin has come into possession of a series of letters from Thomas Hutchinson, governor of the colony of Massachusetts, to Thomas Whatley, a London influence peddler and confidant of British Prime Minister Lord North. The letters had, among other things, expressed contempt for the Massachusetts Assembly. Franklin had forwarded them to friends in the colonies who gave them to Sam Adams. Adams, in a move that the reserved Franklin probably would have shrunk from, went public with the letters. Now Franklin was haled before the Council and called to account for the leak.

Franklin was now sixty-eight years old, a man of personal eminence with powerful friends in Britain. He was of an age and stature where it could be forgiven for a man to choose comfort over principle, and he could have settled permanently in Britain if he chose. Indeed, Franklin's son, the governor of New Jersey, took the Tory side during the Revolutionary War. Benjamin Franklin, grown to be more than an American, had more than other Americans to lose by choosing the Continental cause. Yet something—the harsh struggle of his early indentured years, his reflex resentment of arbitrary power, the parallel between the colonists' contemporary struggle to break their bonds—stirred in him the feelings of his youth. The apprentice boy counseled the worldly master. Forced to choose between the British community where he was intellectually at home and the colonies, where his earliest feelings and his heart lay, he announced that he alone was responsible for exposure of the letters, adding that he felt the colonists should know that the hated taxes and influx of British troops had come at the urging of Governor Hutchinson, supposedly one of their own number.

Franklin now found himself vilified before the Privy Council as a thief, fraudulent and corrupt, a man who "has forfeited all the respect of societies of man." The British press called him an "old snake," an incendiary, "Old Traitor," "Doubleface." His apartment became known as "Judas' office."

Not given to ideology, Franklin seemed to accept these insults without rancor; he would, as always, meet whatever life had thrown at him, and in this matter the correct course to him was clear.

Franklin returned to the colonies. In 1776, he was on the committee that approved Jefferson's draft of the Declaration of Independence. He was one of its signers. During the war that followed, Franklin, now in his seventies, served the crucial function of American minister in Paris.

Unreflective, pragmatic, commonsensical, Franklin trusted his instincts in a way that left him at home wherever he went, and that rarely put him on the side of an issue that opposed or compromised his own feelings. In his crucial choice late in life—his risk of honor and position in behalf of an earlier, stronger bond —we are reminded of another American, Herman Melville, who on his death was found to have written this message to himself on a card taped beneath his desk: "Be faithful to the dreams of your youth."

PART TWO
BOUND

Imagine it, the way it was then, the way it must have been. A wooded country, rocky where it wasn't woods and swamp where it was neither. Stifling in summer, harshly cold in winter, with brief autumns and springs. Roadless, untilled, un-cleared in all the years since life scrambled up out of the sea. Imagine such country cleared without multiplied power, not CATS and graders and loaders and scrapers, but without simple work animals, oxen and horses and mules, so short in supply they amounted to an absence. Imagine timber being felled and hauled, stumps upended and boulders wedged out by main strength, using tools as old as ancient man: wedge, axe, chisel, adze, mattock. Without even such a simple amenity as decent work gloves. Now imagine the people set to such work as figures out of Hogarth: gaunt, toothless, rachitic, tubercular, malarial. And every one of them a temporary, without equity in the work and of no permanent value to any boss. Without even the main-tainable resale property value of an ox or a horse or a slave. Imagining all this, think of yourself now as an owner, land devel-

oper, or tobacco planter, with mortgage payments to meet or neighboring land you need to acquire, a poor crop, maybe, or the prospect of a rich one, with low prices. Where do you trim? Whose food rations do you cut? Whose clothes make do for another season? For whose quarters postpone repairs? Of course. It's the people whose work you only own awhile. Whose eyes you won't have to look into afterwards.

6

JOHN LAWSON

THE PAMPHLET first appeared in London about the middle of the eighteenth century, but it was probably written earlier. In the overwhelming predominance of white indentured servants in the plantation life it describes, it suggests the colony of Virginia prior to 1676. Whatever its true date of origin, it seems to have been intended to serve as a warning to adventurous or unruly boys or young men—an admonition of the perils awaiting those who disobeyed constituted authority; a vivid depiction of an alternative life so harsh and unrelenting that clerks and apprentices with an eye for adventure would thank their lucky stars that they lived in England, the civilized center of the world, instead of running off to some remote colony on the rim of the Empire, where

> *Some who in England had lived fine and brave,*
> *was there like horses forc'd to trudge and slave.*

Yet something in this work, *The Felon's Account of His Transportation at Virginia in America,* overrides its moralistic purpose: the voice of a man determined to make his anonymous suffering count for something; an individual who has decided to restore his abused feelings by keeping faith with what he has seen and heard; the degraded man trying to isolate that last uncontaminated part of himself.

Probably the work has been polished. It is written in verse and few of the rhymes seem forced. It's not the exclusive work of an apprentice-barrelmaker-turned-thief who spent fourteen years on the end of a hoe in Virginia. Yet the literary veneer is thin and undistorting. There is an absence of the mannerisms which characterize the fiction of the era: rambling digression, a picaresque tone, coincidence, claims of noble birth. Instead we get—clear, close, and strong—the acute detail and underlying anguish of earned experience.

His name was John Lawson, or Lauson, in the casual spelling of the time, born in the seaport city of Bristol, where "In virtue's path I for sometime did run."

The son of parents who were "honest, tho' poor," Lawson was sent to school, where he learned to read and write and "cast accounts." At the age of thirteen he was bound out as an apprentice, a practice common at the time, even among upper-class English families. His master was a cooper, a maker of barrels who seemed, at least in retrospect, a decent man who "lik'd me well"; and so, says Lawson, "my business I did mind."

In the custom of the time, an apprentice worked not for wages but for his keep, so that in practice the boy often lived on the master's business premises. For John Lawson, this meant that he was near to "broad-street," the wicked main stem of Bristol, a source of temptation that was to prove the apprentice's undoing. "Here," he confesses, "unto wicked company I fell."

With a gang of toughs, Lawson "rov'd about the streets both night and day," running off meanwhile from his master, whom he'd left shorthanded. He turned to crime and "Did with a gang of thieves a robbing go." His master finds him and considerately takes him back; there is no mention of whipping or chaining, and Lawson's father offers him understanding and support.

Yet,

vice when once it taints the mind,
Is not soon routed out we find.

The boy is soon out "a thieving once again," following "courses that were most wild." Thoughts of fear, including the death penalty, which was the punishment prescribed for all felonies in England, are "banished by strong liquor."

And yet, Lawson observes, "Thieves cannot one another trust." One of the gang is captured. He "peaches": snitches on the other five. All five are arrested. Three of the gang are hanged. "I was one of the Five that was tried and cast," recounts Lawson, "Yet transportation I did get at last."

Probably he pleaded "benefit of clergy." Throughout the seventeenth century, according to Abbott Smith, a person convicted of a felony in England might "call for the book." Under the theory that all who could read were in holy orders, a person who was able to read from a book, usually the Bible, would thereby be exempted from the penalty of death. Instead, the convict would be branded in the thumb. By the Act of 1717, this punishment was amended to provide for transportation to the tobacco-growing colonies, desperately short of plantation help.

"In vain I grieved," Lawson laments, "in vain my Parents wept,/For I was quickly sent on board a ship."

Within a few days the ship has cleared the river and lost sight of land. There are, in all, about sixty convicts, as "Wicked and cruel lousy crew as ever went over." The voyage lasts seven weeks, during which the convicts are confined below decks, "kept under lest we should rebel."

The Virginia that John Lawson was landed in was a plantation society governed by an aristocracy who lived dependent upon, and in fear of, forced labor. The earliest attempts to colonize Virginia had ended in starvation, disease, and death. It wasn't until the province, settled by a joint-stock company, became devoted to the cultivation of tobacco that Virginia began to return a profit to its investors. From the start, the colony was short of labor. Skilled English freemen were understandably unwilling to uproot themselves and hazard a voyage across the Atlantic, only to live in a remote wilderness where they were expected to work for someone else. The planters, only marginally independent men themselves at first, lacked the capital to invest in slaves. The countryside, prone to typhus and other diseases, with a climate that was brutally hot in summer, carried off about half the arrivals within the first year.

The solution seemed to lie in indentured servitude, a system which provided planters with a source of labor that was cheap (for less than one year's wages for a freeman, you could own a servant for four); obedient (the penalties for sassing a boss or running away were severe and had the force of law); and above all replenishable.

Even though bound servants had to be fed, clothed, and sheltered, the Virginia planters' demand for them was insatiable. In the boom-or-bust one-crop economy, where land was at first limitlessly available, a tenant could almost overnight become a landowner, a small farmer, or a plantation aristocrat simply by increasing the number of servants he employed. Indeed "Our principall wealth," admitted the prominent Virginian John Pory, "consisteth in servants."

The same ships that hauled away tobacco would regularly make their way up the wide, deep Virginia rivers to dock and display their human cargo at inland ports like Jamestown, Williamsburg, and Henrico.

"At Virginia," resumes Lawson, "all were put ashore." The convicts are bathed and given clean linen,

> *Our face shav'd we comb'd our wigs and hair,*
> *That we in decent order might appear.*

When the merchandise has been suitably prepared, the local planters come to examine the stock. The convicts stand, women separate from the men, as the planters walk among them inquiring as to their trades and names, inspecting the more promising physical specimens:

> *Some view'd our Limbs turned us around,*
> *Examining like Horses we were sound.*

Asked his trade, Lawson replies that he is a cooper. "That will not do for me," the planter replies. The job interview continues:

> *Some felt our hands others our Legs and Feet,*
> *And made us walk to see we were compleat,*
>
> *Some view'd our Teeth to see if they was good,*
> *And fit to Chaw our hard and homely food.*

When a planter finds a servant whose limbs, looks, and trade are suitable, the captain and the planter bargain over terms. These might include not just the purchase price of the servant but the payment coming on completion of his assigned time. These "freedom dues," awarded according to "the custom of the country," could vary from fifty acres of land to a set of clothes, some seed and tools. With convict servants it was often considered fair to skip paying freedom dues at all.

There is a distinction made, Lawson observes, between servants obligated for seven years and those required to serve fourteen. Those with longer sentences are definitely preferred. The reason was that the people who as servants were Virginia's most valued form of property became on securing their freedom a threat to the colony's stability and order.

Servants who became free after about 1660 found it increasingly difficult to find arable land that hadn't already been claimed. They often had to rent land, thus risking running into debt and sinking back into servitude, or else move to the frontier, where they had to contend with the Indians. This growing class of freed indentured servants, or "freedmen," armed, landless, often idle, had a growing sense of injury, of having been cheated out of the better life they had expected in the New World, and their resentment toward the wealthy planters who controlled the great estates, the House of Burgesses, and the colony increased as the lot of the small freeholders worsened.

In 1676, these feelings exploded in Bacon's Rebellion, the largest uprising of any kind in America prior to the Revolution itself. A group of small freeholders, led by Nathaniel Bacon in what started as an anti-Indian crusade, turned on the government, expelled the royal governor, plundered the planters' estates, and

burned the city of Jamestown to the ground. The revolt degenerated into an orgy of drunkenness and looting, and sputtered out
when Bacon died of dysentery; but the planters never forgot the
violent effectiveness of the attack by freed indentured servants.
Restored to power, the planters quickly imposed new legal restrictions on servants and, flush with tobacco wealth now, began
to replace them by importing Negro slaves.

In Bacon's Rebellion, manned by freed indentured servants,
we can see the first appearance of the elements which were to
sustain the American Revolution a century later: the widespread
sense of shared grievance; the broad resistance to legally constituted authority; the feeling of justification in expelling it; the
effectiveness of irregular troops on their own ground against
professionals; the refusal to recognize or respect the privileges
of rank and position; and above all a resentment at having been
exploited or cheated out of an anticipated New World freedom.

The realization of unfair treatment began for indentured servants at the shoreline, where, the newly arrived Lawson observes:

> *Those that has Money shall have favor show'd,*
> *But if no Cloaths nor Money got,*
> *Hard is their fate and hard will be their lot.*

Lawson finds himself, unfortunately, in this latter category.
Passed over by other, perhaps more prosperous or sanguine
planters, he is at last approached by a "grim old Man" who asks
him his age, which was now eighteen, his term, which is fourteen
years, and the circumstances which have brought him to Virginia.

> *And when from me he thus did understand,*
> *He bought me of the Captain out of Hand.*

Secured in chains, Lawson is led back to the harbor and put
aboard a sloop. His new master, "a man but of ill fame," was
originally a transported convict himself. He heads his ship inland,
up the Rappahannock River, twenty, fifty, seventy miles,

The weather cold and hard our fare,
My lodging on the deck both cold and bare.

A hundred miles up the Rappahannock, they come to the master's house, near a town called "Wicowoco." Lawson's remaining European clothes are taken from him, most likely to be sold; he is given in their place a canvas shirt and drawers "a hop-sack frock in which I was a slave."

No shoes nor stocking had I for to wear
Nor hat, nor cap, my hands and feet went bare.

Thus outfitted, the servant is sent out into the fields to work. The conditions imposed on indentured servants, who were often owned by men living in hovels themselves, were so severe that in the early days of the colony stiff penalties had to be imposed to discourage servants and freedmen from going off to live with the Indians. Later, other acts were passed further binding the servants to the land. Servants who arrived without an indenture were required to serve three extra years. The laws against running away were expanded so that once caught the servant not only had to work off an additional term but was also charged for the cost of apprehending him, a figure which he almost inevitably would have to pay in work. And to discourage men from living freely in the woods, the killing of the wild pigs in which the colony abounded was a punishable offense, subject to a fine amounting to twenty times the value of a pig. The fine was to be split between the servant's owner and the man who had informed on the servant.

Overworked, abused, entrapped, the servants were exploited out of what became America's largest colony's industrial base.

Thus dressed unto the fields I did go,
Among Tobacco plants all day to hoe.

Though land suitable for growing tobacco was abundant, at least to the great planters, the crop could be grown on a piece of land for only three or four years before the yield and the quality of the tobacco began to diminish. As a result, new land was continually brought under cultivation, and the arduous, man-breaking work of land clearing was never entirely finished.

John Lawson's workday began at dawn, and he stayed in the fields until sunset. His fellow workers were five other white transports like himself, plus eighteen blacks. In his house, Lawson's master used four more transports, all women, to serve his wife and daughter. White servant and black slave are treated alike; they sleep and eat together and share the same tasks. Required to grow their own food, black and white together cultivate the same patch of ground. There seems to be an absence of the racism introduced into black-white relationships later, probably by the planters in the interests of discouraging the white freedmen from making common cause with black slaves. Special, severe penalties were instituted for whites who associated with blacks, and racial intermarriage, once a matter of no particular consequence, became strictly forbidden and a violently emotional issue. This too probably originated in the interest of divide and rule. It has been observed that black slaves came to be disparaged in terms identical to those earlier applied to indentured servants: as inherently lazy malingerers, ungrateful and treacherous, fond of drink, and with inherent criminal tendencies.

The work, according to Lawson, didn't stop at sunset. In the evening, servants and slaves were required to go into the mill, where they were again put to work,

> *Till twelve or one o'clock a grinding corn,*
> *And must be up at day break in the morn.*

If a servant gets in debt to any man, his name is posted in a public place, where anyone can claim "their just demands," which usually means additional required work: in effect, extension of term.

Under such hard usage, with years of servitude and laws designed to entrap you into more, with small prospect of ever gaining your own independent farm when your time at last was served, it's no wonder that servants were prompted to run away. The severity of the penalties for those who did testifies to how serious a threat it represented to the planters. "If we offer once to run away," says Lawson,

For every Hour we must serve a Day,
For every day a Week, they're so severe,
Every Week a month, every month a Year.

Originally the punishment for running had been double the time of the servant's absence. An additional penalty for the cost of apprehending the servant was added later. This was extended to include compensation to the owner for his loss of crop. Three Virginia servants who had been gone for thirty-four days were sentenced to serve sixty-eight days for the time they were absent, plus eight months for the master's loss of crop, plus four months and ten days for the costs of bringing them back. On his second offense, a runaway servant could have an ear cut off.

And yet, despite the severity of the penalties, servants continued to flee. The periodicals of the time are full of ads for runaways, and often include elaborate descriptions of the servant's manner and dress, as well as a reward offer and occasionally the opinion of a provoked owner. "Last Wednesday noon, at break of day," begins an ad written by a woman in Philadelphia,

From Philadelphia ran away
An Irishman named John McKeoghn,
To fraud and imposition prone;
About five feet five inches high,
Can curse and swear as well as lie.

Recovery, to the owner, was clearly worth considerable time, money, effort, and thought.

For John Lawson, isolated in a strange country, a convict, probably branded in the hand, the odds against successful escape seemed overwhelming. By the "Rigor of that very Law," he is "kept under and do stand in awe." Yet the term he is required to serve and the harshness of the work he is made to do in the disease-ridden plantation lands amount to a sentence of death. Even when he falls sick, there is no relief:

For I was forc'd to work while I could stand,
Or hold the Hoe within my feeble hands.

His master shows him less pity than do the black slaves. Suffering, ill, at the end of his rope, fully contrite at last, Lawson, in what he interprets as an act of God, finds his health suddenly restored.

> *It pleas'd the Lord to grant to me such grace,*
> *That tho' I was in such a barbarous place,*
> *I served the Lord in fervancy and zeal.*

He has, in short, experienced the kind of religious awakening or conversion endorsed by the publisher and distributors of his pamphlet.

Sustained by his religious faith, possessed of an "inward comfort," Lawson has now served twelve years in Virginia. Now, with just two years of his term left, his cruel master dies. "But that," reports Lawson, "was no Relief to me at all."

The master's widow decides to sell the plantation; Lawson and the other servants and black slaves are among the property to be disposed of. A man comes down from Jamestown, inspects the plantation, and decides to buy it. He purchases the Negroes, who are property for life, but declines to buy any of the transported felons. Lawson, along with the others, is put up for auction:

> *Put like sheep into the fold,*
> *Unto the best bidder for to be sold.*

In the auction lot Lawson is approached by a gentleman who seems "very grave." He asks Lawson how long he has left to serve. Not quite two years, Lawson admits. For a planter, purchasing a servant for such a short term is no bargain.

> *He asked my trade, name and whence that I came,*
> *And what vile fact had brought me to this shame.*

Lawson tells the man the story of his fall from grace, his years of suffering, his true repentance. His greatest regret, he concludes, is the pain and disappointment that he, an only child, has caused his parents. To the convict's surprise, at the end of his story his eyes are filled with tears.

The gentleman meanwhile has approached the overseer and is talking with him. After a brief conversation, he returns to Lawson:

> *I have bought you of this man, said he,*
> *Therefore prepair yourself for to go with me.*

The gentleman says he does not intend to use Lawson for a slave but as a servant, if the convict behaves properly. He will not have to work in the fields. Moreover, when his remaining time has expired, the new owner promises to send Lawson home again, if that is his wish.

Lawson's new master is a cooper, living at Jamestown, where for the first time since he set foot in America John Lawson is allowed to work at his trade. "Thus," concludes Lawson, "God unlook'd for raised me a friend."

Secure in the reasonable treatment of a fair master, confident in the exercise of his own craft, Lawson now lives in "plenty, peace and ease." He rides out with his master and sees for the first time in all his years of captivity the Virginia countryside:

> *And in my heart I often griev'd to see,*
> *So many transported Felons there to be.*

At last, his term expired, Lawson is offered return passage by his master, who has indeed become his friend. As good as his promise, the man gets Lawson shipped and he comes home again "With joy and comfort, tho' I went with pain."

His parents are alive and overjoyed to see the son they had written off as dead, not only returned but reformed. Their troublesome boy has become a dutiful, even religious man.

Lawson ends his tale with a warning to his countrymen, lest they share his unhappy fate. Although the crimes they have committed may be petty ones, he urges them to consider the harsh reality of seven to fourteen years' transportation:

Forc'd from Friends and Country to go
Among the Negroes to work at the Hoe;
In different Countries void of all Relief,
Sold for a Slave, because you prov'd a thief.

Out of John Lawson's Virginia, founded on indentured servitude, with planters living in fear of a repeated uprising of a resentful class of armed, cheated freedmen which they had attempted to counterbalance by the introduction of black slaves, came much of the animating thought and action of the American Revolution.

The irony of a group of planters and descendants of planters whose personal fortunes rested on forced labor agitating in behalf of human liberty was not overlooked by the British. Many, like Samuel Johnson, derided such sentiments as sheer hypocrisy; a few, among them Edmund Burke, detected something more complex and enduring. Where men lived amid slavery, Burke suggested, those who were free were more proud and jealous of their freedom. Not associating it with the required toil and misery of lands where freedom was common, the people of the Southern colonies idealized liberty all the more.

"In such a people," Burke concluded, "the haughtiness of domination combines with the spirit of freedom, fortifies it, and renders it invincible."

In the years that followed, from this one colony there were to come 1) the author of the Declaration of Independence; 2) the commanding general of the American army during the Revolutionary War; 3) the man most responsible for introducing the Bill of Rights into law; and 4) the men who were to serve as President of the new Republic for thirty-two of its first thirty-six years.

All these were men who knew intimately the environment John Lawson describes. Who understood the manifestation of arbitrary power. To whom words like tyranny and enshacklement were neither exaggerations nor abstractions but precise terms potent with imagery for their countrymen. Who understood that there was in America a century and a half of servitude, redeemable by the promise of freedom.

Voices

As we ascended the side of this hulk, a most revolting scene of want and misery presented itself. The eye involuntarily turned for some relief from the horrible picture of human suffering, which this living sepulchre afforded. Mr. ——— enquired if there were any shoemakers on board. The captain advanced: his appearance bespoke his office; he is an American, tall, determined, and with an eye that flashes with Algerine cruelty. He called in the Dutch language for shoe-makers, and never can I forget the scene which followed. The poor fellows came running up with unspeakable delight, no doubt anticipating a relief from their loathsome dungeon. Their clothes, if rags deserved that denomination, actually perfumed the air. Some were without shirts, others had this article of dress, but of a quality as coarse as the worst packing cloth. I enquired of several if they could speak English. They smiled and gabbled "No Engly, no Engly—one Engly 'talk ship.' " The deck was filthy. The cooking, washing and necessary departments were close together. Such is the mercenary barbarity of the Americans who are engaged in this trade, that they crammed into one of those vessels 500 passengers, 80 of whom died in the passage. The price for women is about 70 dollars, men 80 dollars, boys 60 dollars.

—HENRY BRADSHAW FEARON,
Sketches of America

7

JOHN HAMMOND

"THE LABOR servants are put to, is not so hard, nor of such continuance as . . . in England . . . little or nothing is done in winter time . . . In the summer they rest, sleep or exercise themselves five hours in the heat of the day."

This workingman's paradise, the Big Rock Candy Mountain of its time, turns out to have been the colonies of Virginia and Maryland circa 1650, as described in a pamphlet written by John Hammond and published in London in 1656, titled *Leah and Rachel, or, the Two Fruitful Sisters, Virginia and Mary-Land: Their Present Condition, Impartially Stated and Related.*

According to Bernard Bailyn, whose *Ideological Origins of the American Revolution* is considered the authoritative examination of the subject, pamphleteering had become by the time of the Revolution the dominant means of colonial political discourse. For the Revolutionary generation, as for its predecessors back to the early sixteenth century, the pamphlet—topical, polemical, brief—had peculiar virtues as a means of communication. It was in this form that the basic elements of American Revolutionary thought were first expressed.

Hammond's pamphlet was intended as a rebuttal to earlier, unfavorable accounts of life in the colonies which, Hammond claims, so exaggerated conditions in America that "odiums and cruel slanders" were cast on Maryland and Virginia to such an extent that settlement was discouraged, and the colonies "are in danger to moulder away and come in time to nothing."

The original settlers of the colony of Virginia, the people who had arrived at Jamestown in 1607, were largely merchant adventurers, gentlemen and ladies. They were investors who could affort to buy land, who were bred to rule or at least oversee, and who, it was expected, would assume management of vast tracts worked by willing natives. Instead, finding themselves marooned in the wilderness, surrounded by hostile savages and bereft of practical skills, they nearly perished. Living among rivers that swarmed with fish and woods that were thronged with game, standing on rich untilled land in the shade of uncut timber, they clustered, cold and hungry, near their original landing place. Unused to fending for themselves, accustomed to ordering others to carry out practical everyday chores, they were unequipped for life on a new continent whose size and climate and strangeness threatened to overwhelm them.

What was needed were people who could *do* things, those with the common skills that the upper classes so depended upon, and demeaned, in England. These ordinary workingmen and women, with their limited knowledge of the world and small financial resources, were also the people least likely to want to emigrate. Hence the development of a system which induced the marginal members of the working class—the unemployed, the impoverished, or the simply unlucky—to uproot themselves from all they knew and bind themselves to a distant land.

Originally, the plan developed by Sir Edwin Sandys for the settlement of Virginia had an element of social justification in it. The landless poor of England, crowded into London and the other cities as the small freeholds were incorporated into great estates, would, after an initial term of bound labor, at last have the room and the opportunity to free themselves from hunger and the oppression of the landed rich. To encourage the broadest possible emigration, there would be bondage of several different sorts.

Tenants, or sharecroppers, would be sent out under an agreement with either the Virginia Company or an association that had founded a plantation. Under the supervision of agents, they would work on the company's or plantation's lands and be entitled to half the return on the work they did. When they had acquired capital enough, they could purchase freeholds of their own.

Ordinary bond servants were men and women who belonged entirely to their masters for a required term of service. In exchange for supplying the servants with food, clothing, and shelter, the master was entitled to everything the servant earned. Apprentices, in an extension of the apprentice system in England, were boys bound as servants for seven years to anyone who would pay ten pounds for them. When an apprentice had served his seven years and had not committed a crime he was then required to become a tenant for seven more years. If convicted of a criminal offense, the apprentice was to begin his seven-year term as a bond servant all over again.

Sandys's program failed to take into account the profiteering greed of the individual planters and local officers. What happened in Virginia was unique in human settlement. With at first an almost limitless abundance of available land and a desperate shortage of people to work it, profit immediately went to those who controlled the most labor. This produced instead of a land rush a kind of "man rush" in which, according to Edmund Morgan, men staked out claims to men, stole them, lured them, fought over them, and bid up their price to five or six times the initial cost.

In a free-labor economy, this scarcity would have enhanced the individual's negotiating power, and along with it his personal and financial independence; but in the forced-labor society of Virginia a tenant, servant, or apprentice was vulnerable to the demands of just about any planter or company officer. Men were money in Virginia, just as tobacco was money, to be seized and used and exploited, if not by one owner then by another more enterprising, more greedy, more ruthless.

In practice, the tenant's lot was difficult to distinguish from the servant's. A company officer was allowed great latitude in commandeering tenants as part of his quota. If a tenant arrived short of provisions, he could become the property of anyone who could feed and shelter him; and men who arrived without adequate food, tools, and clothing were often in fact treated as servants. The company officers profiteered in the inflated labor market by hiring out tenants, who were supposed to work on company lands, to private planters. Even if a tenant had provided for himself well enough to survive on his own, he could quickly be forced into service by a poor harvest, acquired debts, or an Indian attack. These were so common among the small frontier settlers that, according to Morgan, men were forced for fear of Indians to forsake their houses and join themselves "to some great man's plantation."

For the servant or apprentice, this panting thirst for labor would produce on the death of his master an heir, real or fraudulent, who would quickly lay claim to the servant—and a legal system which protected the right of the servant-as-property as if defending civilization itself. Some planters grew so desperate for help that they would ransom white captives from the Indians, returning them to a servitude which, according to one complainant, "differeth not from her slavery with the Indians."

Even Hammond concedes the all but universal exploitation of indentured labor in Virginia of the tobacco-boom years. "Then were Jayls emptied, youth seduced, infamous women drilled in . . . their labor was almost perpetuall, their allowance of victual small . . . no civil courts of justice but under a Marshall law, no redresse of grievances, complaints were repaid with stripes, moneys with scoffes and tortures made delights."

Yet amind this chaos there were all the while "divers honest and vertuous inhabitants, who observing the general neglect and licensiousnesses . . . caused Assemblies to be call'd and Laws to be made tending to the glory of God."

"Then began the Gospel to flourish, civil, honorable and men of Great estates flocked in: famous buildings went forward, Orchards innumerable were planted and preserved; Tradesmen set on work and encouraged . . . Staple Commodities attempted on, and with good successe brought to perfection."

Order is established, trade and agriculture encouraged, vice suppressed, the country enters upon a Golden Age. Meat is so plentiful that the excess kill is gratefully shared; if a man should fall sick, his neighbors willingly pitch in to see to his chores; travel is without charge; and at every house a stranger is entertained free as if a paying guest at an inn. "And therefore," says Hammond, "those that shall blemish Virginia any more, do but like the Dog bark against the Moon."

"I have undertaken," Hammond insists, "to give the true state of those places . . . and therefore can by experience, not hearsay (as lying Writters have done) . . . but truly let ye know, what they are, and how the people there live."

Perhaps. Yet, like the pamphleteers of the Revolutionary era, John Hammond was adept at applying the conditions and imagery of servitude to his own political purposes. Hammond, at the time he wrote his pamphlet, was under sentence of death in Maryland, and the former Maryland governor he lionizes as a reformer, William Stone, was also the man he was petitioning for rehabilitation.

A nineteen-year resident of Virginia, Hammond had joined a punitive expedition led by Stone against the Independents, an insurgent group of Protestant freedmen and indentured servants who had challenged the authority of Maryland's Catholic Lord Proprietor. Stone had sailed up Chesapeake Bay with a force of 130 men; but as they approached the four inhabited counties along the Maryland shore, one of Stone's own captains opened fire on the commander's ship, forcing it ashore. The following day, the governor's boats, provisions, and ammunition were seized, and the governor, "being shot in many places," was forced to yield on quarter.

Sentenced to die by the rebels of the Bay, John Hammond fled in disguise to Virginia, where he came aboard the ship *Crescent* under an assumed name and threw himself on the mercy of the commander, Thomas Thoroughgood. Living up to his name, Thoroughgood had charitably brought Hammond to England, "otherwise I had causelessly been put to death." For which act of charity Thoroughgood was put under indictment "by an act of Assembly made against masters of Commanders of Ships that shall carry away any of the inhabitants of your colonie without a pass."

This law's true purpose was to discourage Virginia's precious indentured servants from attempting to escape by sea.

Exiled in London, Hammond ponders his former life in the colonies, projecting the condition of the working people he saw around him onto the memory of the limitless distances of Virginia and his ease of access to its high officials.

"The other day," Hammond observes, "I saw a man heavily loaden with a burden of Faggots on his back . . . he travailed much ground, bawled frequently, and sweat with his burthen."

Hammond follows the man for some three hours until the exhausted wood peddler stops to take a drink; then he interviews him. How much does he make by this labor, Hammond asks the man, how much a load? A day? It is, he concludes, a pitiful life. He wonders how the man could live on it. "And yet it were dangerous to advise these wretches to better their condition by travel." So wary are people of being inveigled against their will into going to America that Hammond, self-conscious at the thought of being accused of kidnapping, holds back "for fear of the cry of 'A spirit! A spirit!' "

Instead he sits down to write this pamphlet, to set the colonial record straight and, not incidentally, remind Stone, now governor of Virginia, and the Virginia Council of services rendered.

"As I have done your Country of Virginia justice in standing up to its defence," he reminds them in a postscript, "so I expect and entreat the like from you." He requests that the charges against Thoroughgood be dropped, and that his own name be cleared, so that the true story "may scatter in Virginia amongst my friends, whos good opinion I covet, and that they may know in many odiums I have been wronged, and that I am the man that have seene affliction."

In the colonies, Hammond insists, "those Servants that will be industrious may in their time of service gain a competent estate before their Freedoms." The master will let the deserving servant plant a tobacco patch for himself and get a sow-pig or two. As for accommodations and treatment, "We are Christians . . .

living under a law, which compels as well the Master as the
Servant to perform his duty."

Servants' complaints, he maintains, are "freely harkened to,"
and if justified, "there Masters are compelled either speedily to
amend," or the servants are transferred, on a second complaint,
to another owner, "and often times not onley set free (if the
abuse merit it) but ordered to give reparation and damage to their
servant."

Yet sanguine as he is toward the practice of indentured servitude, Hammond offers revealingly strong advice for any luckless
Englishman considering submission to it.

"Be sure," Hammond warns, "to have your contract in writing and under hand and seal, for if ye go over upon promise made
to do this or that, or to be free, it signifies nothing." A law of the
country waives all promises, so that anyone coming in without
paying his own passage is bound to serve four years no matter
what has been agreed to in England.

Even if the servant has his terms agreed to in writing, the
language of contracts can often be obfuscatory, misleading. The
usual allowance is "a year's provision of corne, dubble apparell,
tooles necessary, and land according to the custome of the Country."

This last promise turns out to be "an old delusion," for there
is no land customarily due to the servant but to the master.
"And therefore that servant is unwise that will not dash out that
custom in his covenant, and make that due of land absolutely
his own."

What the prospective indentured servant needs, Hammond
seems to be suggesting, in negotiating his contract, is nothing less
than the services of a modern corporation lawyer. Little wonder
that these people—poor, mostly illiterate, dealing hat-in-hand
with their social betters—ended up in the vast majority of cases
betrayed, taken advantage of, physically and financially broken,
and occasionally worked to death.

By 1660, according to Abbott Smith, though indentured servants constituted three-quarters of all the emigrants to Virginia,
former servants amounted to less than a third of the landowners.
Climate, disease, working conditions, unequal contracts, and the

desire to give up the new land and return home had taken care of the rest.

The poorest workingman or woman in England was guaranteed by law and custom protection that did not exist for indentured servants in the American colonies. Even English agricultural workers, who could be bound to serve their masters for a year and had to give three months' notice before leaving, were entitled to similar notice in return. Moreover, once each year, in sessions held by local constables, English servants could renew their contracts or make new ones with other masters, which had the force of law. In America, terms were for so long and the death rate among servants was so high that there was little incentive for a master to treat his servant well in order to renew his services. Nor was there any positive reason for a servant to do his job well, since freedom, not rehiring, was every servant's goal. In practice, indentured servitude was a structure supported by a framework of unequal contracts, resting on a foundation of punishment.

In Maryland, the causes for popular discontent were the same as those in Virginia: A plantation economy dependent on cheap labor had produced a class of restless men, servants or former servants with a lingering grievance toward the authorities. All the minor complaints—against the poll tax, the amount of taxation, restrictions on suffrage, lack of protection against the Indians— sprang from the one great grudge, the sense of injury of a class of people cheated out of the rewards of a society built on their work.

When, some twenty years after Hammond's pamphlet, his peaceful Virginia erupted in Bacon's Rebellion, Maryland erupted along with it, even though Maryland's freedmen and servants had no leader as formidable as Bacon. Here too the revolt sputtered out.

It is his account of the treatment of servants, their admitted early exploitation and alleged later indulgence, the contrast between their lot and that of the poor in England, that gives Hammond's pamphlet its documentary conviction and emotional force. Here was an institution unique to the colonies, at the center of colonial personal, political, and economic life, capable of generating great profit and great resentment, which had spawned both a class of fiercely independent planters and an angry mass of disenchanted freedmen who could, properly called upon, be led into rebellion.

These were lessons that were not lost upon the pamphleteers, politicians, and orators of the coming Revolutionary era. It was in the plantation colonies, where tobacco had become a staple under the system of indentured labor, where the importation of bound workers had been greatest, that the urge for independence pulsed strongest. The end result of British corruption, British taxation, religious restrictions, and the presence of a standing army was enslavement of a kind particularly vivid to men and women who had known, owned, been, or were descended from servants themselves.

"Single acts of tyranny may be ascribed to the accidental opinion of a day," the Virginian, and planter, Thomas Jefferson declared in a pamphlet in 1774, "but a series of oppressions, begun at a distinguished period, and pursued unalterably through every change of ministers, too plainly prove a deliberate and systematical plan of reducing us to slavery."

Voices

In the morning the captain ordered public notice to be given of a day of sale, and the prisoners, who were pretty near an hundred, were all ordered upon deck, where a large bowl of punch was made, the planters flocked aboard; . . . Their inquiry was, if the captain had brought them a good store of joiners, carpenters, blacksmiths, weavers and taylors.

When all of the best tradesmen were bought up, a planter came to Mr. Carew, and asked him what trade he was of; Mr. Carew, to satisfy him of his usefulness, told him he was a rat-catcher, a mendicant, and a dog merchant; what the devil trades are those, replies the planter, in astonishment, for I have never heard of them? Upon which the captain, thinking he should lose the sale of him, takes the planter a little aside and tells him, he did but jest, being a man of humour, for he was a great scholar, and was only sent over on account of having disobliged some gentleman; that he had no indenture with him, but he should have him for seven years, and that he would make him an excellent school-master.

—The Life and Adventures of
Bamfylde-Moore Carew

8

MARY MORRILL

IN 1635, a widower named John Foulger emigrated from Norwich, England, aboard the ship *Abigail,* bound for the New England colonies; he was accompanied by his son, Peter. The Foulgers were Anabaptists, members of a religious sect considered radical at the time in England for their insistence that people must be adults before being baptized, and for their unfashionable belief in the legal separation of church and state. Also aboard the *Abigail* were Sir Harry Vane, a dashing English peer of twenty-two, soon to become governor of Massachusetts, and the Reverend Hugh Peters, a clergyman on his way to assume the duties of pastor of the Puritan Church at Salem. Both men were to return to England, and following the Restoration both were beheaded.

Among the Reverend Peters's party aboard the *Abigail* was a young indentured servant, a woman by the name of Mary Morrill. Probably she was an orphan who had been apprenticed out to learn to sew and knit and spin, just as boys were apprenticed out to learn a trade. Serving a family of Puritans, she would have been more tolerant toward radical sects like Anabaptists and Quakers than were most English people, and the voyage, usually an arduous twelve weeks at the time, tended to wear down not only the passengers, but also the formal social and political barriers that prevailed in England.

What seems to have happened aboard the *Abigail* is that amid some of the least romantic surroundings imaginable—cramped quarters, seasickness—Mary Morrill and Peter Foulger, John Foulger's seventeen-year-old son, fell in love.

Young Foulger wished to marry the girl, but to do so he would first have to purchase her indenture from the Reverend Peters, a transaction requiring the sum of twenty pounds, the equivalent of a year and a half's wages for a free workingman.

So Mary Morrill went with the Peterses to Salem, while Peter Foulger went off to work at a fishing weir in Watertown. He became an Indian missionary's assistant and a schoolteacher on Martha's Vineyard; she remained with the Peterses, mastering the "art, trade, and mystery of housewifery." When the Reverend Peters returned to England in 1641 to serve as agent for the colony of Connecticut, Mary Morrill remained with his family in Salem.

Though indentured servants were in greatest demand in the tobacco-growing plantation regions to the south, they were used at the beginning stages in all the colonies, including New England. A dozen indentured servants had arrived on the *Mayflower*. For many years, servants outnumbered free hired labor everywhere. There was, for proprietors, simply no other practical source of employees. The urge of an unencumbered free man to become the independent owner of his own estate was too powerful for him to remain a laborer for hire.

Neither John Foulger nor his son had crossed the Atlantic with the aim in mind of working for someone else. By 1642, Peter Foulger had acquired a certain independent status as a teacher, lay preacher, and interpreter to the Indians. Yet he was still strapped for money. When he heard that the Reverend Peters, back in England, had become the most influential preacher in the revolutionary new order of church and state, and that having been granted by Parliament an annual retainer of two hundred pounds, Peters could now send for his wife and family, young Foulger realized that he must now make his bid for the woman he wanted or lose her forever. Scraping together what he had managed to save, and borrowing the balance from his father, Peter Foulger appeared in Salem and concluded what he later referred to as his best bargain.

By marrying a former indentured servant, Foulger had compounded his outsider status as an Anabaptist. The settled colony of Massachusetts Bay promised only social slights and economic hard times. So Foulger looked to new territory, not the lands to the west, but to where his closeness to the island Indians of Martha's Vineyard had given him a valuable skill.

In 1659, Peter Foulger accompanied Tristram Coffin, a freedman, formerly an indentured servant, to the island of Nantucket "to ascertain the temper and disposition of the Indians and what inducements for emigration thither were offered." Foulger was the Indian interpreter who witnessed, in 1662, the deed of purchase of the island from the chief, Wanackmamak, for five pounds "in English goods or otherwise."

There was now, in Massachusetts Bay, the additional possibility of political difficulties. After the execution of Reverend Peters in 1660, his wife and daughter had returned to New England; and who knew what reprisals might follow those known to have associated with regicides? In 1663, Peter Foulger and his former-servant wife moved to Nantucket.

Although not an original proprietor of Nantucket, Peter Foulger was a "half-share man" or limited partner. Standing at last on his own land with his wife, freed by their union, he flourished, became accomplished, respected, versatile in a way that foreshadowed the career of their famous grandson: mill operator, weaver, surveyor, blacksmith, keeper of the island records, Indian interpreter. "An able Godley Englishman," Cotton Mather described Peter Foulger, "who was employed in teaching the youth in Reading, Writing and the Principles of Religion by Catechism."

And a man with a certain firm sense of principle. Disturbed by what he considered the increasingly domineering nature of Tristram Coffin and his five sons, Foulger allied himself with Coffin's

political rival on the island, John Gardner. When the Coffin party
gained control of Nantucket, Gardner and Foulger were arbitrar-
ily disfranchised and denied any participation in the town's affairs. Peter Foulger was subsequently arrested for contempt of
His Majesty's authority and for "contemptuous carriage."

Arraigned before his prosecutors, he refused to answer questions and, charged with contempt, was bound over for his appearance at the Court of Assizes in New York, with bail set at
twenty pounds. In default of this last order, Foulger was sent to
jail, where he remained the greater part of the time for more than
a year.

While appealing these acts to the governor in New York, Foulger was waging a stubborn non-recognition campaign against the
Coffins on Nantucket. When ordered, as the former clerk of the
court, to deliver up the court records, Foulger refused on the
grounds that he did not recognize the authority of the Nantucket
court as now constituted. The books were lost or hidden so skillfully that they have never been recovered.

Meanwhile, resentment was rising among the island's Indians,
who knew and liked both Gardner and Foulger and objected to
their treatment by the Coffins. The Coffin faction, increasingly
irritated, had Foulger jailed again, fined five pounds, and disfranchised. Finally, in 1677, the governor intervened. Following a
hearing, both Foulger's and Gardner's penalties were declared
null and void. At a town meeting in 1678, both men were voted a
formal apology; Coffin's grip on the island was broken. In 1680,
John Gardner was appointed chief magistrate and chosen the
island's representative in New York. The next year, Tristram
Coffin died.

Peter Foulger continued his trifurcated career: miller,
preacher, public official. Old grudges with the Coffin faction were
resolved. In a community as small and isolated as Nantucket, it
was impractical for families to avoid one another. The choice
was blood feud or intermarriage; Tristram Coffin's grandson married John Gardner's daughter.

For Mary Foulger, life became in many ways an extension of
the work she'd done in servitude: cooking, cleaning, spinning,
mending, collecting feathers to make pillows, and sewing coun-

terpanes for quilts. And child care; she bore Peter Foulger nine children, eight of whom survived childhood. Their youngest, Abiah, was born on Nantucket in 1667. Through her, Mary Morrill's story becomes a tributary flowing out upon other, wider tides.

There is, first of all, the greatest of Nantucket stories, Melville's *Moby-Dick*. Mary Foulger's closest friend was Mary Starbuck, the lineal Quaker antecedent of Ahab's Quaker first mate. There were Folgers (the old spelling was changed) in the New England whale fishery just as there were Starbucks and Greenleafs and Bishops and Pikes. A certain case can be made for the worldly practical preacher Peter Folger as the model for the Nantucket preacher Father Mapple. The figure of Melville's great invention looms behind everyone on Nantucket, lives imagined bigger, truer, deeper somehow than lives lived. Until there, in Chapter 24 of Melville's great work, they meet:

"No good blood in their veins?" Melville challenges those who would "declare that whaling has no aesthetically noble associations connected with it."

"They have something better than royal blood there," he thunders. "The grandmother of Benjamin Franklin was Mary Morrel; afterwards, by marriage Mary Folger, one of the old settlers of Nantucket, and the ancestress to a long line of Folgers and harpooneers—all kith and kin to noble Benjamin—this day darting the barbed iron from one side of the world to the other."

It is a nobility born out of the orphanage, the poorhouse, the jail. From among people of whom the British *Critical Review* once warned its readers: "Beware the complicated cunning of that race whose Adam and Eve emigrated from Newgate."

It was his grandparents that the grandson, Benjamin Franklin, sought to emulate. As the youngest child of a tallow chandler, who bound him out as an apprentice to his own older brother, Franklin was a boy who had to look beyond his father for a model. His "Grandsir Folger" was simultaneously plain and eminent in a way Franklin must have aspired to be. Franklin admired his "unflinching courage under persecution. Going to prison for the principle of law as a moral sanction."

In jail, determined not to be denied his reading, Peter Folger had even managed to devise for himself a primitive pair of spectacles. He wrote a book, in verse, a set of brief admonitions to the young, not unlike those later published by Poor Richard. The book, Franklin thought, "Is in familiar verse agreeably to the taste of the times and country. The author addresses himself to the governors for the time being, speaks for the liberty of conscience, and in favor of the Anabaptists, Quakers and other Sectaries, who had suffered persecution. To this persecution he attributes the wars with the Natives, and other calamities which afflict the country."

In England, as a member of the Royal Society, director of the colonial postal system, agent for the colony of Massachusetts, and the most renowned American in the world, Franklin spent considerable time pursuing his genealogy, tracing his emigrant forebears back to the origins of the Foulger family in Flanders. On Nantucket, he had researched among the parish records.

During his long and resented indenture to his brother, Franklin must have contemplated what it had been like for his grandmother, an emigrant carried across the ocean and eventually sold by her owner. It was a system he declared his opinion of by fleeing it.

More than most thinkers and writers of the Revolutionary era, Franklin understood the unifying emotional potency of the American colonists' broad and deep experience of servitude. Franklin, who was president of Pennsylvania's first abolition society, knew from his own life that enslavement was a threat that transcended race. "A Slave, according to my notion," he wrote in a letter printed in the Philadelphia newspaper in 1770, "is a human Creature stolen, taken by Force, or bought of another or of himself with Money . . . He may be sold again, or let for Hire, by his Master . . . who must wear such Cloaths as his Master thinks fit to give him and be content with such Food or Subsistence as his Master thinks fit to order for him; . . . who must never absent himself from his Master's Service without Leave; . . . who is subject to severe Punishments for small Offences, to enormous Whippings and even Death for absconding from his Service or for Disobedience to Orders."

In his sensitivity to the voice of conscience, his enduring belief in the practicality of ideals, and his instinctive resentment and resistance toward arbitrary power, in these things most of all, Benjamin Franklin was his grandparents' heir.

He never knew them. Peter Folger died in 1691, an honored Early Settler of Nantucket. Mary Morrill Folger survived for fifteen more years, dying, an old woman, in the house of her eldest daughter. Her youngest child, Abiah Franklin, was there at the time. Abiah's son Benjamin was born just a few months later, in 1704, *"almost,"* it is said on the island, "in Nantucket."

Voices

March 8, 1765: Early in the morning, I was obliged to give to the city authorities an account of the *status controversiae* with regard to a German orphan girl whose father died in the (FRENCH AND INDIAN) War. The girl had been bound out to English people for a term of six years and seven months and was supposed to learn to read and write. Now the term of servitude has elapsed and she can neither read a letter nor pray a single word and has been so completely debauched that she prefers to remain with her mistress because she is satisfied with her brutish life.

Where can we get help? And where can we find men who are adapted to the circumstances? As yet we have no *seminarium* here, and the dearly beloved laborers who are called and sent from Europe with so much care and trouble are for the most part, especially in their first years here, not in a position to put up with our work and manner of life. It is impossible to have a clear conception of this in Europe.

—HENRY MELCHIOR MUHLENBERG
*The Notebook of a Colonial
Clergyman*

9
GEORGE ALSOP

"HERDS OF Deer are as numerous in this Province of Mary-
Land," an indentured servant named George Alsop wrote to his
parents in 1658, "as Cuckolds can be in London, only their horns
are not so well drest and tipt with silver."

An apprentice boy in England, an ardent Royalist during the
great Civil War, Alsop grew so disgusted at the sight of "the
Annointed of the Lord tore from his throne by the hand of Patri-
cides" that he decided at the age of twenty to emigrate to America. He had no money. His parents were aged, feeble, probably
poor. He arranged to leave from Gravesend, his passage paid by
Captain Thomas Stockett of Baltimore County, in exchange for
four years' servitude in Maryland.

Alsop's master, Stockett, appears to have been an exception
among the Maryland proprietors of the time. His lands were close
to the Indians, with whom he traded instead of depending on the
enforced drudgery of the tobacco-growing districts. A pious man,
with a reputation for dealing humanely with others, Stockett employed his servants as artisans and as assistants in the Indian

trade, was delegated by the Assembly to treat with the Susque-
hannas, served as sheriff of Anne Arundel County, and until his
death was deputy surveyor general of the province. Treated decently by a master he respected, Alsop served out his indenture
and, he declares, would willingly have served four years more. It
seems he had entered upon earthly paradise.

"The Servants of this Province, which are stigmatiz'd for
Slaves by the clappermouth jaws of the vulgar in *England*,"
Alsop maintains, "live more like Freemen than the most Me-
chanick Apprentices in *London*."

It was not freedom itself that particularly interested Alsop.
Indeed, when he had earned his own, Alsop found himself un-
comfortable with it, exposed as he suddenly was to the boom-
and-bust cycle of what was essentially a one-crop economy.

"While I was linckt with the Chain of a restraining Servitude,"
he confided in a letter to his brother, "I had all things cared for,
and now I have all things to care for myself."

"Liberty without money," Alsop concludes, "is like a man
opprest with the Gout, every step he puts forward puts him to
pain."

With the Restoration of 1660, the rebellious and traitorous government that had prompted him to leave England was gone, and
Alsop was free to return home when his term of servitude ended.
Which, his affections for the colony of Maryland and his kind
master notwithstanding, he did in 1663. Before he left, however,
he experienced a period of physical and perhaps mental illness,
during which "distempers crowded into the main-guard" of his
body.

A portrait of George Alsop survives from this time: a young
man with a steady gaze, thin-faced, with a flowing dark peruke
and a thin, patchy mustache; a bow is at his throat, and he is
wearing a rich coat of folded cloth: a figure with a certain acquired hauteur, a self-made Tory, someone out of the wings of
Restoration comedy, lacking only the long walking stick in one
hand, the flowing kerchief at the opposite wrist, apparently feeling his time has come to stride center stage in London.

He wrote a book before he left, which was published in London
in 1666, helped along, one suspects, by the promoters of the

settlement of the colony of Maryland, which now included just about everyone from the lord proprietor on down to the thugs on the press gangs. *A Character of the Province of Maryland* is such a strange, almost self-cancelling mixture of faithful observation and shameless promotion, conviction and posturing, bawdiness and piety, pastoral rhapsodizing and choleric anger that one suspects Alsop himself could no longer distinguish what is imagined in it from what is fact. As indeed, in his original preface, Alsop warned the reader: "If I have wrote or composed any thing that's wilde and confused, it is because I am so my self, and the world, as far as I can perceive, is not much out of the same trim; therefore I resolve, if I am brought to the Bar of Common Law for anything I have done heare, to plead Non Compos Mentis."

Men of so humble an estate that they cannot afford the pittance required for passage to Maryland, about six pounds sterling at the time, should, according to Alsop, have no misgivings about accepting the alternative of servitude, since "they may, for the debarment of a four years sordid liberty, go over into this Province and there live plentiously well." What's a four-year servitude anyway, when it gains a man advantages which will last him all his days?

As for the passage itself, standards are so high that the prospective servant need not even trouble himself with investigating the merchants with whom he arranges for his voyage. "For there is such an honest care and provision made for them all the time . . . that they want for nothing that is necessary and convenient." On arriving in Maryland, the servant retains the privilege, "if they dwell not with the Merchant they made their first agreement with . . . they may choose whom they will serve their prefixed time with." Alsop neglects to mention the servant's alternative: that unless he finds someone to accept his indenture, he is kept aboard ship till he dies.

As for the labor itself, says Alsop, "let those whose chaps are always breathing forth those filthy dregs of abusive exclamations," exuded by "their sottish and preposterous brains . . . that those which are transported over thither, are sold in open Market for Slaves, and draw in Carts like Horses" . . . be known as liars "of the most antient and damned stamp." The truth is that the servants of Maryland, "of all colonies, distant or remote, have the least cause to complain either for strictness of Servitude, want of Provisions, or need of Apparel."

Five and a half days is the required workweek for servants in summer, and in the two hottest months, presumably July and August, "they claim an antient and customary Priviledge, to repose themselves three hours in the day within the house, and this is undeniably granted to them that work in the Fields."

In winter, which lasts through the months of December, January, and February, "they do little or no work or imployment, save cutting of wood to make good fires to sit by, unless their Ingenuity will prompt them to hunt the Deer or Bear, or recreate themselves in Fowling, to slaughter the Swans, Geese and Turkeys (which this Country affords in a most plentiful manner)."

Every servant, says Alsop, has a gun, powder, and shot. Moreover, servants recruited as artisans are never required to work in the fields "or do any other imployment save that which their Handicraft and Mechanick endeavours are capabile of putting them upon."

In these descriptions of servants' working conditions generally, Alsop, if not intentionally dissimulating, has at least based conclusions too exclusively on his own treatment by the considerate Captain Stockett. The fact is that Alsop, a servant for all but a few months of his time in Maryland, saw little of the province outside his immediate circumstances. Two men who did, who traveled the same territory extensively a few years later, viewed life and servitude in Maryland less benignly.

Jaspar Dankers, or Danckaerts, and Peter Sluyter were Dutch Labadists, members of a quietist sect dedicated to simple living and holding goods and children in common. Some thirteen years after Alsop's book was published, Dankers and Sluyter visited the plantation lands as part of a settlement-scouting expedition that included visits to New York, New Jersey, and Pennsylvania. They found Alsop's Maryland a place of privation, hard work, and hunger.

"The dwellings were very badly appointed," they conclude of the home of their plantation-owner host. "There was no place to retire to, nor a chair to sit on, or a bed to sleep on." Yet there are servants everywhere; and hard times for the masters mean ever harder times for the men and women whose work they depend upon. "For their usual food, the *servants* have nothing but maize bread to eat, and water to drink, which sometimes is not very good and scarcely enough for life, yet they are compelled to work hard."

The servants are "by hundreds of thousands" compelled to spend their lives "here and in Virginia, and elsewhere in planting that vile tobacco, which all vanishes into smoke, and is for the most part miserably abused." With land so abundant, the planters could grow everything necessary to sustain life comfortably, "but this insatiable avarice must be fed and sustained by the bloody sweat of these poor slaves."

With all attention concentrated on the growing of tobacco, the only food available is corn, which requires attention of its own after normal working hours:

"The servants and negroes, after they have worn themselves down the whole day, and gone home to rest, have yet to grind and pound the grain, which is generally maize, for their masters and all their families as well as themselves."

Dankers and Sluyter describe one servant in a sick condition "and there are many so," whose master decided he was going to die. Since there was no probability of the master's enjoying any more service from him, the master "made him sick and languishing as he was, dig his own grave, in which he was laid a few days afterwards, the others being too busy to dig it, having their hands full in attending to the tobacco."

This is the life, of the great majority of Maryland servants, for which George Alsop urges poor English men and women to give up the "care and trouble" that attend "that thing they call Liberty, which according to the common translation is but Idleness, and (if weighed in the Ballance of a just Reason) will be found to be much heavier and cloggy than the four years restrainment of a Mary-Land Servitude." The man who serves but four years "by the Custom of the Country," becomes on expiration of his term a freeman.

"There's a Law in the Province," insists Alsop, "that enjoyns his master whom he hath served to give him Fifty Acres of Land,

Corn to serve him a whole year, three Suits of Apparel . . . and Tools to work withall; so that they are no sooner free, but they are ready to . . . live passingly well.''

How men who themselves lived so poor that they could afford neither a bed nor a chair, who according to Dankers and Sluyter could offer, as the only comfortable object for a guest to recline upon, ''a heap of maize,'' could be expected to endow their freed servants, whom they would now have to replace by further purchase, with land, tools, wardrobe, and a year's provisions, is a contradiction Alsop neglects to even contemplate, let alone resolve.

It is on the subject of women that Alsop's writing, which runs a temperature several degress above normal anyway, grows downright feverish. Perhaps his term of servitude, which was hardly characterized by exhausing physical labor, included a strict and involuntary celibacy; or he may have been anticipating his return to the pleasures of Restoration London. One has the feeling of edging close here to the source of the ''distemper'' that ''crowded into the main-guard'' of his body.

''The Women that go over into this Province as Servants,'' Alsop pronounces, ''have the best luck here as in any place of the world.'' No sooner are they ''on shoar, but they are courted into a Copulative Matrimony, which some of them, had they not come to such a Market with their Virginity, might have kept it by them until it had been mouldy.'' Of course, this might have been prevented if ''they had let it out by a yearly rent to some of the Inhabitants of *Lewknors-lane*''—a disreputable part of the parish of St. Giles, in London—''or made a Deed of Gift of it to *Mother Coney*''—a phrase which seems to be a euphemism for taking up residence in a whorehouse—''until the Gallows or Hospital called them away.''

Indentured men, he concedes, have not altogether quite the same good luck as women in this respect, ''without they be good Rhetoricians, and well-versed in the Art of perswasion.'' Then, in time, they may ingratiate themselves with their proprietors ''ryvet [rivet] themselves in the time of their Servitude into the private and reserved favour of their Mistress, if Age speak their Master deficient.''

To George Alsop, it is the system of servitude itself that is the land of opportunity, a means of physical and moral uplift that offers the individual a better means of keeping himself "from sinking into the Gulf of a slavish, poor, fettered and intangled life, then all the fastness of their prefixed time did involve them in before."

At no time in his discourse does Alsop attempt to explain or justify the practical reason for the existence of servitude in the colonies in the first place: as an essential source of replaceable cheap labor. Instead, it is presented as part of the natural order of things, as obviously correct as the divine right of kings.

"As theire can be no Monarchy without the Supremacy of a King and Crown, nor no King without Subjects," Alsop trumpets, "nor any Parents without it be by the fruitful off-spring of Children; neither can there be any Masters, unless it be by the inferior Servitude of those that dwell under them, by a commanding enjoynment." Indeed, says Alsop, such is as it should be, "since it is ordained from the original and superabounding wisdom of all things, that there should be Degrees and Diversities amongst the Sons of men, in acknowledging of a Superiority from Inferiors to Superiors."

Servitude is not, then, an improvised expediency; it is the backbone of colonial society itself. "Good Servitudes are those Colledges of Sobriety that checks in the giddy and wild-headed youth from his profuse and uneven course of life, by a limited constrainment, as well as it otherwise agrees with the moderate and discreet Servant." Indeed, one gets the opinion that were Alsop to have his wish the colonial system of indentured servitude might be imported in its entirety to England's home counties, in place of the "levelling doctrine we here of England in this latter age (whose womb was truss'd out with nothing but confused Rebellion) have too much experienced."

The connection between monarchy and servitude—its conditioning people to authority, its association with the divine right of kings, its humbling of many for the exaltation of a few—was also seized upon by people who opposed both institutions. If there could be no monarch without servitude, then perhaps it was the king who ought to go. If servitude was the backbone of colonial government, then maybe it was time to cast off that government. Surely it is no coincidence that the same historical epoch that witnessed the gradual elimination of servitude also saw the final decline of the real power of monarchy.

"What are these arguments?" said Abraham Lincoln of the Alsopian, or Tory, view of the natural order of society in an anti-slavery speech in 1858. "They are the arguments that kings have made for enslaving the people in all the ages of the world . . . they always bestrode the necks of the people, not that they wanted to do it, but because the people were better off for being ridden. That is their argument . . . the same old serpent that says: 'You work and I eat, you toil and I will enjoy the fruits of it.' "

At the time of George Alsop's idyllic term of servitude in Maryland, there were men working in the tobacco lands of Maryland and Virginia, or edging close to debt servitude on marginal Indian-endangered frontier farms who just ten years after the publication of Alsop's book would be in bloody revolt against the great master, expelling Virginia's royal governor and attacking and looting the plantations of the great landowners of both colonies. And a century later, in the plantation lands where, according to Alsop's reasoning, the lessons of loyalty to authority and the crown should have been ingrained deepest, there arose instead the leadership of the kingless republic that was to begin the disestablishment of His Majesty's colonial empire.

Voices

RANSOM, SARAH, otherwise BICKLEY, otherwise CHICKLEY,
otherwise SARAH THE COCK CUTTER;

ARMSTRONG, ELIZ., alias LITTLE BESS;

ARNOLD, CATHERINE, alias ONYON;

BURTON, ELIZ., alias BLACK BESS;

JOHNSON, SAMUEL, alias CABBAGE;

PRICE, SARAH, alias COCK HER PLUMP;

HUDSON, WILLIAM, alias THICKHEAD;

GEORGE, DANIEL, alias LITTLE JOHN;

GOAT, MARY, otherwise FATTY;

GILLET, JOHN, alias MOUTH;

GRIFFITH, WM., otherwise SHOVEL;

HUNT, MARY, alias SPY;

LONG, RICHARD, alias FROST, alias FLEABITE;

TREVIS, JOHN, otherwise MOCO JACK;

MILLS, JOHN, otherwise MOLLYING JACK;

STEWART, HANNAH, alias YORKSHIRE HANNAH.

—FROM ORIGINAL LISTS OF
EMIGRANTS IN BONDAGE FROM
LONDON TO THE AMERICAN
COLONIES, 1719–1744

10

THOMAS HELLIER

IN JULY of 1678, a man named Thomas Hellier was convicted of murder and sentenced to be hanged in Westover, Virginia. An indentured servant, twenty-eight years old, Hellier had been charged with using an ax to batter to death his master, his master's wife, and the mistress's chambermaid. The incident, following on the heels of Bacon's Rebellion, had shaken the colony to its core, not only because of the brutal nature of the killings but because of what they implied about the Virginia plantation society and the forced-labor system on which it was based.

Almost since its earliest days, the Virginia Company had encouraged the transportation of vagrant children and criminals of various sorts, in order to staff the chronically shorthanded plantations. Although the colony was desperately in need of cheap labor, the transportation was justified as an important step toward rehabilitation, and in the case of the children funds to cover the cost of passage and clothing were appropriated by the Common Council of London. In the clear air of a new continent,

removed from the temptations of their old companions and surroundings, their energies absorbed in useful physical work, the
vagrant boys and girls and formerly criminal men and women
would at last have a chance to break old habits, acquire useful
trades and create new lives. For each servant, child or adult, the
right to fifty acres of land would be set aside, which the servant
would be given when his or her term was up. Here was a system
which, in theory, would benefit all concerned.

The problem was that the system, in practice, made exploitation all but inevitable. To encourage the servants to work out
their terms, the fifty-acre headrights were entrusted in blocks to
the owners, to be deeded to each servant when he became a
freedman. A planter who imported six servants acquired, in trust,
the right to three hundred acres of land, a trust which could be
converted into an ownership deed simply by buying the headrights from the freed servants. Since many of the servants wanted
nothing more than to return to England when their time was up,
a disgruntled and unhappy servant could represent to a planter
not just cheap labor but the opportunity to add substantially to
his estate. A planter could thus profit twice from the same human
investment.

At the other end, in Britain, the idea of encouraging vagrant
children and criminals to resettle in America led some people in
positions of authority—police, magistrates, agents, ship captains
—to greatly stretch the definition of what constituted a vagrant
child or a reformable criminal. Though some colonists grew
alarmed at the continuing importation into the colonies of men
and women convicted of crimes, and at the corresponding increase in the occurrence and seriousness of colonial violence,
there were always others who felt the acquisition of new hands
and headrights justified a certain amount of risk.

By the time of Thomas Hellier's arrest and trial, the presence
of former convicts and runaways was commonplace in both Virginia and Maryland. According to Ebenezer Cooke, in *The Sot-
Weed Factor:*

> *You'd blush if one cou'd blush for shame,*
> *Who from Bridewell or Newgate came.*

Servants with a dubious past and potentially violent tendencies were not only plentiful, they were on intimate terms with their masters. Isolated on the plantations, they worked in the master's fields, tended his stock, mended his tools, prepared his food, instructed his children. They had access to the things the planter valued most. That was why the penalties for a servant who attacked a master were so severe: death if he struck the master.

Also, people with an interest in servitude, not just profiteers but advocates of convict reform as well, continued to stress the positive aspects of the system. "There is not the poorest, and most despicable Felon that ever went over," wrote Daniel Defoe in *Colonel Jack*, "but may after his time is serv'd, begin for himself, and may in time be sure of raising a good Plantation."

Now Thomas Hellier, a servant, had been tried and convicted of a crime that reinforced the worst fears of the most alarmed colonists, while at the same time, challenging the best hopes of the most optimistic British reformers.

Though he was accused of having been a highwayman in England, Thomas Hellier denied it, insisting that he had on one occasion only relieved a beggar of an insignificant amount of coins, when he was desperate and penniless himself. During his trial, Hellier made no statement whatsoever. It was only after his conviction that he asked that a minister be sent for, promising that he would tell the clergyman the entire story. The following morning, a Mr. Williams appeared at the Westover jail and wrote down what Hellier, standing in chains in the shadow of the gallows, related to him.

"I was born at Whitchurch near Lime in Dorsetshire," Hellier began, and "I liv'd with my own Parents till I was ten years old." Taken by his grandfather to the village of Marshwood, Hellier lived the kind of rustic life idealized by the advocates of colonial transportation, and even attended school. His grandfather "bred me up till fifteen or sixteen years of age; who loved and tender'd me very indulgently." He was, in short, neither a vagrant nor a slum child stunted by breathing foul air in narrow darkened city alleyways.

At sixteen, Hellier was apprenticed to a barber-surgeon in the town of Lime for a term of seven years. While serving this apprenticeship, he also acquired from his master's son the trade of stationer, or bookseller. During his term, Hellier admitted, "I had plaid some frolickish youthful Pranks, which were mildly conniv'd and winked at, through the gentleness of indulgent Relations; which yet I had not the grace to make a good use of." After Hellier had served six years with this master, the barber-surgeon died. Deeded, as part of the estate to his master's widow, Hellier sued for his freedom and was released from his term before it had expired. Shortly after this, his grandfather died, bequeathing to Hellier fifty acres of land, which the old man had intended to give to three of his descendants, two of whom were now deceased. For the second time, Thomas Hellier had been granted liberty through the death of someone close to him and in a position of authority over him. The experience marked him deeper than he realized.

A man of property now, Hellier lived on his estate, an embryonic country squire. He married the daughter of a wealthy farmer, who brought with her an income of fifty pounds a year. Within a year they had a child, a daughter. Hellier found himself in the peculiarly disconcerting position of a young man who discovers that, perhaps too early, his wildest hopes have been fulfilled.

"My own and Wife's Friends both loved me very well." Hellier admitted, "and would have done very well for me, had I not taken bad courses; but I could not contain my self within the due bonds of Sobriety and Moderation."

Entrusted by his father with the sum of twelve pounds sterling which, as collector of the royal aid money, the father had evidently received for the poor, Hellier absconded with it. There seems to be no logical explanation for this, other than a youthful impetuosity combined with a more serious lack of connection on Hellier's part between actions and their consequences. Without saying anything to his wife or his father, Hellier, "taking horse, rode away to London," leaving behind him farm, income, wife, and daughter, none of whom he referred to again.

In London he proceeded to squander the money drinking and gambling. "I ranted out my twelve pounds in Companykeeping" is how Hellier phrased it. "I lived but too much at ease, I knew not when I was well: I was all on fire to set up in the world, to make a bustle abroad to and fro, and be doing that I might seem somebody.''

Impatient, disinclined to take a long view of things, Hellier decided to set up in the trade of stationer. On credit, he acquired twenty-four pounds' worth of books from one bookseller and similar stock by the same means from several others and opened his bookshop in the town of Crewkerne. "Now it was high Noon," he rejoiced. "I thought it would never be Night with me; I seem'd to have the World in a string, and thought I could hale it which way I listed at my pleasure."

Hellier continued at this trade in Crewkerne for nearly two years, by which time, thanks to continued drinking and gambling, he had run himself deeply in debt. The business he worked hardest at was that of keeping up appearances. "If six or eight pot-companions had sate tipling with me, had they but bestowed their Compliments liberally upon me, let such flatterers drink night and day, there was nothing for any of them to pay."

As he had run out on his father and his wife, Hellier now ran out on his creditors, another character trait which was to surface again significantly later. Taking his horse and ten pounds, Hellier "tripped up to London, resolving there to seek my fortune." Though trained in several useful trades—barber, chemist, engraver, wood-carver—he remained fixated on adventure: "I could fancie nothing but a Voyage to Sea."

"After much fruitless rambling to and fro," Hellier met a German captain who had a French commission as a privateer. Agreeing to go aboard the ship as sea surgeon, Hellier was to be outfitted by the captain with a full set of drugs and medications. But before the ship could sail, the captain was haled before the admiralty court, convicted of piracy, and fined a thousand pounds. Unable to raise the amount of the fine, the captain could neither set sail nor furnish Hellier's medicine chest. In August of 1677, Hellier went ashore, "having just one poor sixpence in my pocket."

Having used up his ten pounds, plus the money from the sale of his horse, Hellier was reduced to selling his clothes. At an inn near Towerditch, where he inquired if there was any ship captain present, Hellier was approached by a man who said that, though he was no captain himself, he was concerned about seafaring matters. Apparently the man was a crimp.

"I enquired to what parts he was concerned. He answered, to Virginia." If he was of a mind to go to the colonies, the man told Hellier, he would have "Meat, Drink and Apparel, with other Necessaries" provided him.

In his wanderings about southern England, and from his gambling and tippling companions, Hellier had heard about Virginia. "I replied, I had heard so bad a character of that Country, that I dreaded going thither, in regard I abhorred the Ax and the Hoe." The man assured Hellier that he would promise him that he would only be employed in trade or in such "Employments to which I had been bred, if they were here used."

Hungry, broke, unable or unwilling to return to his family and his farm, enticed perhaps by the immediate prospect of a full belly and the adventure of a voyage to sea, Hellier agreed to go to Virginia, and in August of 1677, "I being over-perswaded, went on board the *Young Princess*, Captain Robert Morris, Commander."

On September 5, the ship weighed anchor from the Downs, "and on the 25th of October following, she arrived within the Capes of Virginia, and dropt Anchor at Newpersnews [Newport News]."

Hellier was delivered into the custody of a merchant or agent at Bermuda Hundred, Virginia, who sold his indenture to "one Cutbeard Williamson" of Westover Parish in Charles City County, "living at a Plantation call'd Hard Labour."

Williamson promised Hellier that he would be employed as a teacher, instructing the planter's own children. He would not be assigned to any hard physical tasks, the planter assured him, "unless necessity did compel now and then, merely for a short spurt." Nevertheless, Hellier soon discovered that both plantation and planter were to live down to their names.

"Though I wanted not for Cloaths nor Victuals," Hellier conceded, "yet I found their dealings contrary to their fair promises." His schoolhouse turned out to be a tobacco field, his means of instruction a hoe, and his task the cultivation of tobacco plants instead of children's minds. Though both difficult and disappointing to Hellier, the work was bearable; what he could not endure was the ceaseless nagging of the master's wife, "who would not only rail, swear and curse at me within doors, whenever I came into the house casting on me continually biting Taunts and bitter Flouts; but like a live Ghost would impertinently haunt me, when I was quiet in the Ground at work."

Nothing that he did could satisfy her; no work was good enough to allay her criticism. Even diligent silence produced no respite. "And although I silently wrought as fast as she rail'd, plying my labor, without so much as muttering at her, or answering any thing good or bad; yet all the silence and observance that I could use would not charm her vile tongue."

The woman's carping so grated on the mercurial ex-barber's helper and bookstore owner that she "embittered my life, and made everything I took in hand burdensome to me." Once again, Hellier's desperation prompted thoughts of flight. He had left his father, his family, his farm, and his business behind without serious consequence; why not cut again and run?

"These things burning and broyling in my Breast, tempted me to take the trip, and give my master the bag to hold; thereupon I vamped off." Hellier made his way to Warwicks-Creek Bay, where he got on board a ship under a Captain Larimore.

What Hellier had failed to take into account was that as a runaway indentured servant in Virginia at this time, he was the equivalent of a prisoner in a penal colony, a fugitive—worth a bounty to anyone who captured him, who made an accomplice, guilty of a felony, of anyone who helped him. So wary were the authorities of the desire to escape, that Captain Larimore simply by harboring a servant without a pass was subject to indictment. Hellier was still not a man inclined to take the longer view.

He lasted almost three weeks as a runaway. "But at length my Master hunting about, and searching to and fro, had discovered where I was, and so sending a Messenger, fetched me back home again." For the first time, Thomas Hellier was faced with the consequences of running away, and this time the penalty was compounded by the strict laws of a forced-labor society: extension of his term by a month for every week absent, plus a time equivalent to the cost of catching him, plus compensation in the form of additional labor time to the owner for any loss of crop. By running off, he had only placed himself deeper under Cutbeard Williamson's—and worse still, Mrs. Cutbeard's—control.

Hellier's first response was characteristically rash. "As I was upon my return homeward, I had a design to have knock the Messenger on the head." To that purpose, he picked up a "great stone, and carried it along in my hand a good way." Eventually his nerve failed him and he dropped the rock along the roadside.

Returned home to Hard Labour, Hellier begged pardon of his master for his fault, and initially "all seemed pretty well again." Perhaps a small seedling of responsibility, a sprouting sense of consequence, was growing in Hellier's heart after all.

If so, it was quickly withered by blasts from the "odious and inveterate Tongue" of Mrs. Williamson. "Do all I would and strive all the ways whatever I could, she, I found, was no whit pacified toward me. Whereupon I began to cast about and bethink my self, which way to rid me of that Hell upon Earth, yet still seeking if possible to weather it, but all in vain."

Twice before, early in his life, good fortune had burst like unexpected sunshine on Thomas Hellier through a cloud of death. The abrupt death of his first master had freed him from his indenture as an apprentice; the death of his grandfather had brought him financial independence. Perhaps good luck required propitiation: Someone must be sacrificed.

"At last, Satan taking advantage of my secret inward regret, suggested to my vicious corrupt minde, that by ridding my Master and Mistress out of the way, I might with ease gain my Freedom." Again there was a recurring lack of any sense of consequence, an inability to profit from his own experience. Convincing himself that "when they were dead, I should be a Freeman," he had forgotten where he was, ignoring the law and nature of the society where he was living.

"Which said execrable Project," he resumed, "I attempted . . . May 24, 1678."

Rising before dawn that morning, Hellier dressed himself in his best clothes, then took his hated ax, the tool he had least wished to wield in Virginia, and headed for his master's bedroom. Two or three times he approached the door. His heart failed him and he stepped back. "But however at length in I rushed." A servant maid, who slept every night in the same room, passed by him, her bedding on her shoulder. Intent upon killing his master now, Hellier let her pass untouched. "From her I passed on to my Master's bed, and struck at him with the Ax, and gave him several blows, as near as I could guess, upon the Head."

Hellier had killed Cutbeard Williamson instantly. "I do believe I had so unhappy an aim with my hand, that I mortally wounded him the first blow." Meanwhile, Mrs. Cutbeard, his great antagonist, had stirred. Rising from bed, she grabbed a chair, which she hoped to use to defend herself. Hellier came toward her; they struggled. "She begg'd me to save her Life, and I might take what I would and go my way. But all in vain, nothing would satisfie but her Life, whom I looked on as my greatest Enemy; so down she went without mercy."

Now the servant maid, whom Hellier had previously let pass, "to whom I intended no hurt," returned, presumably to assist her mistress, "whereupon she suffer'd the same cruel Fate with the other two."

Breaking open a closet and rummaging through a chest, Hellier gathered up an armload of provisions and "loaded a good lusty horse." While the horse stood loaded at the door, Hellier went back inside to take up his master's gun. When he returned outside, a neighbor was there who had come to borrow the horse. Hellier, refusing, threatened him, arousing the neighbor's suspicions; one of the Williamson's children ran off to spread the alarm, but before anybody else arrived, Hellier was off, "with my Master's Horse loaded, and his gun in my hand."

Finding himself in an armed and hostile country, Hellier wandered in the woods. Finally he decided to head for the plantation of a man named Gilly, near the Chickahominy Swamp, where there lived an indentured servant Hellier knew, a shipmate from the *Young Princess*. At the planter's house, Hellier asked his shipmate the nearest way to the falls of the James River. The servant told Hellier he didn't know the way but offered to go inside and find out, "so he called his Master's son, who asked if I would not walk into the house, and eat before I went." Hellier tried to beg off going inside, but the master's son, joined now by his brother-in-law, insisted that he come in, "I being as shie of them, as they were watchful over me."

Assuring Hellier that if he accompanied them, they would show him the way, the two brothers-in-law led him to a small bridge, "one walking before me and the other following me."

As he passed over the bridge, Hellier took his hand from his gun, "Whereupon one laying hold of the Gun said, This is a compleat Gun, and withal fired it off: Whereupon I discern'd myself surprised."

They told Hellier to go no further. "So they seizing me, I struggled a while, and had like to have been too hard for one of the men." But Gilly, the master of the plantation, had heard the gunshot. He now rushed down to the bridge and helped his son and son-in-law subdue Hellier.

"So being overpower'd, I was forced to submit to have my hands bound." It was at this point that Hellier fell silent, "not having power either to confess or deny the Fact." Brought before the justice of the peace, he refused to make any statement until after his trial and conviction, when he unburdened himself to the Reverend Mr. Williams.

In the Virginia of his time, Thomas Hellier was regarded as an exception, someone who was "criminally disposed": base, loathsome, unreformable. He was, in fact, reckless, irresponsible, and with an alarming lack of any sense of consequence. Had he stayed in England, where as a thief he had already committed a capital felony, he might well have been hanged anyway. Whether he would have murdered anyone or not is quite another matter.

It was his feelings of resentment, his sense of injury over being cheated and betrayed, and his desperation at finding himself confined that prompted Hellier's turning on the people he most immediately associated with his plight. In these feelings of resentment and betrayal, his frustration at finding himself confined in the land whose strongest promise was personal independence, Thomas Hellier did not represent a departure from the common feelings of indentured servants so much as he typified them. The goal in America was not a pleasant servitude under an easy master, or avoidance of a harsh one, but freedom from the caprices of any master at all.

From a widespread frustration that was individual, deep, and personal came a fear of arbitrary authority as limitless in its hunger to expand its power at the expense of individual liberty.

It was not the vague, abstract, and never quite manifested tyranny of George III that the Revolutionary pamphleteers threatened their readers with so effectively as the American experience—their own, their parents', their neighbors'—of being completely at the command of another person.

"They who have no property can have no freedom," wrote Stephen Hopkins in *The Rights of Colonies Examined,* an anti–Stamp Act pamphlet of 1764, "but are indeed reduced to the most abject slavery. . . . For one who is bound to obey the will of another is as really a slave though he may have a good master as if he had a bad one."

The Reverend Williams, after he had written down Hellier's statement, read it back to him. "After he had heard the same read over," Williams related, "he acknowledged this to be the true sense of his own Intentions, and the very same which, he desired, might be published to the world. So I promised him I would take so much care as to have it transported for England." Instinctively, Hellier seems to have grasped the fact that the feelings that moved him had a significance beyond his immediate situation. That others might profit by the experiences which had cost him so much.

His statement was taken in early August of 1678. On August 5, in chains, he was hanged.

Voices

Run away from the Subscriber living at Annapolis, a servant man named John Powell, alias Charles Lucas, a Londoner born, by trade a clock and watch maker; he is a short, well-set fellow, has full goggle eyes, and wears a wig: He had on when he went away, an osnabrigs shirt, a pair of buckskin breeches, a pair of short wide trousers, two pairs of white hose and a well-worn broadcloth coat with metal buttons.

Whoever secures the said runaway so that he can be had again shall have 3 pounds reward, besides what the law allows; and if brought home, reasonable charges.

—MARYLAND GAZETTE,
August 27, 1745

Whereas John Powell was advertised last week in this paper as a runaway; but being only gone into the country a cyder-drinking, and being returned again to his Master's service, these are therefore to acquaint all gentlemen and others, who have any watches or clocks to repair, that they may have them done in the best manner, at reasonable rates.

—MARYLAND GAZETTE,
September 3, 1745

11

JENNEY VOSS

IN APRIL of 1684, a woman named Jenney Voss was convicted in London of stealing a silver tankard, in that time and place a capital felony. To avoid the sentence of death for this and the long list of other larcenies, she "Pleaded her Belly," claiming to be pregnant, and heightening the effect by drinking in advance "a Gallon of New Ale and Honey." This ruse was only the latest in a remarkable career which stretched from England to America and back to Europe, and which included the abandonment of so many admirers of varying classes, nationalities, and even sexes that Jenney became known as the "London Jilt."

Jenney Voss's first significant departure took place at the age of fourteen, when to avoid punishment for a series of petty thefts she climbed out of her bedroom window and ran away from home. In the first of a series of elaborate deceits, worked mostly upon men, that were to characterize her life, she next passed herself off as the child of a deceased mother, abandoned by an indifferent father, and was taken in as a servant by a wealthy Middlesex farmer. Within a matter of months, she had also run off from the farmer to join up with a local drifter or "Gypsy," "for some time afterwards her Doxy," after robbing her benefactor of forty pounds' worth of money and plate.

This theft qualified Jenney for initiation into a Gypsy gang whose company she found congenial. A quick study, "she was soon perfect in their manner of Conversation and Gibberidge"; and by the age of sixteen she was pre-eminent among them as a "Crafts Mistress in the Art of Deceit." A ringleader of the gang, she was already possessed of ambitions beyond her associates' vision. Having thrown over her first companion, she had replaced him with the brightest of the troupe as her new bedfellow. Now Jenney conspired with this new lover to break from their companions and head as a team for the rich pickings rumored in the West of England. Here they performed an armed robbery on a reportedly rich man who had misguidedly given them food and lodging for the night.

While fleeing from this robbery the following morning, Jenney and her partner decided that in order to avoid discovery they had to adopt a disguise. To this end they assaulted two gentleman travelers, and, Jenney using a pistol and her fellow a quarterstaff, they forced the two men to strip, took their clothes, and left the two travelers bound in the woods.

Dressed in "Manlike Garb" now, "travelling in the Country as a Gentleman of Fortune," Jenney rode about the countryside with her comrade "rejoyceing in their Good Success, every Day committing some new Robbery or other." Feeling luck was with them, they pushed it to extremes. Riding into the market town in Wiltshire to sell a horse they had stolen, they were spotted by its owner, who had the two "Gentlemen of Fortune" clapped into jail.

Imprisoned, in irons, Jenney remained "in Mans Cloaths and her Sex undiscovered," an impressive tribute to her skills in the Art of Deceit. Moreover, "having the Beauty of Woman to add to the appearance of Manhood," she began a flirtation with the wife of the "Old and Peevish" jailer. The jailer's wife, "being very eager to bring her supposed Gallant to her Embraces," arranged an assignation. On an evening when her husband would be conveniently out of the way, the young gentleman was to come to the jailer's wife's bedchamber and "fearing lest the same should come to a Discovery," she "ordered the meeting to be in the Dark," and insisted on "the strictest Silence Imaginable."

When the hour approached, Jenney dispatched her companion to service the jailer's wife, whom "he gave the greatest satisfaction she could hope for, apprehending it all the while to be Jenney's own Person." So smitten was the jailer's wife that she agreed to help her lover escape disguised in a set of her own clothing. A set of woman's apparel was provided, and Jenney "at the Hour appointed . . . found the Door Opened and the Gaoler's Wife ready to discharge her." Instructed to head for a safe house where she would be brought a horse and pistol, Jenney, intent on avoiding a change of heart by the jailer's wife, and leaving her partner to stand trial for robbery, went off in the opposite direction on foot for London. She thus performed the remarkable feat of jilting at one stroke not only two lovers but two of different sexes.

Using a false name, Jenney next got work as a servant for a "Family of Reputation," whom she proceeded to rob at the first opportunity, running away "carrying with her a considerable quantity of Plate and Goods." Searching for a way to dispose of the booty in a strange city, she was put in touch with a pawnbroker who doubled as a fence. Through him, she became acquainted with "all the Cheats and Pickpockets in Town: Of whom she not only learned the Mastery but was soon after matriculated into their Society and became one of their most applauded Artisans."

Her skills as a pickpocket acquired such a reputation in London's underworld that Jenney was once hired by a gentleman to win a wager from another man who had insisted that his pocket could not be picked. Jenney, swooning at the feet of this man in the customs house, relieved him so deftly of his pocket watch that the man didn't miss it until it was returned to him by the gentleman who'd retained Jenney.

It was through these exploits that Jenney Voss came to the attention of a man named Sadler, a gang leader and thief whose career reached its climax with his successful theft of the mace—the jeweled staff symbolizing authority—of the lord chancellor

of England. Jenney, who was often called in as a kind of consul-
tant when there were things of moment to be done, and who
participated personally in a number of Sadler gang's robberies,
had kept part of the loot from this robbery hidden under her bed,
where it was found during a police search. Arraigned along with
Sadler, Jenney once again let a man take the fall, while she received a favor. Though Sadler was sent to the gallows, Jenney
"by the Favour of the Court, obtained to be Transported."

Sentenced to go "Beyond Sea," Jenney Voss was sent to one
of the plantation colonies, most likely Maryland. She thus became part of a tradition that extended throughout the colonial
era, and is suggested in literature by women like Moll Flanders.

In fact, the transportation of British convicts to the colonies
increased as the colonial period wore on, was vehemently opposed by many people in America, and became one of the sore
points on the crucial issue of the authority of the colonial assemblies as opposed to that of Parliament. Several times the assemblies of Virginia and Maryland either outlawed or severely
restricted the importation of convicts, only to be overruled by
Parliament. It was the same with the slave trade. The issue of
sovereignty was thus laid bare as the stark power to command.
"Parliament," according to the Declaratory Act of 1766, "had
. . . of right . . . full power and authority to make laws and statutes . . . to bind the colonies and people of America," whether
the people were actually represented there or not. This was one
of the acts the colonists considered part of a conspiracy to enslave them.

Transportation was not a punishment that British courts meted
out lightly to women, and it was generally assumed that anyone
so sentenced was either guilty of a serious crime or was a repeated offender. Unlike men convicts, women couldn't simply
be sent out into the tobacco fields and worked in gangs. Taking
such people in as household servants represented to many planters a grave threat to life and property. Things grew so bad that
during one summer Newgate prison filled up with women convicts awaiting transportation when there was no one willing to
accept them.

Yet despite the reluctance of many colonists to take them,

removal to the New World did represent for many convict women an opportunity to start life anew. In Jenney Voss's time, women were still scarce in America, and it was easy to find a husband, even a man with property, in the overwhelmingly male colonies. By adopting a husband's name, moving to his land, and nurturing their children, a woman convict had possibilities men hadn't for obliterating the tracks of her old career and, like Moll Flanders's mother, inventing a whole new identity in America.

It's somewhat surprising that Jenney Voss, "Crafts Mistress in the Art of Deceit," didn't inveigle her way into some First Family in America. Probably she didn't want to. For Jenney, a change in environment had produced no corresponding change in disposition. The urge to rob and run remained predominant. During her term of servitude in the colonies, we are told, "she could not forget her old Pranks, but used not only to Steal herself, but incited all others that were her fellow servants to Pilfer and Cheat what they could from their Master."

In addition, Jenney, who under any conditions seems to have retained her ability to sexually attract and manipulate any convenient person, entered into an affair with the son of one of the planters "who used to Lye with her and supply her with Moneys, which she was always averse to the want of."

The upshot of all this was that when Jenney's time was out her master was glad to be rid of her. And having no desire to press for an extension of her term by prosecuting her for theft or seduction, he happily saw her off, headed back again to England.

Responding to the stimulus of her old society, Jenney "quickly found many of her Old Comerades with whom she continually associated, resolving not to leave those Courses she had been all her Life bred in." For her, the Old World, with its centuries of accumulated family wealth and jewels, was the true land of opportunity, which she now spiritedly set out to explore.

A voyage to Holland brought her into the company of a Dutch merchant whom she bilked of "3 Great Diamonds and a Pearl Neck-lace to a considerable Vallue." Back in England, she concluded a "Westminster Wedding" with a man named Robinson, who was later hanged as a horse thief: "the Gallows sued out their divorce."

At last, in March of 1684, Jenney was arrested for having stolen "a Silver Tankard from one John Warren of St. Olive Silver-Street in the parish of Cripplegate." She was tried and convicted in April by a court which, in the light of her previous offenses, her association with the arch-thief Sadler, her unsuccessful transportation, was not inclined toward lenience. Sentenced to hang, the London Jilt made her one last attempt to jilt the hangman with the ale-and-honey-aided claim of pregnancy; but there was to be no pardon, "there being no place found for Mercy where so great and Notorious a Criminal was concerned."

In December, the sentence was carried out on a supposedly repentent Jenney Voss at Tyburn gallows. Publicly she expressed regret that she had been the cause of so many persons falling into "Bad Courses which had led them to untimely ends." If true, it was her only expression of guilt or remorse toward the people, mostly men, who had befriended, admired, and been abandoned by her.

Privately, one can't help wondering if she didn't derive some secret satisfaction from having outlasted so many men at what was considered a man's trade in an overwhelmingly male world. "For according to Report, no less than 18 who had been her Reputed Husbands or Friends had suffered for their Robberies."

Voices

TUESDAY 10.

Fourteen transports from Durham, Newcastle and Morpeth, were put on board the *Jenny,* Captain Blagdon, bound for Virginia; at which time ten young artificers shipped themselves for America. One of the indented servants, we hear, who formerly belonged to Newcastle, has inlisted into 46 different regiments, been whipped out of 19, sentenced to be shot six times, but reprieved, confined in 73 different gaols, appeared under the character of Quack Doctor in seven kingdoms, and now is only in the 32nd year of his age.

—THE GENTLEMAN'S MAGAZINE
London, May 1767

12

ROBERT COLLINS

In 1671, Richard Sprague, master of the ship *Arabella,* brought an action in the court of Suffolk County, Massachusetts, against one Robert Collins, whom Sprague had brought to America as an indentured servant. Acting on behalf of the *Arabella's* owner, Thomas Kinghts, Sprague charged Collins with absenting himself from his owner's service and with disowning any obligation to serve any master whatsoever. Collins, vigorously contesting the case, conceded the accuracy of the charge of nonperformance but insisted he was not bound to serve, since he had, in effect, been kidnapped.

In order to enforce the system of servitude, colonial courts were not at all hesitant about ordering the return of a reluctant servant to his master or fining or imprisoning a servant who displayed insubordination. A system so dependent on individual authority could and occasionally did degenerate into chaos, with undisciplined servants simply refusing to exert themselves at tasks for masters under whom they were essentially only serving time anyway. Though the impoverished servants were practically judgment-proof in damage suits, the penalty or runaway time often awarded owners represented property which the owners could make use of themselves or sell to someone else. In the chronically shorthanded colonies, it was therefore in the interest not only of the individual master but the forced labor system as a whole that challenges such as Collins's be dealt with firmly.

For Collins, the trial represented an overwhelming mismatch in terms of time, money, and skill. He had neither the leisure, the funds, nor the legal talent at his command to match those available to a New England shipowner. If defeated, he would be stuck with court costs, which translated into a further extension of his term. His one hope was that it was to be a jury trial, before individual men who could be convinced, as he was convinced, that Robert Collins and not Richard Sprague or Thomas Knights was the wronged party in this action.

Pitching his argument to the individual feelings of the men on the jury, all of whom as Massachusetts men had either known, owned, or been servants themselves, Collins related his story.

Captain Richard Sprague could never have recruited Robert Collins as an indentured servant, Collins began, because the two men had never met until after Collins was already aboard the *Arabella*. Nor had Collins met or heard of any Mr. Knights. He had instead encountered, in London, presumably in some grog shop or deadfall, "a suttle Fellow who sayd he was Botswaine of the ship *Arabella*." This impostor, taking notice of Collins's "weakness & infirmity," most likely an inclination to overindulge in strong drink, saw in this an opportunity for himself. Representing himself as the boatswain, he asked Collins if he would like to go to sea. If Collins came aboard the *Arabella*, he was assured, he would be paid eighteen shillings immediately and in addition disbursed the same sum each month until he arrived in New England. What was more, the boatswain himself, his newfound buddy, would be there at his side to see to it that everything was done as promised.

To this proposition the flattered, naive, and presumably somewhat drunk Robert Collins agreed. He accompanied the boatswain to the wharf, where the two men haled the ship's boat to take them to the *Arabella*. It was only at the last moment that the boatswain begged off, telling Collins to go ahead on board by himself, and that he, the boatswain, would subsequently follow. Collins dutifully scrambled into a dory and rode out to the *Arabella.*

Once aboard ship, the still-trustful Collins waited patiently for the boatswain to come aboard. Several days passed with no sign of his companion. Finally, Collins asked several of the seamen what had happened to this boatswain who never came aboard ship. "Then the seamen one bord laughted at him & tould him that he was catched by the kidnapper."

He need not fear, however, the sailors assured Collins. At Gravesend, the final stopping place for ships leaving England, the customs searchers would come aboard, and by appealing to them and explaining what had happened Collins would gain his release.

Meanwhile, Collins, living aboard the *Arabella,* ate in the ship's mess, drank the ship's drink, and accepted an issue of clothing, all of which he assumed was chargeable to the eighteen-shilling payment guaranteed him by the pretended boatswain, but which Sprague later contended represented an incurred indebtedness to the ship's owners. He had to eat and drink or else starve, maintained Collins, and he was not permitted to go ashore. It was not until the ship sailed and stopped at Gravesend that Collins was allowed shore liberty at all "and that was with 3 or 4 to look after him, and that was in such blind Corners, and uncoth places, that he knew not which way to go if he had been at liberty."

It was at Gravesend that the promised customs searchers came aboard. Collins "did in their presents refuse to give them his name & tould positively that he was not willing to go the voyage." Yet apparently there were papers verifying Collins's willingness to go, testified to by the clerk of the voyage, a man Collins also denied ever knowing or seeing.

It was these papers, most likely an indenture with Collins's mark or signature, that convinced the customs searchers to permit the *Arabella* to sail away with her unwilling passenger still on board.

In making his case, Captain Sprague maintained that Collins's

objections to the voyage had come only after its completion, that
he had signed the indentures; accepted food, drink, and clothing
to the value of three pounds; and had cheated both Sprague and
ship owner Knights out of the price of a passage to the New
World, under a contract which Collins had never intended honoring.

Such swindles were not at all unknown, partly because actual
kidnapping was not all that uncommon. The whole enterprise of
transporting people—free-willers, redemptioners, convicts—to
the New World was so unregulated, as the merchants themselves
preferred it to be, that it invited racketeering, not only on the
part of shipowners, crimps, sea captains, and agents, but by
blackmailers, who saw opportunities to shake down merchants
with the threat of denunciation for real or contrived crimes. According to a petition of July 14, 1664, the custom of kidnapping
or "spiriting" "gives the opportunity to many evil-minded persons to enlist themselves voluntarily to go the voyage and, having
received money, clothes, diet, etc. to pretend they were betrayed
or carried away without their consents."

According to Richard Sprague, this was exactly what Robert
Collins had done, intending to bilk him and Mr. Knights out of
the price of a passage, with maybe even more in mind. A payment of money to keep the matter quiet perhaps. Or if this judgment went against the shipowner and captain, a suit for damages
by the litigious Collins.

During the course of the trial, it was revealed that while
Sprague had indeed invested some three pounds in feeding and
clothing Collins, he had also paid forty shillings to the false boatswain Collins had accused of "manstealing" him. There was also
some dispute over whether Collins's signature on the indentures
was genuine or forged. And a claim that Collins had offered the
sum of ten pounds to Sprague and Knights's side in order to be
set free.

The trial had arrived at a stalemate, with both sides offering
contradictory testimony, none of which had been corroborated
by any third-party witness. It was at this point that Collins's
defense introduced William Hearsy, an indentured servant.
Hearsy, twenty-one years old, had also been aboard the *Arabella*

and was present when the customs men had come aboard at
Gravesend to record the names of those about to leave the country.

"The said Robert Collins," Hearsy testified, "did then declare
himselfe to the Said serchers that he would not goe in that said
Shipp to New England to be a Servant to Mr. Sprague or to be
disposed of." What was more, Hearsy said, Collins had earlier
made the same vow in the most emphatic terms to Captain Sprague himself. Noting that Collins had been living aboard the *Arabella* for some time, eating ship's food and wearing ship's-issue
clothing. Sprague threatened to strip Collins naked and put him
ashore. To which Collins, apparently to the captain's astonishment, promptly agreed. The captain, refusing to believe that Collins would actually accept this dare, said that this being the case
they would drop the clothesless Collins when the *Arabella*
stopped at Torquay.

When the ship arrived at this spot, said Hearsy, Mr. Sprague
ordered Collins to remove his clothes, which Collins, standing on
the deck of the *Arabella,* proceeded to do. "And when his clothes
was ofe, the said Mr. Sprague would not suffer him to goe on
shore, notwithstanding all the seamen tould the said Collins with
the passengers that if they were not willing to goe the said voyage
when they came to Graves End, they might be cleared."

Hearsy's testimony, convincing in the vividness of its detail,
seemed to put to rest Sprague's depiction of Collins's refusal to
be an indentured servant as a sentiment that had bloomed only
on American soil. Apparently the jury agreed. They found for
Collins, the defendant, and awarded him court costs of thirty-five
shillings and twopence.

Collins's victory in this case suggests several things: the early
stirrings in Massachusetts of individual resistance to the abuse of
arbitrary power; the awakening sense that there was a body of
experience among the public, familiar enough with the practice
of servitude to recognize its abuse; and the possibility of using
the traditions of English law to gain recourse. These were the
issues—the insistence on the full protection of English law guaranteed to British subjects—that the American colonists were de-
manding in far greater numbers a century later.

Collins's case also illustrates the conviction—already strong in New England and spreading throughout the colonies by the Revolution—of the tendency of power to expand itself at the expense of liberty. Power was brutal, ceaselessly active, heedless. Liberty was delicate, passive, sensitive. Liberty was therefore not the interest and concern of governors but only of the governed. "The one must be resisted, the other defended, and the two must never be confused."

How the seemingly naive and impoverished Collins was able to present such a defense is a mystery. He may have had the services of an especially dedicated or sympathetic lawyer. He was certainly lucky in finding a servant who was able and willing to testify against his former owners in another servant's behalf. At any rate, Collins's victory was something of an exception. Though from time to time in Massachusetts and in the other colonies servants were acquitted of charges by the courts, and though occasionally servants even brought suit against their masters and won their freedom, the odds were heavily in favor of the men who owned the ships, stores, plantations, and in many instances the magistrates.

The verdict was not one that Captain Sprague accepted gracefully. At the following session of the county court six months later, a lawyer named Lidgett, representing Sprague, again brought suit against Collins, this time for the value of his passage and expenses. The jury brought in "a spetiall verdict" in which they found for the plaintiff, Sprague, in the costs of the voyage, some nine pounds. And for the defendant, Collins, in all costs of court. Sprague's lawyer, still unhappy with this split decision, announced that he would appeal to the next court of assistance. There is no record of this appeal ever being made.

Voices

Negroes being a property for life, the death of slaves, in the prime of youth or strength, is a material loss to the proprietor: they are, therefore, almost in every instance, under more comfortable circumstances than the miserable European, over whom the rigid planter exercises an inflexible severity. They are strained to the utmost to perform their allotted labour; and, from a prepossession in many cases too justly founded, they are supposed to be receiving only the just reward which is due to repeated offences. There are doubtless many exceptions to this observation, yet, generally speaking, they groan beneath a worse than Egyptian bondage.

—William Eddis
Letters from America, 1774

13
DAVID EVANS

In 1747, David Evans, a New Jersey Presbyterian divine, began writing his autobiography. Though so fluent in English that he preached to an English-speaking congregation and was the author of three books of religious admonitions, he reached back now into his childhood land and language to compose his life story in Welsh, and in verse.

Born in Carmarthenshire in South Wales in 1681, Evans lived for a few short years under his parents' care,

> Leading a youthful life of folly,*
> Like a wild ass's foal.

The family was poor and moved often from one unpromising spot to another. At the age of only eight or nine, the boy was sent off to work as "a feeble shepherd," although "for an amia-

---

* David Evans's poem has been translated from the Welsh by Elvyn Jenkins of the University of Wales, Aberystwyth.

ble master." After a year he moved to a place called Glyn Coch near the town of Pencader, where he was reunited with his parents. "During this time," he recalled,

> *I was sent*
> *To a solemn school to learn reading.*

The boy seems to have taken to both scholarship and religious instruction; but his parents lived in the chronic itinerance of rural poverty, and after two years in this religious school he spent the next five years moving from place to place, tending sheep in one bleak landscape after another. At length, the family moved to a valley "above Rhyd y Bennau"; here the boy was sent to an educated weaver,

> *Where I learnt the craft of weaving,*
> *And to read books in the bargain.*

This was at a time when the idea of the poet-craftsman was becoming popular in Wales. Evans spent two years with the weaver, and the experience transformed his life. It was this time and this tongue he was reaching back to in telling it,

> *Learning to weave, sometimes studying*
> *Books, with every intention*
> *Of becoming a scholar.*

It was here that he felt the first strong stirrings to emigrate to America.

As in Virginia, the opening of land for settlement in Pennsylvania had brought with it an insatiable hunger for cheap labor to work it. In the North however, the indenture system under which people were recruited and signed to contracts before emigrating from England was replaced by the redemption method: People, usually non-English, were encouraged to go to the New World by ship captains who in exchange for passage would sell their charges into service when the passengers arrived in America.

This removed the few remaining safeguards of English law and put life-and-death authority into the hands of the ship captains and owners, and led, as we shall see, to some of the cruelest abuses of the transportation of human beings to America.

The Welsh settlement of Pennsylvania had begun as early as 1682, before William Penn himself had seen the land he had designated for the Quakers. A vast parcel known as the Welsh Tract, originally thirty thousand acres and later doubled, covering parts of Pennsylvania and the present state of Delaware, was to be set aside as a sort of national redoubt where the Welsh would enjoy religious freedom and establish cultural independence through use of their mother tongue. Neither dream was realized, as the Welsh in America became Anglicized to a degree they had been able to resist in Britain.

Nevertheless, the place names in certain parts of Pennsylvania —Merion (Merioneth), Radnor (Radnorshire), Newcastle, Pencader—took on a strong Welsh flavor. It is through these early ties with Wales, and through the preaching and writing of Iaco ab Dewi, a Welsh Quaker convert who returned to his homeland to preach the quietist faith, that David Evans first came to believe the promises of religious freedom and a better life in America.

There was also the matter of the books. America was the land where a poor man could acquire not only land but learning; there was room and tolerance for the cultivation of one's mind in a place where the weaver's combination of craft and scholarship could be nurtured, extended, and deepened, where a boy was not confined to the prison of reliving his father's life. What to other men was the promise of streets paved with gold was to David Evans a vision of endless shelves lined with books:

> *I sailed across the wide ocean*
> *To Pennsylvania to earn money*
> *So that I could purchase many books.*

First, however, there was the passage and the payment exacted for it. In his poem, Evans does not describe his crossing; if it was unremarkable, then he was fortunate compared to later redemptioners, particularly the Palatine Germans. Perhaps

Evans emigrated early enough and from close enough to England to avoid the extreme privation which prevailed later. The passage price, however, was fairly typical of the prevailing rate throughout the eighteenth century. For a ticket worth about six pounds, or approximately a half-year's wages for a free laborer in America, Evans was bound to indenture himself for four years.

This time, there was to be no study, not even the simple craft pleasures of weaving. Sold to a master in Merion, near Philadelphia, Evans was put to work "hewing and uprooting trees"— land clearing, the most arduous of colonial labor, work that was spared black slaves because they were too valuable.

"I did not," admitted Evans, "find much happiness."

Observing the shortage of men in the skilled manual trades in the colonies, Evans decided "during this period of hard labor" to become a carpenter. The way to the bookshelves was by means of the plane and the level, and "though I had little instruction . . . God helped me wondrously."

When he had served out his term, Evans traveled "as soon as possible" to the town of Newcastle, Pennsylvania, where he worked for a time as a carpenter. Always a man of a strong religious bent, Evans found that "the loose morals of the townfolk caused me loathing." In time, the devout young carpenter left Newcastle and headed for Philadelphia, "hoping there to find happiness."

For a while he worked at his trade cheerfully, earning "some money and also some respect"; but tiring of city life, he moved to nearby Radnor, where he spent more than a year practicing carpentry. As yet he had neither land nor business of his own, nor any real intention of acquiring either:

> *Through all these journeyings, know*
> *That books were my chief source of pleasure,*
> *So that, between the books and carpentry,*
> *My poor mind became completely wearied.*

He was a scholar in a land with scant respect for scholarship, a reluctant carpenter in a country with an insatiable appetite for the skills of people in the building trades.

Meditating sadly on my condition,
God put it in my mind to put everything aside.

He became a preacher, self-ordained, ministering among the Welsh. And like that other, greater carpenter, he soon attracted the attention of the established authorities. In September of 1710, the Presbytery of Philadelphia, on being informed that "David Evans, a lay person, had taken upon him publicly to teach or preach among the Welsh in the Great Valley, Chester County, it was unanimously agreed, that said Evans had done very ill, and acted irregularly in thus invading the work of the ministry, and he was thereupon censured."

Still, what Evans had preached was only the accepted word. He was twenty-nine, obviously devout, and was fluent in both English and Welsh. The ministers of the Presbytery, in their wisdom, decided that the proper method for dealing with David Evans was that he lay aside all other business for a twelvemonth, "and apply himself to learning and study," under the Reverend Jedediah Andrews of Philadelphia.

According to Evans,

I spent six years learning languages
And the arts with their plentiful riches,
Sometimes pursuing my studies in schools,
Sometimes a teacher to scholars.

In September 1712, the people of the two adjoining congregations of the Welsh Tract and the Tredyffrin, or Great Valley, petitioned for his ordination as their pastor; but though the Presbytery, after examining Evans, concluded that he had made considerable progress, it was recommended that he pursue further study.

After special examinations, Evans was admitted to Yale College, where in 1713 he was awarded the degree of master of arts. It was and is a remarkable achievement of intellect and will. A man who began his working life as an eight-year-old shepherd, who emigrated to a foreign country where he worked as a bound laborer, had made himself into an educated man.

He was grudgingly accepted, after being again examined "by infallible divine preachers," who gave him permission to preach, though only on probation.

A year later he was ordained in Pencader, "as a poor minister to my fellow countrymen." He was now thirty-three years old.

What David Evans had earned had come to him too late. The process had taken so long, had asked so much of him in terms of patience and in deference to men he clearly did not respect, that it embittered him and made him defensive. He was a scholar on whom judgment was being passed by men who were nothing more than provincial preachers, not one of whom had started with as little or achieved as much on faith as Evans had. He never got over the reluctant acceptance of the legitimacy of his vocation.

As a member of a nonconformist faith, Evans was part of a tradition of dissent that extended beyond the religious realm into politics. Here in America, in the absence of an established church, there was a constant fear that political and religious mastery might be instituted at the expense of colonial freedom. Settlement in the colonies had been so scattered and shifting, involving so many people of dissenting faiths, that the establishment of any broad system of religious orthodoxy had been impossible. Laws officially recognizing the Anglican faith tended to be winked at, and taxes imposed for its support led to public protest, while the appearance in New England of the Anglican Society for the Propagation of the Gospel aroused fears of an ecclesiastical conspiracy against all American liberties. Resistance to one kind of oppression was easily translated into resistance to all, and in the colonies pulpits became sources of expressions of dissent.

"Some have thought it warrantable and glorious to disobey the civil powers," declared the Presbyterian minister Jonathan Mayhew in 1750, in the most widely printed sermon of the pre-Revolutionary era, "in cases of very great and general oppression . . . to rise unanimously even against the sovereign himself . . . to vindicate their natural and legal rights, to break the yoke of tyranny, and free themselves and posterity from inglorious servitude and ruin."

As a dissenting preacher, Evans found himself plagued by dissenters within his congregation. It was the same problem that was to haunt the American colonies under the Articles of Confederation: Once one authority is rejected, what is to prevent people from rejecting subsequent authorities? In a time of intense religious feeling, when people had founded entire communities upon flight from persecution, where new congregations were spinning off from old like spiral nebulae over doctrinal disputes, Evans's was not the consoling temperament ideal for reconciling feuding factions. Excitable, high-spirited, Evans remained at his first church for four years, "Preaching the Holy Gospel, and administering the Sacraments of Christ according to the Rules of Scripture." Then gradually among his congregation certain differences of opinion began to assert themselves:

> *Until the Devil by crooked means*
> *Kindled a blaze of devilish plots.*

The devil's incendiary in this instance appears to have been a parishioner named Samuel Jones, whose differences with the redeemed minister became both heated and irreconcilable,

> *So that there was no sign of peace,*
> *Alas! nor hope of a quiet life.*

The quarrels so aggravated and exhausted Evans that he sank into despair:

> *My poor heart faltered,*
> *So that I could not minister*
> *On account of the sorrow that pained me.*

It was with both resignation and rancor that Evans, after four years at Pencader, accepted the call to be pastor of the Welsh church at Tredyffrin. Here he was to remain more than twenty years. It was also where he was to complete the work most closely associated with his name.

Evans published two books while at Tredyffrin. The first, a catechism called *A Help for Parents and Heads of Families,* appeared in 1732; *The Minister of Christ*, first given as a sermon, was published some months later. The printer of both volumes was Benjamin Franklin. Here, it seems, was Evans's great opportunity to connect with the intellectual life of his time. Franklin was the most advanced thinker of that place and time; in that same year he had founded the Library Company of Philadelphia, the colonies' first free library. Regrettably, his and Evans's was never more than a business relationship.

While at Pencader, Evans had married "a beautiful girl full of grace,

> *Fair and tender, full of gentleness,*
> *To take care of me in the wilderness.*

There and at Tredyffrin they had six children, four of whom, three daughters and a son, died in childhood. The two surviving sons, both intending to enter the clergy, graduated from Yale, but one died at the start of his ministry.

At Tredyffrin, Evans preached the gospel of Christ and his virtues,

> *An all-sufficient Saviour*
> *To every repentant sinner.*

Still even here he was unable to avoid the doctrinal disputes that split the churches of the eighteenth century. The differences in America, as in Wales, arose from the same sources: the nature of Christ and the nature of God's grace, the power of sin and the power of salvation, God's hold and the hold of the devil.

This was at the full flood tide of the Protestant discovery of direct communication with the Almighty, and the role of the clergy—indeed, the justification for their existence—was a matter of almost constant dispute and redefinition. In Tredyffrin this issue was personalized by the reappearance of "the father of strife," Samuel Jones, who "there found

> *Skillful and crooked means*
> *To cause contention and disagreement.*

Evans found himself once again on the defensive, "bitter and sorrowful against wranglers

> *Until their unceasing disputing*
> *Weakened my strength and all my mental faculties.*

Once again, he slid into depression. "The sadness of Melancholy disheartened me greatly,

> *Apart from revealling that there was no sign of an end*
> *To this erroneous and bitter quarrelling.*

In the fall of 1740, Evans was dismissed as pastor, the majority of his congregation sympathizing with the "New Side" branch of the denomination, while Evans remained with the "Old Side." He was charged with heterodoxy, not preaching enough in the Welsh language, and church tyranny.

Before he left Tredyffrin, however, Evans had his moment. Addressing his fickle congregation, he confined his farewell sermon to a single sentence: "Goats I found you, and goats I leave you."

At Pilesgrove, in New Jersey, it was never quite the same. He was preaching entirely in English now, to a congregation of English, Irish, and Germans; there were no longer the Welsh family and place names to suggest his youth and early ambitions. His surviving son, also a minister to a Welsh congregation, found himself caught in the same web of disputes, and fell also into depression,

> *So that in sorrow he crossed the ocean*
> *To seek the haven of peace.*

Evans must have felt at times like this that he was cursed, with the worst aspects of his own life, the things he'd already suffered through, being reincarnated in his son's.

He continued his work. Removed from his countrymen, he was absolved at last of their quarrels. He published a third book, *Law and Gospel: Or, Man Wholly Ruined by the Law, and Recovered by the Gospel.* Drawn from his sermons, it was printed, also by Franklin, in 1748.

His wife remained his "great mercy"; his comfort on his difficult pilgrimage,

> *During all the strife and tribulation,*
> *And up to the present she has continued to succor me*
> *Lovingly in my grey-haired debility.*

Evans was a complex man, more intelligent and driven and volatile than the simple, stalwart immigrants of American folklore. Like the stick-figure colonial settler, he had crossed the ocean, worked the land, risen from humble beginnings, and transformed himself by achievement. Yet disappointment dogged him all his days; a resentment not present in his published religious works suffuses his memoir, written in the verse he had learned from the Welsh weaver when both Evans and his dream were young.

In the intensity of this feeling, this linking of religious and political liberty, Evans resembles the orators and pamphleteers of the coming era of Revolution. One of them, Patrick Henry, in the speech that made his reputation, defended the Virginia civil authorities' right to tax the salaries of Church of England ministers, by attacking the British Crown. The king who had disallowed the colonial act had, said Henry, "from being the father of his people degenerated into a tyrant, and forfeits all rights to his subjects' obedience."

David Evans didn't live to turn his rage against the British Crown. He died in 1750. He was a man who bitched about his job, who complained of bad luck. He was quarrelsome and disputatious and balked at putting up with what he felt he shouldn't have to. He consoled himself increasingly as he grew older with reveries of a simple, independent, rustic existence. In these things most of all he had become an American.

Voices

Is it because you have left your native land at the risk of your lives and fortunes to toil for your mother country, to load her with wealth, that you are to be rewarded with a loss of your privileges? Are you not of the same stock? Was the blood of your ancestors polluted by a change of soil? Were they freemen in *England* and did they become slaves by a six-weeks' voyage to *America?*

—JOSEPH GALLOWAY
*A Letter to the People of
Pennsylvania, 1760*

14

WILLIAM MORALEY

IN 1725, a young Englishman named William Moraley was browsing outside the Royal Exchange in London, reading the notices posted on the columns there advertising ships bound for America. This was at a time when, according to one Londoner, advertisements for emigration to the colonies were all but impossible to ignore, "offering the most seducing encouragement to adventurers under every possible description; to those who are disgusted with the frowns of fortune in their native land; and to those of an enterprising disposition, who are tempted to court her smiles in a distant region." Moraley's mental state at the time seems to have represented a blend of both emotions.

He was a man who felt cheated, done out of his father's remnant of what had once been a substantial Moraley family estate by the indifference of his own mother. Remarried, living in Newcastle, she had obliged her son William to go off to London to seek his fortune on a stake of twelve shillings, "she assuring me," Moraley recalled later, "she could not raise any more, by reason of her Marriage."

Once in the city, Moraley found the money was quickly spent, and he was soon reduced to going about unshaven, wearing a worn-out, uncombed wig, a torn, unwashed shirt, and stockings riddled with holes. Not surprisingly, he was unable to find regular work, though trained as a watchmaker after an earlier, unsuccessful apprenticeship as a lawyer's clerk. Informed by "a Gentleman" of her son's pinched circumstances, Moraley's mother replied that she had done all she could for him, and when threatened with legal action countered with a promise to leave her son out of her own will if she was not left alone. The gentleman, intent on pursuing the matter, was determined to take it to court. Moraley, meanwhile, grown despondent over this combination of poverty and rejection, had utterly lost heart.

"Not caring what became of me," he remembered, "it entered into my Head to leave England, and sell myself for a Term of Years into the American Plantations."

From the earliest days of settlement, the American colonies represented to various elements in Europe a new and hopeful alternative to what was seen as an increasing and dangerous Old World corruption. Founded at the high-water mark of the assertion of English individual liberties, used by writers like Locke and Voltaire as examples of man and society in a simpler and therefore more desirable state, the colonies were also propagandized by the promoters of emigration—the producers of the pamphlets and posters that Moraley was now studying—as preserves of a simple, upright social life and unique political freedom.

As he stood outside the Royal Exchange dressed in his shabby clothes, gawking at the ads about America, an almost classic country bumpkin, Moraley was approached by a crimp. Having sized up Moraley as a man in search of better circumstances, the stranger offered himself to be of service. And though Moraley might suspect the man of having a design to inveigle him, the stranger assured him of his sincerity and offered to treat Moraley to a mug of beer while he imparted what he proposed.

"The man appearing sincere," said Moraley, "I gave Ear to him."

The crimp in turn gave Moraley, in addition to a mug of beer, a shave. While sprucing up the down-at-heels youngster, Moraley's new friend outlined his plan. There was a ship at Limehouse, sailing in three or four days for Philadelphia, in Pennsylvania, "a Country producing everything necessary for the Support of Life." When Moraley's time was expired, he would be free to live in any of the provinces of America. And while watchmakers were not as much in demand in the colonies as bricklayers, carpenters, bakers, tanners, and weavers, all of whom were traditionally indentured for a term of four years, the agent said he could probably get Moraley admitted if he would consent to serve for five, thus taking for his own advantage a year beyond what the law required. After the men had another beer, Moraley agreed to go.

The agent then took Moraley to the office of the lord mayor, "where I was sworn as not being a married Person, or an Apprentice by Indenture." The agent paid the clerk the obligatory shilling tip. Next the two men went to a stationer's shop near London Bridge, where an indenture of servitude was drawn, which Moraley signed. He and his companion then headed for Billingsgate, where they boarded a boat which headed down the Thames for Limehouse, where they arrived just before noon. The ship was the *Bonetta*, of about 200 tons, James Reed, master. There were twenty men on board, all indentured servants, all headed for the same destination. "As soon as I entered," said Moraley, "my Friend left me to think better of it, and wished me a prosperous Voyage, and a good Wife."

Alone, standing on deck, Moraley noticed several of his fellow bondsmen in a state of extreme dejection, as though repenting the rashness of their decision. He was soon distracted however by a lunch of mutton chops, the first meat the hungry youth had seen in four days, and which he washed down with two more quarts of beer. In the afternoon there was more free beer for the taking on deck, and the master and mate were gone for the day. Prowling in one of the cabins, Moraley found some raisins and made off with two pounds. In the warm glow of mutton, beer, and a private stash of snacks, Moraley settled into his first night of servitude.

The following day, while the *Bonetta* still lay at anchor, Moraley sent a letter by way of the mate's wife to the gentleman who was pressing Moraley's legal case against his mother, informing him where the young man was, "and whither bound." The counselor sent a return message saying that Moraley "deserved all possible Hardship for my Imprudence, in leaving him at a time when he was doing me Justice, by prosecuting my Mother."

Three days later, while the ship was under sail, the *Bonetta* was hailed by a boatman, who asked if there was one Moraley on board. When told there was an order from the lord mayor to bring him back, the mate insisted that Moraley had been discharged by the captain and was gone. Accepting this, the boatman turned away and headed back. Moraley was actually fast asleep, kept below along with the rest of the bondsmen to prevent them from hearing what was going on. Moraley seems to have interpreted this unheeded order as a great missed opportunity of his life, for when he was informed about the boatman's inquiry, "I curs'd my Fate ten thousand times."

Here, as elsewhere in his narrative, Moraley displays a disappointing passivity; in any situation, he is the one acted upon rather than the initiator. He suggests that he has been taken advantage of, yet he refuses again and again to act in his own behalf or even oppose or condemn his exploiters. He expects to be victimized, and writes off as bad luck the repeated instances of this, thus disclaiming his responsibility for what has happened to him. The title of his account of his adventures gives him away: *The Infortunate*. He is playing for sympathy.

After a hard but otherwise uneventful voyage of some fourteen weeks, the *Bonetta* docked at Philadelphia on the day after Christmas. The men were given liberty to visit the town, where Moraley traded his coat for a quart of rum and also bought a quart of cider. Back aboard ship, the 'Voluntary Slaves" were sold off one by one. Moraley's turn came last, when he was sold for eleven pounds to Isaac Pearson, a clockmaker and goldsmith who lived at Burlington, New Jersey. "He was a Quaker," noted the bibulous Moraley, "but a Wet one."

Leaving Philadelphia, Moraley headed for Burlington by boat, "where I got myself Drunk for the first time after my Arrival, and first experienced the strength of Rum." Arriving at his master's house. Moraley was served dumplings and boiled beef, stripped of his rags, and given in their place a torn shirt and an old coat. This confusing mixture of indulgence and privation was to characterize his term of servitude.

Moraley's master, Isaac Pearson, "a humane man," employed him in his business. He worked at his trade of watchmaker, and "I continued satisfied with him for sometime." When they clashed it was over the issue of personal liberty.

"Being desirous to settle at Philadelphia during the rest of my Servitude," Moraley told Pearson that he would stay no longer and wished to be sold to some other master. Pearson refused. Moraley insisted until his demand made his master "cross to me." Moraley was now up against the harsh limits of the forced-labor system, subject to the arbitrary power of a single man backed by the authority of the law. Moraley attempted to run away but was recaptured and put in prison. Upon consenting to serve out his time with Pearson, Moraley was released. He and Pearson appeared before the mayor of Philadelphia, who officially reconciled them. "So I returned back to Burlington," Moraley recalled, where he remained for three years. The clockmaker, his authority over Moraley now firmly established, promised to release his servant from the obligation of the final two years of his indenture. "I was ever after perfectly pleased with my Master's behaviour to me, which was generous."

His collision with the wall of the colonial indentured-labor system seems to have knocked the spirit out of Moraley. He withdrew into the routine of his tasks. There were no more attempts at escape. He also seems to have abandoned all thought of an autonomous future in America. There is no mention of plans to set up in the clockmaking trade on his own when his term is over. Nor does he seem to consider acquiring land. There is an air of defeat about Moraley. If he cannot be a free, autonomous man here, perhaps he cannot be one anywhere.

The thought of the colonies as the preserve of traditional liberties under attack in England was an idea increasingly popular up to the time of the Revolution with Whigs on both sides of the Atlantic. A combination of ministerial corruption, effeminizing luxury, and slothful negligence, it was argued, was unraveling England's moral fiber, so that the prime safeguard of individual liberty, an independent Parliament, was being undermined by administrative manipulation on the part of people immediately around the king. The preservation of individual liberties in England might well depend on people standing up for them in America.

"O let not Britain seek to oppress us," Benjamin Franklin, a man intimately familiar with British politics, wrote in 1753, "but like an affectionate parent endeavor to secure freedom to her children; they may be able one day to assist her in defending her own."

All this came too late for William Moraley. Yet Moraley was an able man and on occasion a brave one. While crossing the Delaware River in a canoe with a Mrs. Lambert, a relative of his master's, Moraley and the woman were thrown into the current when the canoe overturned. "So being in Danger," Moraley recalled, almost as if in surprise at his own capacity for action, "I forgot my own for her Safety." Taking the woman about the waist with one arm, Moraley swam with the other, carrying her across to the other side. The woman and her family never forgot this incident. Moraley was rewarded with five pounds by the girl's father, and from then on, whenever Moraley was in that part of the country, "I generally made his House my resting Place, where I was very civilly treated."

As a watchmaker, Moraley was often sent by his master on house calls, dispatched to clean clocks and watches in various parts of the countryside. "Almost every Inhabitant, in the county," he observed, "have a Plantation, some two or more." There were no leaseholds as in England, and no idle class of gentlemen living on the labor of farmers. The plantation owners worked the land themselves "with the Assistance both of bought Servants and Negroes." The land was not only abundant, it was fruitful, producing in addition to "almost every Fruit, Herb and Root as grows in Great Britain, but divers Sorts unknown to us." The country was well wooded, rich with game and fish, and the inhabitants generous and hospitable. "I have travelled some Hundreds of Miles at no Expence, Meat and Drink being bestowed upon all the Subjects of Great Britain; for they strive to out-do one another in Works of good Nature and Charity."

"In short," Moraley concludes, "it is the best Poor Man's

Country in the World; and, I believe, if this was sufficiently known by the miserable Objects we have in our Streets, Multitudes would be induced to go thither."

Yet he failed utterly to heed his own advice. Here again Moraley seems to have been undermined by his fatal lack of confidence. Even in the ideal poor-man's country, with land and food and opportunity for everyone, he did not see himself as the owner of a farm or the proprietor of a business. In the same self-abnegating way, his narrative keeps skittering away from his own story, his feelings and observations. He not only includes long and crowded descriptions, amounting to lists, of colonial animal and plant life, but meanders off into the as-told-to adventures of certain rogues he has met. These pastoral interludes and fashionably picaresque episodes seem inserted apologetically, as if Moraley were not convinced at heart that his own story deserved the attention of others.

Among the natural occurrences that Moraley observed was a flight of what seems to have been passenger pigeons, a species eventually eliminated by its own abundance and tameness. As Moraley watched, "a prodigious Flight of Pidgeons" appeared, so dense that it "almost darkened the Air." The pigeons infested the fields and villages, alighted in flocks, "and rested upon the Tops of Houses and Barns in a starving condition, being by Necessity drove from some other Country." So tame were the pigeons that they became the food of the inhabitants for an entire month.

The American planters, free from the rack renting which cursed the English farmer, with their land worked by indentured servants and Negro slaves to whom they paid no wages, "are become the richest Farmers in the World." As they lived "in Affluence and Plenty," said Moraley, "you will taste of their Liberality."

In contrast was the condition of the Negroes, which was "very bad, by reason of the Severity of the Laws." For the least offense there was the severest sort of punishment; and while some amends were offered by their being allowed to marry, this also had the effect of discouraging running away. Worst of all, "their posterity are slaves without redemption." Slaves who attempt to

run away and are caught "are unmercifully whipped," and there
is no law against murdering them. Should a man kill another
man's slave, he is obliged only to reimburse the owner for damages.

Though theoretically within the protection of the law, bought
servants also learned that conditions in America could be "very
hard." While the indentures drawn in England stipulated that
servants on their arrival were to be given the "Necessaries . . .
such as Clothes, Meat and Drink," collecting from a master who
welshed on the deal was quite another matter. According to Moraley, when a servant protested against his master for noncompliance before a magistrate, the master's word was generally
accepted over the servant's, "and it is ten to one if he does not
get his Licks for his Pains, as I have experienced upon the like
Occasion, to my Cost."

Servants who attempted to escape had the entire legal machinery of the colonies against them. There was a reward for
taking up any person who traveled without a pass, an offer which
extended throughout the colonies, plus the additional reward offered by the master. Printed ads were also set up "against the
Trees and public Places," as well as in the newspapers. This
vigorous enforcement made successful escape all but impossible,
yet servants were perpetually running away."

"A hot Pursuit being made, brings them back, when a Justice
settles their Expences, and the Servant is oblig'd to serve a
longer time."

In addition, though the legal codes in the colonies had the same
basis as those in England, local by-laws allowed for certain vari-
ations which, in the name of efficient justice, repressed individual
liberty. Nothing was more common, said Moraley, "then to see
Men committed to Prison without a legal Warrant, by the Arbitrary Authority of the Magistrates." He had himself, he claimed,
"been twice committed in this Manner."

The colonial America Moraley shows us is a country of people
at odds with themselves, or perhaps with their system of government, beckoning the poor and dissatisfied with one hand, offering
hospitality and the prospect of abundance, while the other hand
remains closed, a fist of retribution ready to strike down anyone

who gets out of line or who challenges the forced-labor system on which the country's wealth is founded. The desire to be virtuous is in conflict with the necessity to be firm.

"Being of a Temper not easily cast down by Adversity," Moraley continued, "though down," to "wait for a Trump Card to repay me what I had lost." Following his reconciliation with his master, Moraley was sent to an ironworks in which Pearson had invested, some seven miles from Burlington. Here he spent his time at a pleasing variety of tasks, sometimes as a blacksmith, at others "in the Water, stark naked, among Water Snakes"; he sometimes hunted "Cows" in the woods, "and sometimes I got drunk for Joy that my Work was ended."

When the ironworks was completed, Moraley's term of servitude had expired, and he became free. " 'Tis impossible to Express the Satisfaction I found," Moraley exulted, "at being released from the precarious Humour and Dependence of my Master." Outfitting his former servant "in an indifferent Manner," the clockmaker gave Moraley his discharge "to find out a new Way of Living." There was no new suit of clothes, no land, no money, seed, tools, or provisions. And no complaint from Moraley. After three years' servitude in America, he was as broke as the day he arrived.

In keeping with his earlier, frustrated wish, Moraley went to Philadelphia, where he "served with one Edmund Lewis, a brisk young Clock-maker." The two did not get along, Lewis "being unsettled, and of a roving Temper (like Master, like Man!)," noted Moraley, who left him and moved on, though he may have signed some sort of indenture first; at least Lewis was to claim he did.

Moraley now drifted from job to job until he was reduced to sleeping in a hayloft and living on handouts from some of his old London companions. They put him up to courting "an old ugly Maid" who owned a "good store of Pewter and Brass." A match was made, and the wedding day was set. The night before the marriage, Moraley's intended gave him a gold ring. Later that night he encountered some of his acquaintances, who got the ring from Moraley, sold it, and spent the money. "So," he concluded without any real regret, "I lost my Sweet-heart."

"This Life not being likely to last long, and the People's Good-nature beginning to cool," Moraley "set my Wits to Work how to get home." Not hearing of a ship bound for England, he wandered the countryside cleaning clocks and watches and working, not very competently, as a tinker. Without a steady job or a place to live, but possessing the authorized freedom of signed, fulfilled indentures, he lived in the present, wandering from odd job to odd job, "always endeavouring to ingratiate myself into the People's Favour by a modest and decent Behaviour." He tells people stories and gives them his account of England, acquiring a certain reputation for perception and intelligence, "though upon Occasion I could rake with the best of them, and change my Note as a proper time offer'd."

In his account of this part of his life, Moraley seems to have decided to depict himself as a rogue and an adventurer, his own picaresque hero, a role that doesn't suit him, as it almost always turns out that he is the person suffering the greater disadvantage.

While passing through Trent-Town (Trenton), New Jersey, Moraley discovers the young lady whom he had saved from drowning. On the death of her father, she has inherited a fortune of three thousand pounds. The heiress invites Moraley to have dinner with her; it seems as if his long-awaited hour has struck, that he will become the fulfilled hero of his own adventurous tale, an American country squire settled in New Jersey on the strength of his own daring; but when the dinner is over and the lady has satisfied her curiosity about how things are with Moraley, she offers him tea and gives him three pounds to assist him in returning home. As if heaping dishonor on disappointment, on his way back from Trenton, Moraley encounters a mountain lion which chases him up a tree, where the would-be adventurer is left stranded for two hours.

Returned once again to Burlington, working for a blacksmith, Moraley "now began to be heartily tir'd with these Ramblings, and endeavour'd to make Friends with Masters of Ships, in order to get my Passage." Through a Quaker friend, he is referred to a "Capt. Peel, whose Ship then lay at the Key, and would sail in about five Weeks."

As Moraley was without experience as a sailor, Peel offered to take the former clockmaker, blacksmith, and tinker on as ship's cook—further indication why ship's food during this era was universally regarded as vile. "I immediately struck a Bargain," Moraley crowed happily, "and at his Desire assisted the Crew in stowing the ship."

Always conscientious, Moraley worked hard at his new job, apparently to his skipper's satisfaction. The day before the ship was to sail, Peel invited all his friends aboard, after ordering Moraley to prepare a dinner of mutton and beef for forty. Accepting compliments "for my good management," Moraley made his way to the Punch Bowl, where "I made a shift to get myself drunk before Three O'Clock."

After a stop for provisions at Philadelphia, the ship headed down the Delaware, where the following day the vessel paused at the town of Chester. Here, while Moraley was admiring the town, with its "Pleasante Gardens and Orchards," he was over-taken by Edmund Lewis, the "brisk young Clock-maker" Mor-aley had worked for in Philadelphia. Claiming Moraley was still under indenture to him, Lewis demanded that the captain give him up. The ship by this time was already under sail. Faced with a choice of going to sea or giving up his claim, the indignant Lewis scrambled back into his boat, "and so," says Moraley, "I escaped being carried back." Getting into servitude was nothing compared to getting out of it.

It was December by the time Moraley set foot in England again, three years and eight months after his departure, looking like anything but a man who had found his fortune in America. He had worn the same shirt for fifteen weeks, was in a "misera-ble" pair of breeches, torn waistcoat and stockings, an old hat, and a pair of shoes held together with pack thread. "I looked," he admits, "not unlike the Picture of Robinson Crusoe."

In this sorry state, Moraley set out for Newcastle. After his experiences in America, he had made up his mind to reconcile himself with his mother, evidently preferring the known to the unknown devil. Cadging meals, traveling on foot, staying one night in a hall and the next in a hovel, he arrived at last at Newcastle, where he "met with a very kind Reception" among his relatives, with whom he stayed for some three weeks. After this he returned to his mother's, where he lived for three years until her death, when once again, as he tells it, he was swindled out of his rightful estate.

"He was an easy and good-natured fellow," an anonymous postscript describes Moraley, "whose wants were few, and cares, less." Yet there was much more to him than that, an ache of unfulfillment that suffuses every line he writes, and undoubtedly prompted him to set down his memoir.

A man who left and returned to England in rags, he was described as a "spend-thrift," and perhaps he was, but not in the sense intended. What Moraley wasted was not money but himself. His life was a series of concessions in the name of necessity, as though, lacking in examples, he didn't know what to demand of himself or others, or who to blame for his frustrating inability to achieve personal independence or material success. He lacked the animating confirmation of a shared sense of grievance.

The other elements were there: the sense of injury; the intimate experience of the abuse of arbitrary power; the civilizing hunger not for vengeance but for justice; the fundamental optimism and diligence; the steadfastness rising occasionally to courage; the tolerance for hardship and disgust at unearned privilege; the awareness of posterity and the yearning for some achievement to catch its eye; the implicit willingness to accept limitations on power including, if required, the opportunity for his own.

He was a generation too early. In the heightened atmosphere of the American Revolution, the pressures within him would have been equalized. He could have transcended himself, found resonance for his grievances, applications for his diligence and self-sacrifice and occasional courage, and personal justification in the great adventure he so obviously sought.

The Virginian George Washington understood the potential of feeling among men like Moraley. When at the beginning of the Revolutionary War Virginia's royal governor, Lord Dunmore, offered freedom to indentured servants and slaves who embraced the British cause, Washington branded him "the most formidable enemy of America if some expedient cannot be hit upon to convince the servants and slaves of the impotency of his designs."

William Moraley didn't live to see, in the conception of a new nation, fortune pass him by yet another time. He died in 1762, in Newcastle, where, we are told, "he contrived to make a livelihood as a Watch-maker." His hunger for justice remained unsatisfied.

"Whatever hardships I may lie under in This life," Moraley wrote at the conclusion of his narrative, "They are infinitely preferable to an Estate got by illegal means; for tho' ill Persons may and do thrive for a while; yet a time will come that will bring to light the hidden Things of Darkness, when everyone will be rewarded according to his Works."

Voices

My mother was born in Scotland. When twelve to fourteen years of age, she was, with many others, forcibly taken,
carried on board a ship, and brought to Pennsylvania. She
was here sold as a servant to Caleb Pusey, near Chester,
and served her time out. When free, she married William
Coles, and settled at Nottingham. Some time after, my father married her.

—JOSHUA BROWN,
"BIOGRAPHICAL SKETCHES,"
The Friend, Philadelphia,
Volume XXXIV

15

SALLY DAWSON AND SALLY BRANT*

IN 1793, a nine-year-old girl named Sally Dawson was brought by her father to the home of a well-to-do- Quaker family in Philadelphia. After a fifteen-day trial period, the girl was indentured to serve the family for eight years. In return for her eight years' work, Sally would by contract have received, in addition to "meat, drink, lodging and washing," and instruction in the "art, craft and mystery of housewifery," a total of about six months' instruction in reading, writing, and elementary mathematics.

Though born in America, Sally Dawson faced the same sort of individual restrictions as laborers imported from abroad. Probably her parents had been indentured servants; her father may have been working for someone else and have sold his daughter off in a desperate attempt to raise the capital necessary to acquire his own piece of land; for while in the earliest years in Virginia,

* People and incidents in this narrative are adapted from "Female Servants in Eighteenth Century Philadelphia," by Sharon V. Salinger, in the *Pennsylvania Magazine of History and Biography*, January 1983.

Maryland, and Pennsylvania servants had been granted tracts of land as part of their freedom dues, as the colonies' population increased, and the more easily accessible and cultivable land grew scarce, freedom dues came to mean only the *right* to purchase up to fifty acres of usually remote and uncleared frontier territory. The capital had to come from somewhere else.

In a study of 158 men brought as indentured servants into Maryland, Russell R. Menard observed that not one was able to become a freeholder within two years after completing his term of servitude. To own land, the freed servant either had to pay surveyor's and clerk's fees for a patent or buy existing property from a landholder. The freedman would then have to find some way to live while the land was cleared, adequate shelter erected, and a crop planted and harvested. He would have to buy tools, seed, and livestock. All in all, it represented an enterprise severely overstretching the standard freedman's resources of a suit of clothes and three barrels of corn.

As a result, freed servants trying to start their own plantations were forced to hire themselves out as wage laborers, work as sharecroppers, or lease land in hope of acquiring the necessary capital. At the same time, they ran the risk of falling into debt, and thus sinking back into servitude. Little wonder that men like Sally Dawson's father chose to indenture a child in order to pocket the bonding fee while escaping the burden of another mouth to feed.

Opportunities for indentured women were both greater and more limited than those for men. A woman servant who was fortunate enough to marry a settler or even a planter could escape her class origins almost immediately, with the possibility of rising into the highest reaches of colonial society. There were women like Eleanor Stevenson, a runaway servant girl who married William Branthwait, Lord Baltimore's relative and deputy governor of Maryland. The very strenuousness of the efforts to establish an aristocracy of arrival in Virginia, the insistence on the social significance of the First Families, suggests the widespread need to kick over the traces of an earlier, less exalted existence. As writers such as Boswell and Defoe have suggested, and as the heavy immigration figures into early Virginia attest, a considerable quantity of colonial blue blood flowed at one time through Newgate.

The woman household servant who didn't manage to marry, and do so rather soon, could find herself slipped down the social ladder to as great a degree as her more fortunate sister had climbed up. A housemaid who spent her peak childbearing years living with and working under the supervisory eyes of her master and mistress and who obeyed the colonies' strict legal and moral rules against sexual relations with men could find herself cast out in old age, childless and alone, and forced on public charity. The option of acquiring land, clearing it, erecting buildings, planting crops, or raising stock didn't realistically exist for colonial servant women. The sole escape route was that of exchanging the labor bond for a marriage bond. It was probably for this reason that the market for women servants fluctuated so wildly, going from desperate demand at one time to what amounted to exclusion at another.

In the earliest existing account of kidnapping to the colonies, a man named Owen Evans confessed, in 1618, to insisting in the king's name that several constables assist him "to press him divers maidens to be sent to the Bermudas and Virginia." Evans's activities had so alarmed people in one area of England that more than forty young women were reported to have fled the parish of Ottery "and were not yet to be found." The women were considered so essential to establishing domestic life in Virginia that Evans, a minor official, had been willing to resort to illegal means to recruit them.

There was a limit, however, to the number of women servants a household could absorb. Women were not worked in the fields in Virginia unless, according to John Hammond, they were "nasty, beastly and not fit" for other work. The various trades, the construction and commercial crafts which were in such great demand throughout the colonial era, were by tradition closed to women. And there was as yet no colonial industrial employment of any consequence. For colonial indentured women, the choice was between domestic work and no work; and as immigration to the colonies expanded and the household jobs filled up, the demand for women servants shrank.

By the 1760s, colonial merchants were instructing ship captains and European agents to "send us no more women." Female servants, they had concluded, were "very troublesome." Women convicts had become so unpopular that at one time, a minor scandal arose when Newgate authorities, frustrated by a prison jammed with female convicts and with no colony willing to accept transportation of them, had instead simply released some of them.

Those women who did find work as household servants often discovered that servitude could turn out to be a trap even more cruelly illusory for women that it was for men. Like military personnel, women household servants were never entirely beyond the reach of command. Often owned by financially pinched people who couldn't afford either hired servants or slaves, indentured household help were commonly required to sleep in the kitchen or at the foot of their master's bed. This made it temptingly easy when a strange sound or a cry of fire occurred in the night to dispatch the nearest servant to investigate. All but devoid of privacy, household servants were required to nurse the sick, deliver messages, transmit gossip extracted from tradespeople or other families' servants, and attend services at church of their master's choice. And the best way of securing reliable help, who would accustom themselves to the master's ways and whose service would be unlikely to be interrupted by marriage or pregnancy, was to indenture them as Sally Dawson had been, as children.

In the master and mistress she drew, Sally Dawson turned out to be far more fortunate than most household indentured servants. Henry Drinker and his wife Elizabeth were people "of quality" and Quakers, with both the means and the moral admonition to treat people of every station humanely and decently. Elizabeth Drinker especially was a person of unusual perception and sensitivity, who kept a personal record covering more than forty-five years of her daily life, a diary which gives us among other things the clearest guide to what life for women indentured servants was actually like.

The Drinkers treated their servants, who included both indentured and hired workers, paternalistically. Servants were "family'' but were treated as children rather than adults, given certain special consideration in return for accepting extensive personal control. When Sally Dawson fell sick with the yellow fever that commonly struck Philadelphia in the summer, Mrs. Drinker was overwhelmed with guilt because, being ill at the time, she couldn't nurse the girl herself. Instead, Sally was sent to the hospital, which, the doctor assured Mrs. Drinker, was the best alternative to her mistress attending to her at home. Yet at another time, when Mrs. Drinker decided that Sally had misbehaved, she didn't hestitate to punish her by administering a whipping. Nevertheless, the bonds of affection between the Quaker mistress, who was given to lecturing servants on their shortcomings, and her young servant seem to have been genuine. When her term of servitude expired, Sally Dawson remained with the Drinkers as a hired live-in maid. And though Mrs. Drinker criticized Sally for having "a great call for money—to purchase finery,'' she wasn't above withholding wages from the girl at a later time when the Drinkers were short of cash.

Servants like Sally who remained with one family for a long period of time were exceptions. The Drinker household was for the most part plagued by a continuing turnover in women servants. In addition to indentured servants, the Drinkers employed free wage-earning household help, short-term live-in specialists like day nurses and wet nurses, and women hired day-to-day for piecework such as sewing and ironing. Over a period of forty years, according to Sharon V. Salinger, fifty different women worked for the Drinker family, only eight of them for more than one year. It was in the interest of the Drinkers, as it was of other well-to-do colonial families, to find reliable household workers and keep them attached to the family if possible. Nothing served this interest as well as servitude. It provided labor that was cheap, amenable to discipline, and was not free to seek more favorable employment elsewhere.

For this reason, it was very much to the master's interest to keep his women servants from marrying. A servant married was a servant lost, with her freedom purchased by some ambitious settler anxious to establish a plantation of his own, or with work interrupted and perhaps permanently impaired by pregnancy or childbearing. For the same reason, sexual relations involving women servants were strenuously discouraged and were punished with extremely rigorous penalties. In most colonies a woman indentured servant who was guilty of "bastardy" was not only required to pay the civil fines required of free unmarried mothers but was also obligated to reimburse her master for any loss of service he had suffered because of her pregnancy and confinement. Since maidservants rarely had access to independent funds, the almost invariable alternative was an extension of the term of service. It was a punishment frequently, widely, and often unfairly employed.

"From Pennsylvania down to the Carolinas," observes Richard Morris, "the master was often enriched far beyond his actual losses." In Maryland, a woman servant was sentenced to an additional year for giving birth to "a mulatto bastard," plus six months for a second child. The second child's father was required to serve six months or pay a fine, and to serve an additional nine months for the child's maintenance. A Virginia law mandated a penalty of a year's extra servitude whenever a man servant was convicted of having illicit relations with a woman servant. And in Maryland, any white woman marrying a Negro was required to become a servant for seven years, while the Negro, if he was free, would become a servant for the rest of his life.

Even servants who had actually married did not escape the intrusion of masters into their personal lives. Eleanor Bradbury, sold with her three sons to a Maryland owner, was separated from her husband, who was bought by a man in Pennsylvania. Roger Bradbury, when he had served out his time, apparently fled the colony entirely in order to rejoin his family. Nicholas Millethopp and Mary Barton, a servant couple who claimed to have been married in England, were actually prosecuted for fornication. They claimed that they had concealed their marriage on the advice of their importer, who sold them into servitude without informing their owners. Unable to provide documents or witnesses to back up their claim, they were condemned and enjoined from living together as man and wife until they had served out their terms.

The entire relationship of women household servants with their owners was rampant with sexual and social opportunity and opportunism. While a woman maidservant could be at the mercy of the attentions of her master's predatory son, an ambitious housemaid might well capitalize on the same situation to make herself an advantageous marriage or at least acquire a handsome cash settlement. Of course, such negotiations were tricky, and the advantages were overwhelmingly on the master's side. A Virginia statute of 1672 admitted that there were masters who had demanded additional time of service as reimbursement from women servants whom they had themselves made pregnant. Other than the requirement of the posting of a bond for maintenance of the child, no punishment was applied to the master for such an act. And if the unwed mother happened to have a criminal record, the master, in Virginia at least, was entitled not only to an extra year of service from her but to the child's servitude as well.

Even in the enlightened atmosphere of the Drinker household the pregnancy of a woman servant represented an ominous moral and economic threat. When in August of 1794 Elizabeth Drinker suspected that Sally Brant, a woman servant, had become pregnant, the tolerant Quaker mistress was deeply distressed. "I could not have thought," she confided to her journal, "that a girl brought up from her tenth year with the care and kindness that [she] has experienced from our family could be so thoughtless."

At such times, it appears that all the old proprietary instincts welled up, and "Our Sally" was guilty not only of a moral breach but of a serious affront to property values.

Even more disturbing was the thought that the pregnant Sally, apparently genuinely in love, seemed to feel entirely guiltless in the matter. She "appears to be full of glee," Elizabeth Drinker grumbled to her diary, "as if nothing ailed her." The Drinkers were embarrassed by Sally's pregnancy, and when the family returned to Philadelphia from their summer home in the country, Sally Brant was discreetly left behind.

With the arrival of the baby came the full moral and legal reckoning of the property-conscious colonies. While Sally Brant returned to work at the Drinker household, her baby remained with a hired nurse. The mother was not allowed to choose the baby's name. Sally Brant had planned to name the child after its father, but Mrs. Drinker, aghast at this, had instead imposed a name of her own choosing, "Catherine Clearfield"—after the Drinkers' summer country house. The father was forbidden to see Sally or his child, though he tried on several occasions, until warned by Henry Drinker that if he "found him sculking about our neighborhood he would lay him by the heels." The father never saw the child; nor, after her return to Philadelphia, did Sally Brant. The baby died.

To repay the obligation to her owners for loss of time during her pregnancy, Sally Brant was required to serve extra time amounting to the expenses of the pregnancy itself, time lost during her confinement, and the wages of the nurse, whom she had not requested and who, in effect, assumed management of the child and lost it. At the baby's death, Elizabeth Drinker expressed sadness and considered that perhaps things might have turned out better if they had tried to raise the baby in their home. Yet it was a time of widespread sickness—yellow fever, consumption, typhus, cholera—and death, untimely and unbidden, was no stranger to any household.

It should be noted that in the Drinkers' eyes and in the view of colonial authorities generally, the penalties imposed on Sally Brant were not harsh. She was the Drinkers' property, after all, whom they had purchased for a certain period, entitling them to certain rights and requiring of them certain firm measures in its defense. To own property, after all, one had to prove deserving of it.

It is also significant that what happened to Sally Brant occurred after both the Revolution and the adoption of the Constitution of the United States. People's attitudes toward indentured servitude didn't change everywhere all at once, and the full implications of what had been said in the Bill of Rights weren't immediately apparent to all. Although in this same society there were people who understood immediately that what had passed with the Revolution was the idea of unrestricted authority and arbitrary power, that notion had not touched the Drinkers, who were now in their advanced years. For this reason, it's not surprising to note Elizabeth Drinker's abiding hatred for one significant figure of the Revolution: Tom Paine. He was in her view a blasphemer, a sinister person whose true appeal was to "the ignorant, the weak and the vicious"—the class of people in which she no doubt included Sally Brant.

More to Mrs. Drinker's approval would have been the women servants who when they had worked for her had remained loyal and chaste, even though in later years a number of them, unmarried, childless, and alone, were reduced to coming to beg at the Drinkers' door. Broke, hungry, sometimes widowed, recalling their considerate treatment at the hands of the Drinkers, these women returned to the house where they had worked, some to demand freedom dues, others to request a letter of recommendation, some simply seeking a referral to the overseers of the poor.

As Sharon Salinger has pointed out, "If the women who served the wealthy Quaker family fared so poorly after gaining freedom, or leaving its employ, others must have been truly desperate."

Sally Brant was not among these returning petitioners. A year after the death of Sally's child, Elizabeth Drinker mentioned in her diary that Sally "left us before tea, 'tis eight years this month that she has been with us."

There is no further mention of Sally or the child by her former owner and mistress.

Voices

For it must be confessed by all men that they who are taxed at pleasure by others cannot possibly have any property, can have nothing to be called their own. They who have no property, can have no freedom, but are indeed reduced to the most abject slavery. . . . For one who is bound to obey the will of another is as really a slave though he may have a good master as if he had a bad one.

—STEPHEN HOPKINS
*The Rights of Colonies
Examined, 1764*

16

HENRY JUSTICE

IN OCTOBER of 1763, Nicholas van Daalen, a bookseller at The Hague, in Holland, published a catalogue announcing the upcoming sale of one of the most remarkable private libraries of the age. "Of all the catalogues of famous & Curious Libraries," van Daalen's copy gloated in what seems, for once, an example of promotional understatement, "the present one, it is apprehended is not the least worthy of your perusal & attention." The learned and curious were advised that the catalogue listed "an exceeding fine and great Collection of Books and Prints" that were intended to be sold by auction at the beginning of the following year. However, any "Prince or Nobleman or others" choosing to purchase the entire list of works, "whose cabinet or collection they will not disgrace," was invited to address himself directly to van Daalen or to the family of the owner in Rotterdam.

The collection was described by van Daalen as representing a labor of more than forty years on the part of its owner, Henry Justice, Esquire, now deceased, "Known among the Litterati for his fine edition of Virgil," and assembled "with a great deal of care, expense and trouble, not only in England and Holland, but also in his travels through Flanders, France, Italy, and Germany, where he collected the best editions of the most famous Printers, such as Aldus, the Junta's, the Stephens, Elzevier, and others.''

Even more remarkable was the fact that works which at the time were scarcely to be met with anywhere were found in this catalogue two and three times over.

Understandably not mentioned by the bookseller was the fact that this prestigious, if unusual, collection originated in theft. And that among the more curious travels undertaken by the "pursuer of Antiquities," Mr. Justice, was a journey to America as one of what were then known as "His Majesty's seven-year passengers."

Henry Justice was a man whose passion for books reached the intensity of lifelong infatuation and who ruined his career over paper and print as surely as the romantic figure who ruins himself in pursuit of a loved one.

A barrister of the Middle Temple in London, a teacher at Trinity College, Cambridge, Justice was a man of such attainments that his education, profession, and circumstances were to count against him in meliorating his sentence when he was judged to have violated not only a trust but the rules of his class.

As a teacher at Cambridge, Justice had free access to the Trinity College Library, a temptation that was to prove his undoing. For like any infatuated lover, Justice's passion was primarily physical; he seems to have been enraptured with the look and feel of books, the paper, the illumination, and typeface, rather than with any moral, ethical, or philosophical content. And he had the jealous lover's insatiable need to *possess*. Giving him access to the Trinity Library was like turning a satyr loose in a harem. Nevertheless, it must have come as a shock to a considerable number of the gentleman class, among them Mr. Justice himself, to learn that in May of 1736 he was to be indicted for theft. Justice was charged with stealing out of the Trinity College Library a Middle English Bible with cuts and Common Prayer, Newcastle's *Horsemanship,* several other books of great value, and several tracts cut out of books. These were apparently only the works that had been seized in his chambers, the tip of a literary iceberg the bulk of which had already drifted off in the direction of Holland, for the prosecution arraigned against him was of the weight usually reserved for crimes against the state. Suit had been brought by the Crown, and counsel on the prosecuting side included the attorney general, the solicitor general, and the counsel for the university.

Justice, electing not to have a fool for a client, retained three lawyers in his defense. They pleaded him not guilty at a trial that took place at the Old Bailey in the first week of May.

Unable to deny that Justice had in fact taken possession of the books, counsel for the defense maintained that they were legally his shared property. As a fellow commoner of Trinity College, to which status Justice insisted he had been admitted two years earlier, he had thereby become a member of the College Corporation, which gave him a property in the books. Justice's lawyers read several clauses out of the college's charter and statutes in support of this position, but in a debate that stretched over several hours it appeared that Justice was in fact not a member of the corporation at all but instead, according to the words of the charter granted by Henry VIII and the statutes of Elizabeth I, "only a Boarder or Lodger," in which case he could be found guilty of a felony.

After an elaborate charge was delivered to the jury, with points of law and fact explained to them in detail, the panel retired for deliberation. In "a little time," they returned, bringing in a verdict of guilty, convicting Justice of a felony within the benefit of clergy: meaning that he could be exempted from the death penalty. Justice was then charged with two other indictments, one in London and the other in Middlesex, for stealing books from the University Library in Cambridge. Though he at first pleaded not guilty to these additional charges, Justice afterward changed his plea to guilty on both counts and threw himself on the mercy of the court.

Though a felony conviction for the theft of library books may seem harsh in this era, it should be kept in mind that the books found in Justice's possession represented only a portion of the total he had taken, and that criminals of less distinction convicted of less serious crimes could expect treatment far more severe. During the same week Henry Justice was convicted, another man was sentenced to death at the Old Bailey for stealing a watch, a second for horse theft, a third for taking a silver tankard, and another for lifting a handkerchief. As rude a turn as life appeared to have taken for Henry, it was not a case of equal Justice under law.

A week after Justice's conviction, he was brought back to the Old Bailey to receive sentence. Anticipating being transported to America, Justice moved that at the discretion of the court he not be sent abroad. This would represent not only an injury to his family, particularly his children, but also to his clients, several of whom had concerns pending which could not be settled in time. In addition, transportation of Henry Justice would not represent the best interest of the university, since Justice had transferred numbers of books belonging to the library either into the hands of friends or to dealers in Holland. Were he to be transported, he could not make restitution. So, though considering his circumstances and having lived in good repute until this "unhappy mistake," Justice might himself prefer to be sent to the colonies, he did hope the university would intercede for him, in which case he would be willing to accept the alternative punishment of being burned in the hand.

The deputy recorder, while commiserating with Justice's situation, maintained that his education and attainments only aggravated the seriousness of his crime, and that the only person to apply to for clemency was the king. He then pronounced sentence: Henry Justice was to be "transported to some of his Majesty's Plantations in America, there to remain for seven Years; and that in case he returned to Great Britain or Ireland during that Time, it was Felony without Benefit of Clergy." He would be hanged.

The ship that Henry Justice was to be transported on was a veteran of the convict trade with a name as unromantic as a present-day containership's: the *Patapsco Merchant*. Her skipper, Captain Darby Lux, had made a dozen voyages with convicts, seven of them in the *Merchant,* and was to retire to Maryland, where he became a convict shipper's agent in 1738. It's doubtful if Darby Lux in all his years encountered another convict of the stature and style of Henry Justice.

On sailing day, a hundred convicted felons were walked from

Newgate prison to Blackfriar's Stairs, where they were put aboard a closed lighter and transferred to the *Patapsco Merchant* at Blackwell. Four more convicts, "Gentlemen of Distinction," including an attorney named William Wreatback, were allowed to go to Blackwell by hackney coach, while one felon, Henry Justice, "had the Privilege of going two Hours after the common Transports, and in a Coach."

Justice was accompanied in his coach by Jonathan Forward, Esquire, who represented to the shipment of convicts to eighteenth-century Maryland something on the order of what Thomas Cook did to nineteenth-century British tourism. A London merchant with connections in Maryland, Forward had jumped at the opportunity to ship convicts out of England on a government subsidy and sell them at a profit in Maryland. Though the previous contract had been for only forty shillings per convict, Forward explained that because of death, sickness, and other accidents, and because of the doubling of charges for irons and prison fees, he required to be paid three pounds apiece for Newgate felons and five pounds for those from the provinces. It has been estimated that up until the Revolution some twenty thousand convicts were imported into Maryland, and Forward had a lock on the business out of Newgate. His contract, renewed annually, was gradually increased, and he continued as contractor for more than twenty years.

Once on board the *Patapsco Merchant,* Justice and the four other distinguished gentlemen were accommodated in the captain's cabin, "which they stored with Plenty of Provisions &c. for their Voyage and Travel." It is, in all, a telling picture of eighteenth-century British social justice: Five gentlemen convicts, one found guilty of grand theft and the other four convicted armed robbers, sharing the captain's cabin and table, while below deck in irons were jammed a hundred "common transports," probably among them men guilty of felonies such as the theft of a watch or a handkerchief, and who had been spared execution only by being fortunate enough to have learned to read.

Objections to this sort of luxury and corruption in England, articulated by writers like Walpole and Gibbon, were enormously popular and influential in colonial America. In the colonies, it was maintained, the spread of independent landholding, broadened representation, the multiplicity of religious groupings, and the existence of a broad constituency of people risen from servitude combined to create what was considered a solid moral base of uncorrupted yeoman farmers, to whom "luxury and extravagance were the certain forerunners of indigence, and servility."

"Both senates and their chosers vote for pay," Lewis Morris, an American visiting in London at the time of Henry Justice's sentencing, observed of the English society around him, "and both alike their liberty betray."

Liberty, he concluded, was not to be found in England, "but lies far distant from this place somewhere, not in this, but in some other hemisphere." Luxury and privilege represented a growing danger to virtue and liberty in colonial America, where on the eve of the Revolution "Venality, Luxury and Effeminacy" were threatening to be established. They constituted another aspect of what was regarded as the growing ministerial conspiracy to expand English power at the expense of American liberty.

"In vain," recalled David Ramsey in 1778, "we sought to check the growth of luxury, by sumptuary laws; every wholesome restraint of this kind was sure to meet with the royal negative."

The *Patapsco Merchant* left London in May of 1736, destined for Maryland. Presumably she arrived in the colony later that summer. Of Henry Justice, there is no record of his arrival in the New World, or of where or how he served out his indenture. Certain things about service in Maryland allow us to make an educated guess, given Justice's attainments and background. According to the Reverend Jonathan Boucher, whose letters provide one of the most accurate descriptions of colonial Maryland and Virginia, there were few schoolmasters in those parts, and of those there were, two-thirds were from the indentured servants and convicts. Not a ship arrived, wrote Boucher, that didn't advertise teachers as well as weavers and other tradesmen. The difference was that teachers didn't sell for as good a price as men in the more practical trades.

To a Maryland planter looking for a schoolmaster to tutor his children, or perhaps for instruction in the Law, or maybe even assembling a private library, Henry Justice, with his Cambridge and Middle Temple credentials and his aesthetic judgment, would have represented a bargain indeed. Combine this with Justice's natural instinct for landing on his feet and his taste for luxury, and we can imagine that Henry Justice probably did well for himself in America. In fact, he may have bought his way out of servitude entirely.

In 1757, there appeared in Brussels the first volume in what promised to be a sumptuous reissue of the works of the Roman poet Virgil. Published at The Hague in a printing of just eighty copies, Volume I included Virgil's *Eclogues* and *Georgics,* engravings by the artist Marco Pitteri, and a foreword in Latin by the edition's sponsor and editor, Henry Justice, "bearer of the arms and Lord of Rufforth." Henry Justice had followed his stolen books into the Low Countries.

The work was dedicated to Francis I, the Holy Roman Emperor and, Justice suggests, worthy successor to Augustus Caesar, the original protector of Virgil's works. The comparison is considerably more flattery than fact; shrunken by various political and religious defections, the Holy Roman Empire at this time consisted of certain Austrian duchies, the Austrian Netherlands (Belgium and Luxembourg), Bohemia, and Hungary. Francis was emperor by virtue of having married Maria Theresa, empress of Austria, who actually governed the territories, assisted by her chancellor, Count Wenzel von Kaunitz. As emperor, Francis seems to have performed mostly ceremonial duties, outside of fathering Maria Theresa's son, later Emperor Joseph II. In saluting Francis as patron of this work, honoring Virgil's name anew, Justice also indicates the emperor's role in the restoration of his own.

"For you were designated . . . as he with Whom Virgil would seek refuge, trusting in the certainty of your protection."

Justice, living now in Rotterdam with the title "de Rufforth," appears to have been under the protection of Francis himself. "I did not have to deliberate at length," Justice declared, "as to the

God at whose feet I should deposit the work." Francis I, a man with a reputation as something of a reformer, and with an interest in celebrating the antiquity of his dwindling empire, had not simply taken Justice under his protection as an endorsement of criminal rehabilitation. There were still the books.

In some ways it seems a shame that Henry Justice didn't decide to settle in America. In his audacity and pretensions, the boundless grandiosity of his ambitions, and the overwhelming irony of his name, he could have been one of Moll Flanders's early colonial magistrates, signing warrants with a gloved, branded hand. Or a frontier figure of dubious European noble associations, like the King and the Duke in *Huckleberry Finn.* There would have been a definite appeal to a man who had cocked a snook at the values of the British ruling class, among a people who were soon about to do the same; but Henry Justice was by temperament neither rustic nor republican, and for a man of his passion for the literary works of antiquity there was really no other home but Europe.

As his beloved Virgil had died before the completion of his great epic poem, the *Aeneid,* about the founding of Rome, so Henry Justice passed away before finishing his reissue of the works of "the most noble of poets." Justice died in his house in the Wine Street, in Rotterdam, in 1763, bequeathing to his son the task of bringing out the second and third volumes of his engraved Virgil, which William Justice took the opportunity of advertising to "the Noblemen and Gentlemen that did his late Father the Honor" of subscribing to the earlier volume.

The notice was included in the catalogue listing the books in Justice's collection and announcing their upcoming sale, which appeared in October of 1763 and provides as clear a picture as we will probably ever get of the extent of the man's thefts, the depths of his passion, and the source of his appeal to a man like Francis I.

In an age when any book was a rare book, Henry Justice's collection at his death consisted of more than seven thousand items. The list alone covers some seventy pages of close-packed type, including books in folio, books in quarto, manuscripts, prints, and drawings. "The late Mr. Justice," explains the cata-

logue, "being always extremely occupied in his pursuit of Antiquities . . . as well as . . . in satisfying his great taste for fine
prints," had never found time to get his books properly bound.
So that while the works might lack "that niceness they really
merited" and not be "outwardly so beautiful to the Eye, as might
be wished," they offered the greater inward merit of large mar-
gins, "which permits the Curious to have them bound according
to their own taste and likeing."

The list of authors and titles reads like a police report of the
sacking of the Great Library at Alexandria. There are bibles,
Duns Scotus commentaries, Julius Caesar's histories, Ptolemy's
geography, Pindar, Horatius, Cicero, Terence, Catullus, Ovid,
Seneca, Homer, and of course his revered Virgil. There are dic-
tionaries, books on architecture, geography, books in English,
German, Flemish, Dutch, French, Italian, Greek, Latin—page
after page, item on item, some articles marked scarce and rare,
but only a few, to "avoid repetition," "some thousands of others, which are also rare, being left unnoticed."

Reading the list, trying to assess the lifetime of theft, finagling,
and horse trading involved in assembling such a collection, one
sees Henry Justice emerging as a kind of William Randolph
Hearst of books, living in a castle of classical literature ruthlessly
assembled from the gaping library shelves of Western Europe,
dedicating himself to the republication and embellishment of his
favorite works of Virgil, and pleading for sanctuary from the
descendant of the emperor who decreed upon Virgil's death that
no other writer would be permitted to "complete" or "improve"
his work.

"Thus the bard," Henry Justice addressed the Emperor Francis, "rising anew in a not unbecoming guise, happily has again
taken up residence under favorable auspices in the innermost
precincts of your temple, O reborn Augustus, and he seeks a
renewal of his ancestral dignity."

PART THREE
SEIZED

A young man or woman of intelligence and sensitivity falls victim to misfortune; he or she is spirited off in reduced circumstances, denied friends and comforts, and is thrown back on individual brains and pluck. Forced to hew a new identity out of the granite indifference or opposition of the world, the captive becomes independent or rich.

These are the epic ingredients, the ordinary opening out onto the marvelous, that began with the coming of the novel. Indeed, the form may have evolved out of the function to serve these stories. For there were such people, they led such lives, and their adventures were closely studied by the writers the age made novelists: Fielding, Smollett, Defoe. There was something in these lives—the expansive stress of the existence of a New World upon an older society's constraints, the sense of a common yearning toward individual liberty, the questioning of an authority no longer regarded as originating with the Almighty, the sense of society as something developed by man and therefore susceptible to change, the interconnections between exploration, settle-

ment, and coercion on the one hand and the urge to resist and rebel on the other—fundamental to the spirit of the age.

They inspired stories and characters that have accompanied us down the decades. Adventures that, through the suspension of the ordinary, suggest possibilities and fears muted in our own lives. And represent an experience at once so broad and deep, an accumulated sense of injury that, appealed to properly, could prompt people to undertake almost any risk in the name of an earned and fragile freedom.

17
HENRY PITMAN

IN JULY of 1685, a young surgeon by the name of Henry Pitman visiting relatives in the south of England was persuaded or coerced into offering medical attention to wounded troops, part of an invading force commanded by the Duke of Monmouth. The illegitimate son of Charles II of England, the duke had become the center of anti-Catholic feeling in Britain following the accession of the Catholic Duke of York to the throne as James II. Exiled to Holland, Monmouth landed at Lyme Regis, Dorset, raised a small force, and had himself proclaimed king.

Motivated initially by curiosity, then by compassion for the wounded, Pitman stayed with the duke's army until it was fatally routed by James's forces at Sedgemoor on July 6, 1685. The somewhat baffled Pitman was among the troops taken prisoner, and was committed to Ilchester Gaol. Here he seems to have passed for the first time in his life under the arbitrariness of absolute authority.

"Certain persons," Pitman later recalled, "called us forth, one after another, and told us that the King was very gracious and merciful, and would cause none to be executed but such as had been Officers or capital offenders.'' In exchange for an account of where and in what capacity they had served in the duke's army, the prisoners would "render ourselves fit objects of the King's grace and favor.'' By confessing to membership in the duke's forces, the prisoners expected to be treated as conquered soldiers; but the lord chief justice insisted that they must now plead guilty to treason and that "If we would acknowledge our crimes by pleading Guilty to our indictment, the King, who was almost all mercy, would be as ready to forgive us as we were ready to rebel against him.''

As encouragement to accept the king's mercy, the lord chief justice quickly tried and convicted twenty-eight of those who had pleaded not guilty, and signed a warrant for their execution the same afternoon. Prompted by the sudden dispatch of these men, the remaining prisoners, all but three or four, quickly pleaded guilty in hope of saving their lives. They were rewarded by the gracious and merciful James II by being condemned to be "hanged, drawn and quartered.'' Two hundred and thirty were so executed. The remainder, Pitman and his brother among them, were ordered to be transported "to the Caribee Islands.''

Sold, along with nearly a hundred more prisoners to George Penne, "a needy Papist,'' Pitman and his brother were informed that if their family could redeem them by paying the price of transportation the sons would be freed at Barbados.

The money was paid, and Pitman and his brother transported, taking ship at London, bound for Barbados, where "we arrived in about five weeks' time; but had a very sickly passage, insomuch that nine of my companions were buried in the sea.''

Anticipating freedom, Pitman and his brother instead found themselves welcomed in Barbados by the governor and the General Assembly with the following official decree:

> Whereas a most horrid, wicked and execrable Rebellion was lately raised and prosecuted within His Majesty's Dominions by James Scot, late Duke of Monmouth . . . for which impious fact, many of them

have since been deservedly punished with the crime of death, according to law . . . and Forasmuch as His sacred Majesty hath signified it, as his royal pleasure, that the said rebels or so many of them as should be transported to his said American colonies, should be there held and obliged to serve the Buyers of them, for and during the space of Ten Years at least; and that they be not permitted in any manner whatsoever, to redeem themselves by money or otherwise, until that time be fully expired.

"Thus we may see," said the distraught, enraged Pitman, "the buying and selling of free men into slavery."

Any person assisting one of the rebels to escape would be fined five hundred pounds, while any servant or rebel attempting to escape the island before the completion of his ten-year term was to be given thirty-nine lashes "on his bare body," and "on another market day in the same town, be set in the pillory, by the space of one hour; and be burned in the forehead with the letters F.T. signifying Fugitive Traitor."

The boundlessness of King James's mercy extended to the owner or keeper of any "small vessel, sloop, shallow, wherry, fishing-boat or any other sort of boat belonging to this island," each of whom was now required to post a bond of two hundred pounds against the use of his vessel for escape by any "Servant, Slave or Debtor." And if any woman on the island might marry any of the said convict rebels for the purpose of freeing him from his servitude, the rebel would be ordered to serve the remainder of his time for some other person, and the woman required to forfeit two hundred pounds and serve six months in prison.

Tricked into confessing guilt for treason, his promise of freedom in Barbados betrayed, facing ten years' servitude on an island where four-fifths of the servants didn't survive the first year, Pitman sustained himself with hope of a pardon. Yet it was his loss of professional standing that finally drove him beyond endurance. Denied adequate food or clothing as well as compensation of any sort for his services as a surgeon, Pitman finally told his harsh master that "I would no longer serve him, nor any other, as a surgeon unless I were entertained according to the just merits of my profession and practice.''

For his trouble, Pitman was beaten with a cane upon his head, arms, and back by his angry master "like a furious fencer," until his skin broke, then confined "close prisoner in the Stocks," in the heat of the sun for twelve hours.

Such "Abusive and unkind treatment" to Pitman and his brother on the part of their master continued for some fifteen months "until by his debauched and extravagant course of life, he had run himself so extremely in debt that he could not pay for us."

Pitman and his brother were repossessed by the dealers who had originally sold them, as goods unpaid for. When he balked at the prospect of resale, Pitman was threatened with horsewhipping.

It was while Pitman was in the hands of these merchants that his brother died. Abandoning hope of a pardon, "perplexed and tired with the great abuses I had received," he resolved to attempt his escape from the island.

Introduced by a friend to a debt servant, a carver named John Nuthall, Pitman confided his plan. Using money provided Pitman by his relatives, Nuthall would buy a boat from one of the Guineamen, slave ships that anchored in the harbor. In return, Nuthall would receive free passage, money for his expenses, and, when they had arrived at a safe port, the boat.

Having bought the boat and posted the two-hundred-pound bond required by the Secretary's Office, Nuthall was accused by the magistrates, who knew he was a debtor, of fronting for another person. They threatened to seize the boat unless Nuthall revealed who the person was. To avoid losing the boat, Pitman had Nuthall sink it.

Meanwhile, Pitman had confided his escape plan to two other indentured servants, Thomas Austin and John Whicker, who agreed to accompany him and give him what money they could spare for the scheme. He continued to meet at night with Nuthall "at some convenient place remote from the town by the sea side" to concoct a plan of escape. Gradually the men assembled provisions and rigging, which were hidden at a friend's house not far from the waterside.

Then an unusual opportunity presented itself. The governor of the island of Nevis was scheduled to visit Barbados, a formal occasion with the militia of the town in arms, "which was attended with revelling, drinking and feasting to excess; the consequences of which, I easily conjectured, would be drowsy security and carelessness."

With the help of "two lusty blacks," John Nuthall emptied the water out of the sunken skiff and set her afloat. The vessel was provisioned and brought to a wharf near the men's secret storehouse. Weighing the drastic penalties for attempted escape—branding, whipping—against the death-sentence certainty of ten years' servitude, Pitman made his choice: "I resolved to hazard a burned forehead and a sore back."

A surgeon, a wood-carver, two laborers—these were hardly the swashbuckling heroes of traditional romantic adventure but rather ordinary men, frightened, emotionally dependent on one another, made desperate by imprisonment and the denial of their rights. Sneaking away to the wharf one midnight, they panicked at the approach of the watch and fled. Pitman was so disheartened by this failure that he had to be persuaded into trying again, and one man grew so fearful of being cast away at sea that he backed out.

Nevertheless, another night about midnight, when the governor of Nevis was still visiting, the men, now eight in all, put out to sea, aiming for the Dutch island of Curaçao.

"We rowed softly forward, within a pistol's shot of the Fort; and there lay at that time a man-of-war in the road: which made us not a little afraid of being discovered by those watchful enemies; but Providence so ordered it, that we passed both without discovery."

Their troubles were only beginning. Landlubbers to a man, they had no sooner got clear of the fort than they discovered that their boat was leaking, taking on water so fast that it was almost ready to sink. With their candles congealed into one mass of tallow and their matches and tinder soaked, they couldn't strike a light to read the compass by. The laden boat wallowed; the men grew seasick. One man while bailing out water accidentally heaved their lone wooden bowl over the side, leaving them to fight the leaks with a single tub.

"My companions now began to wish themselves at Barbados again," wrote Pitman. He told them that it was impossible, that they were now too far to the leeward of the island to reverse course. Only after "great importunity and earnest persuasion" was he able to get them to overcome their misery in the interest of preserving themselves from drowning.

Proceeding in this fitful manner, they were by the morning of May 10, 1687, almost beyond sight of the island. They began to cheer up, feeling that at least they wouldn't be spotted from shore. That night, however, a gale arose which split the rudder, forcing them to lower their sail.

The helm was mended, the sail raised, the seasickness overcome. They began being buffeted by the winds and currents of the Caribbean. After a few days, their water turned foul. They approached several islands, on which they were unable or unwilling to land, and were ultimately struck by a violent storm.

"And now the sea began to foam, and to turn its smooth surface into mountains and vales. Our boat was tossed and tumbled from one side to the other." Once again they wished they were at Barbados; the misery of the storm "confirmed us the more in the certainty of our approaching ruin." Just when all their hopes had been given over, "expecting every moment when the wide gaping sea would devour and swallow us up: GOD, of his infinite mercy and Unspeakable goodness, commanded the violence of the winds to cease, and allayed the fury of the raging waves."

Pitman was a devout Presbyterian, a dissenter in an age of religious dissent; convinced of the efficacy of direct communication with the Almighty, he was opposed on principle to the state establishment of any religion. This was a sentiment particularly strong in the American colonies, where official church authority was weak and scattered and dissenting religions strong among the indentured and other poor settlers. There were colonists who preferred imprisonment and loss of property to paying taxes to support a church that was not their own. Religion, especially in the Northern colonies, represented, according to Edmund Burke, a refinement on the principle of resistance: "it is the dissidence of dissent, and the protestantism of the Protestant Religion."

It was Protestantism, Burke pointed out, "of that kind which is the most averse to all implicit submission of mind and opinion."

On May 16, Pitman and the other battered and shaken fugitive servants were approaching the small Caribbean island of Salta-tudos, or Isla La Tortuga, about forty miles north of the Vene-zuelan coast, when they were overtaken by three men paddling a native dugout canoe, or pirogue. To their surprise, the men turned out to be English and proclaimed themselves also to be supporters of the Duke of Monmouth.

Their new friends helped Pitman and his companions haul their boat up onto the island, showed them the well of fresh water which was by their huts, helped them rig a shady awning of their sail, and shared their provisions with the rescued men. It was only when the fugitives had so rested and refreshed themselves that they were ready to start repairing their boat so they might press on to Curaçao that their hosts revealed that they had other ideas.

"Alleging the insufficiency of our boat, and the dangers we were so lately exposed unto, [they advised] us rather to go with them in their pirogues a-privateering than to hazard our lives by a second attempt."

The men, it was now revealed, were pirates, part of a band originally headed by a Captain Yanche, which had set out to plunder the town of St. Augustine, Florida. In order to equip his men for the raid, Captain Yanche had sent thirty of them to steal canoes from the Indians. Instead, the pirates were set upon themselves by Indians on the Spanish Mainland of South America. By the time they had fought their way free, they had missed the rendezvous with Yanche's man-of-war. They had come to this island hoping to get passage on one of the English ships that occasionally stopped at Saltatudos for salt, but the ships had also gone by the time they arrived.

When Pitman and his men declined to enlist in the pirate band, the privateers tried to compel them by burning their boat. The men now faced being stranded on the island until the next ship arrived for salt, about eight or nine months, while in danger

meanwhile not only of starvation, but of being seized as privateers by the Spanish.

"I continued my resolution," writes Pitman, "and chose
rather to trust Divine Providence on that desolate and inhabitable
island than to partake or be in any ways concerned with them in
their piracy."

To better prepare his band for survival on the island, Pitman
paid the privateers thirty pieces of eight for an Indian they had
captured on the mainland, anticipating that the native would be
helpful to them in catching fish. This arrangement may well have
later suggested the relationship of Robinson Crusoe and Friday
to Daniel Defoe, who is known to have been interested in the
followers of the Duke of Monmouth.

Turned down by the runaway servants, rigging their pirogues
with canvas and nails salvaged from Pitman's burned boat, the
pirates set sail, abandoning the fugitives along with four of their
own men, and a Spanish boat without rudder or sails.

Thrown back completely on their own devices, Pitman and his
companions began by taking stock of their lonely island. Called
by the Spanish La Tortuga, the island was a breeding ground for
the giant sea turtles which came there in certain seasons to lay
eggs in the sand. From the four abandoned pirates, Pitman and
the others learned to walk the beaches at night looking for the
turtles, which they turned on their backs, rendering the creatures
helpless. In the daytime the men returned and cut their throats.

The castaways cooked and ate the turtle meat; some of it they
salted and stored away. Walking the rocks of the island, their
feet grew callused and tough. They built houses with walls woven
of the coarse grass that grew by the seaside. From the Indian
they learned to catch fish. And since "there is no mountain so
barren on which there may not be found some medicinal plant,"
Pitman was able to use his medical eye to make use of a number
of herbs and flowers. They scoured their clothes with the prickly
leaves of the agave, made poultices of balsam, smoked wild sage
in lieu of tobacco. They homesteaded their island.

They had lived in this state of marginal, lonely independence
for some three months, when in August of 1687 "we saw a ship,

attended by a small sloop, steering towards the shore." The men felt a mixture of hopefulness and fear: if it was an English vessel they would get a passage home. If it was Spanish they would be taken prisoner. The four remaining pirates went out to investigate.

At this time and in these waters it was difficult to determine the true allegiance of any vessel. Privateers such as Captain Yanche with his forty-eight-gun man-of-war were as substantially outfitted as an English or Spanish ship of the line. In addition, under letters of marque, private vessels might well be recruited into sailing under one or the other nation's flag. Spotting pirates was not so much a matter of searching out Jolly Rogers, earrings, peglegs, or parrots on the shoulder as distinguishing a nationalized armed rabble from a private-enterprise armed rabble.

The ship that had arrived at the castaways' island turned out to be the latter, a privateering man-of-war run along the lines of a joint-stock company. After the castaway pirates had gone aboard, the captain sent the sloop to the part of the island where Pitman and his companions were. When they came ashore, they asked only one thing: Which man was the doctor?

Directed to Pitman, they invited him on behalf of their captain to come aboard the man-of-war, "where I should be kindly entertained and have liberty to go ashore when I pleased."

Pitman went out to the ship, where he was received with "the trumpets sounding," given a feast with wine and choice provisions in the main cabin with the captain and ship's doctor, and handed "a pair of silk stockings, a pair of shoes, and a great deal of linen cloth to make me shirts."

The men had a long talk about political affairs in England and commiserated with each other over the defeat of the Duke of Monmouth. In the warmth of good madeira and the comforts of the main cabin, Pitman asked the captain whether he would take him and his castaway companions along with the privateers. They could be set ashore at the man-of-war's next port, or perhaps put aboard the next English ship they seized as a prize.

The pirate captain, who seems to have been more like an embattled corporate manager than a cutlass-wielding autocrat, regretfully told Pitman that he could not take the men aboard without the consent of the company, and that he, the captain, had only two votes and as many shares in the ship and cargo.

"The Company were called together," recounted Pitman, "and, after some debates, they voted that they would take me with them, but none of my companions. However, they were so kind that they sent them a cask of wine, some bread and cheese, a gammon of bacon, some linen cloth, thread and needles . . . And the next day they permitted them to come on board, and entertained them very courteously."

And so in about two days' time Pitman set sail, "leaving my companions on the island, not a little grieved at my departure."

They headed north, toward Puerto Rico. From the primitive isolation of the Island of the Turtles Pitman now found himself cast into a society compounded of organization and spontaneity, a sort of disciplined impulsiveness dictated by the random and competitive opportunities offered privateers in the Caribbean.

The pirates steered between Puerto Rico and Haiti, where there were "divers vessels" scavenging a wreck for plate. They chased and overtook a ketch, whose crew told them they were headed for the island of Providence in the Bahamas, where a town had been newly built and improved. The privateers elected to join them. However the weather turned foul, and the men aboard the ketch, drunk on brandy given them by the privateers, ran their boat into the man-of-war, causing both vessels to "unavoidably sink down in the sea." When they arrived at Providence the following day, both ketch and man-of-war were being bailed with tubs.

The town was bright and booming, a tiny independent commonwealth where the privateers were given a kind reception. After they had taken their goods ashore and no doubt called for another company vote, the pirates ran their ship aground and burned her. Giving their guns to the inhabitants to fortify the island, the privateers decided "to divide themselves into small numbers, and to go thence, to some other place where they might sell their goods and betake themselves to an honest course of life."

This tone of rehabilitation, the freshened sense of possibilities, the desire to achieve respectability, the pirates must have ab-

sorbed from the town itself. Formerly "a harbor for privateers
and a nest of robbers," Providence had been pillaged and burned
by the Spaniards and was now being resettled by inhabitants from
"Jamaica and other parts."

Pitman spent some two weeks in the Bahamas, after which he
set sail with the crew of the repaired ketch, bound for "Carolina."

After a near wreck on a shoal in the Bahamas, and being blown
off course by a storm, the ketch arrived off the bar of Charleston,
South Carolina. The captain of the ketch, fearing arrest because
of his dealings with privateers, sent in his boat instead. Finding
no vessel at Charleston bound for England, Pitman elected to
continue with the ketch to New York.

It would be comforting to think that Pitman, having been transported from the Old World in chains, would have been so transformed by his experience of adventure and earned freedom that
he would have cast his lot with the New. He was, however, not
that sort of man. Pitman had seen all he wished of this perverse
New World of democratic pirates and honest men in chains.
Bound by strong family ties, Pitman was a firm Protestant at the
height of Protestantism's surging faith in the power of personal
conviction. To him, James II was a usurper, a Catholic, an ab-
solutist, a threat to English law, parliamentary rule, and individual freedom.

It was religious conviction of this dissenting sort, however,
repeatedly challenging established authority, that was to be summoned up again by the Revolutionary thought of the 1760s and
'70s. What Edmund Burke termed "a persuasion not only favorable to liberty, but built upon it," colonial dissenting Protestantism joined the broad, contagious movement for independence
that was to produce not only political autonomy but the ultimate
disestablishment of religion in the United States.

One morning while walking on a bridge in New York, Pitman
encountered a man he had known in Barbados. Cautious at first,
wary that the man might expose him as an escaped servant, Pitman accompanied him to a house where the man recounted the
Barbados masters' reaction to Pitman's escape.

Pitman's owners had hired a sloop to send after the fugitives. They had forwarded names and descriptions of the fleeing servants to the Leeward Islands. They had listened eagerly to reports that the men had been taken prisoner at the West Indian Island of St. Kitt's.

This last news "made our masters rejoice, and insultingly to boast of the severe punishments they would inflict upon us." They were resolved that Pitman, as the leader of the escape, would be hanged. "But these hopes and insultings of theirs were soon over: for when, at length, they could hear no true account of us, they concluded that we had perished in the sea."

From New York, Pitman took ship for Amsterdam, where under an assumed name he bought passage to Southampton.

"I returned in a disguise to my relations," he concluded, "who, before this time, unknown to me, had procured my Pardon; and joyfully received me, as one risen from the dead."

Voices

kid'nap . . . 1. Orig., to carry off (a person) to enforced labor in the British colonies in America. *Obs*.

—WEBSTER'S NEW
  INTERNATIONAL DICTIONARY,
  Second Edition

18

JAMES ANNESLEY

IN 1743, a man named James Annesley was tried for and acquitted of murder in London. That same year, he was involved in another trial, in Dublin, in which he charged his uncle, Richard, the Earl of Anglesey, with robbing him of his birthright by arranging to have him carried off into indentured servitude in America. The trial caused a sensation, both in Britain and in the colonies, where Annesley had been discovered after serving thirteen years as an indentured servant, with charges of kidnapping on one side and illegitimacy on the other, amid the tantalizing prospect of the simultaneous unmasking and restoration of an English peer.

The story is considered to have inspired two different novels of Smollett, one by Scott, and Stevenson's *Kidnapped,* as well as a less famous work, of somewhat lesser imagination, attributed to the plaintiff himself.

As a family, the Annesleys seem to represent characters out of *Tom Jones.* Of old English stock, originating in Nottinghamshire, the first Earl of Anglesey was a Restoration politician elevated to the peerage by Charles II. He acquired tracts of land, mostly in

Ireland, sufficient to support two baronies, those of Anglesey and Altham. By the time of the fourth Lord Altham, who called himself Arthur Annesley, the transplanted stock appears to have run riot in the indulgent Irish soil.

Arthur, Lord Altham, was a profligate drunk who "swilled brandy and mead with surgeons lost to self-respect," and "parasites of low degree." He is said to have shared his mistress with his butler and his dog boy. He underfed a pack of hounds, "each yearning to sate his maw with the flesh of any other member of the pack," and with them he hunted, accompanied by his riffraff of hangers-on. His house, Liberty Hall, was run with a transitory staff of discontented domestics who were cheated of their wages, abused with rude manners and language, and who never stayed long. Altham had been blinded in one eye by one of his disgruntled tenants, who took a shot at him through a window. He is described as "a little, black, very noisy nobleman," with "a preposterously violent temper, no sense of honor, no self-control, and less brains than a rabbit."

His brother Richard, Earl of Anglesey, was even worse. "Of a blacker heart," we are told, "we have few examples." Surrounded like his brother by parasites, Richard employed his flunkeys so treacherously that even they mocked his cowardice. He shared his brother's mistress, had his nephew kidnapped and sold into servitude, and bribed constables and recruited witnesses who perjured themselves in an attempt to convict the nephew of murder. When challenged by one of his victims, he ran away and set his grooms on the challenger instead. He was the kind of man who resorts to foul means even when fair would be easier, a trait that was well documented in four separate trials between 1742 and 1745. Along with his family, he seems to have epitomized the self-indulgent corruption of certain elements of the British gentry which English Whigs, and the colonists in America, feared would turn England into a tyranny.

Arthur, the older brother, Lord Altham, had married Mary Sheffield, daughter of the Earl of Buckingham, in 1706. Altham squandered his wife's money, the two were on the worst of terms, they separated, and he threatened her with divorce. They were reconciled temporarily in 1713. According to James Annes-

ley, the claimant, he was born of this union in 1715. There were
rejoicings when this son and heir was christened; and when Lord
and Lady Altham quarreled and parted the following year, Lord
Altham kept James with him. He took the boy with him to various
places and treated him as his legitimate son.

In 1722, however, a mistress of Lord Altham's, a Miss Gregory
of Dublin, turned his lordship against the child, who was dismissed from his father's house and "roved about," an object of
charity and curiosity, until Lord Altham died in November of
1727. Lady Altham, partially paralyzed, died in poverty in London in 1729. Richard Annesley, Lord Altham's younger brother,
who had now succeeded to the Altham title and estates, fearing
a challenge to his claim, had the boy James Annesley kidnapped
and sold into servitude in America. Here the story of the "Wandering Heir" begins.

James Annesley's *Memoirs of an Unfortunate Young Nobleman, Returned from Thirteen Years' Slavery in America* is told
in the third person. There are hairsbreadth escapes; people in
extremis make long, declamatory speeches; female characters,
often young and attractive, appear with a frequency not commonly noted in the colonial backwoods of America. Yet, as with
John Lawson, there is a convincing tone of injury just beneath
the literary surface, a lingering indignation at prolonged submission to arbitrary power, the voice of a man challenging all authority by calling to account its flagrant abuse.

"The first step this inhumane Uncle took," James Annesley
accuses his father's brother Richard, "was to agree with the
Master of a Ship bound for Pennsylvania, for a certain sum of
money, to transport James thither." The boy, kidnapped in Dublin and concealed in a conspirator's house, has been told that he
is going to be sent away to a school for gentlemen in Brussels.
Meanwhile, as the boy is held prisoner, his father dies of a sudden illness, and the uncle assumes the title, and with it the father's estate. James finds himself alone at sea, tossed about by a
violent storm and rebuked by the crew when he seats himself at
the officers' mess.

"On his mentioning however that he was going to St. Omer's

in order to study, and that his Father was a Lord, they easily found he was ignorant of his Condition, and some there were who, having Hearts less rugged than their Appearance denoted, very much compassioned him.''

It is by this means that the young James learns of the treachery of his uncle, and that instead of being educated as an accomplished nobleman ''he was going into the worst kind of servitude.'' When he cries out in anguished complaint the captain, fearing the boy might destroy himself, confines him to the ship's hold. James refuses food until, concerned that he will starve, the captain has him brought to his cabin, where he assures the boy that indentured servitude is in reality no worse than serving as an apprentice in England. Moreover, he assures James that once it is discovered that he has been bound his freedom can easily be purchased by his father.

His hopes restored, the boy begins to eat and drink and rapidly regains his health. As a result, he is on arrival in Philadelphia quickly sold for a tidy profit by the treacherous captain ''to a rich Planter in ''Newcastle County'' who takes the young James home ''and immediately enter'd him among the Number of his Slaves.''

James sleeps but one night in the ''House of Bondage,'' when he is called up at daybreak and put to work cutting timber for pipe staves, work at which the boy is so unskilled and for which after his ocean voyage he shows so little strength, ''that he had many Stripes [lashes] for his aukwardness before he had any Meat.'' Setting himself to do his best in hope of gaining an early pardon, he soon finds he is ''as absolutely as an Ox or an Ass, or any other Property . . . made purchase of.''

''There are,'' James observes, ''a Sort of People in the World that are not to be obliged, and the greater your endeavours for that End, the less will be your Effect.'' ''Drumon,'' or Drummond, his harsh new master, is one of this species, a man who seems ''to take a savage Pleasure in adding to the Misery of [his slaves'] Condition by continual ill Usage.'' A condition which Annesley observes is hardly ideal to begin with. There is in addition to the harshness of the labor the constant exposure in a climate more severe in its extremes than anything in Europe, sustained by a diet composed mainly of corn pone, hominy, water, and bacon fat. "The Hardships of an American Slavery," Annesley concludes, "are infinitely more terrible than a Turkish one."

There is among the slaves a woman of nearly fifty who despite her condition has something in her "air and Aspect" of less brutal usage. She is, it turns out, the discarded wife of a "Person of some Consideration" in England, an unfaithful husband who has trapped her into transportation to get rid of her, in much the same way Annesley was kidnapped. The woman has been broken by Drummond from maid service to kitchenwork, where she is required to prepare food and carry it to the distant fields for the slaves. It is she who points out to Annesley that it is not in the planters' interest to treat slaves well, and that it is even more to their advantage to treat them especially harshly when their term has nearly expired.

This, says Annesley, is a "sort of barbarous Policy in these Planters": to use their slaves ill, especially when their service is nearly up. By the laws of the country, those servants who run away, if they are retaken, "as they commonly are, they are mulcted for that Disobedience, and obliged to pay, by a longer Servitude, all the Expenses and Damages the Master pretends he has sustained by their Elopement." By treating the servant harshly at the end of his term, a master has nothing to lose. If the servant dies or is crippled, he represents no loss to the owner, since he will ordinarily be leaving anyway. But if he can be provoked into daring an escape, the master may regain him and turn a profit in the process.

Here again, as with John Lawson, we see the individual consequences of the exercise of arbitrary power. The gross extension of the inequities of the bound-labor system beyond anything known in England, where the maximum term for farm workers was one year. Implicit in the story is the commonplaceness of such treatment and the lack of legal recourse for anyone subjected to it. No one who ran away, legally got to stay away. As with black slavery, such conditions degraded both servant and master, as well as the legal system and the government which supported them.

The only course, the woman counsels Annesley, is patience. "Since in seeking any other, they but prolong their Misery, and give a Shew of Justice to the Persecutions inflicted on them."

The woman becomes first Annesley's friend, and then his tutor, supposedly writing down what information she can recall from her extensive reading on bits of paper, which she slips to her pupil when she brings him his food. This cram course is accompanied by simultaneous instruction in the school of hard knocks, for "in this Employment being often catch'd, he endur'd many Stripes for neglecting his Works. Never any Boy suffer'd more Correction for his little Propensity to Learning."

In his rare free moments, James the servant seeks out the woman to ask her questions arising from his reading. In this combination of involuntary physical, and voluntary mental, labor, he spends the first four years of his required seven years' servitude. Then the woman dies; Annesley now feels "all his Woes with double weight, having none to advise him how to bear them." For the first time, despite the cruel penalties, he begins to entertain ideas of escape. When a fellow servant by the name of Jacob runs off in the night after robbing the master's house, the whole county is aroused to pursue him. He is brought back the next day bound hand and foot—a fate that Annesley, who was invited to join in the escape, has avoided only by oversleeping.

" 'Tis certain," Annesley observes, "that nothing is more difficult than for a Slave or a Servant in America to make his Escape without being re-taken." The master, almost certain to be reimbursed in owed labor, "spares no Expence for that Purpose."

The recaptured Jacob is beaten, confined to a dungeon, and, his term extended by recapture, is resold to a planter in Philadelphia. "Few," Annesley concludes, "know how to make a right Use of Power . . . They shew too great a Consciousness of it, and imagine they cannot be *Rulers* without being *Tyrants;* and it is this mistaken Exertion of Authority that occasions Rebellions in States."

Now seventeen years old, Annesley has spent five years in servitude without becoming inured to it. His resentment against the uncle who entrapped him is "a continual Vulture preying on his Peace . . . and he would have . . . hazarded everything . . . to obtain the Satisfaction of Upbraiding and exposing him."

It is in one of these fits of cornered-rat rage that Annesley at last leaves the House of Drummond "determined rather to suffer himself to be cut to pieces than be brought back." He has armed himself with a "hedging bill"—a staff with a hooked blade at the end used for cutting branches; those who pursue him "should not find him so easy to be taken as Jacob had." Plunging off into the unfamiliar countryside, Annesley strikes out in the direction of the Delaware River, hoping to follow it to the seaport of Dover, and perhaps a ship back to England. Instead he mistakes the Susquehanna River for the Delaware and wanders in the backcountry for three days, where in a thoroughly implausible scene he comes upon a maiden and her lover having a backwoods tryst, befriends them, assists them in a fight against *their* pursuers, and is himself captured, tried, and flung into the Chester Town jail, where he is accidentally discovered and reclaimed by his hated master.

Drummond is surprised, overjoyed, and, when he has brought Annesley safely back to Newcastle, vengeful: "there he let all his Fury loose, and represented the Loss his Flight had been to him, and the Expenses he had been at . . . so that he had now four Years to remain a Slave" instead of two. In addition, Drummond tightens the screws, giving Annesley "Tasks utterly impossible to be performed, gave him Stripes without Mercy for his enforced Disobedience, and Food in such Scanty portions . . . only sufficient to keep him from perishing."

Annesley's treatment, always bad, has now become intolerable. Denied by close watch any possibility of flight, he goes in desperation to the justices and makes a complaint against his master.

As a Christian and a white man, and a servant who was not a felon, Annesley was entitled to protection against arbitrary and unnatural cruelties. According to law in colonies such as Virginia, a servant could repair to the nearest commissioner and make a complaint. Although the penniless servant was at a disadvantage in pressing a suit, and could be held liable to the public as well as to his master for any crimes he might commit, petitions

could be filed, and there is reason to believe that it was possible
for a servant to get a fair hearing. This, at least, seems to have
been what Annesley received. As a result of his complaint,
Drummond was ordered to sell him to another master.

"But the still-unhappy slave," recounts Annesley, finds "no
Change in his Condition by this Change of Hands." The new
master is "of as Cruel and inexorable a Disposition" as the old.
Resigning himself, Annesley endures this treatment for three
more years.

With just twelve months left to go until the completion of his
term, fate again conspires against James Annesley. He falls into
the company of some sailors who, exciting his imagination with
their descriptions of Europe, including Ireland, his home, persuade him to come off with them, stow away aboard ship, and
sail home. They are on their way to the vessel when overtaken
by men dispatched by Annesley's master. The would-be escapee
has been informed on, a constant temptation in a country where
the informer gets half the reward. Worse luck, his recapture
comes at a time following several discovered slave escape attempts; and he is to be made an example of. "For this Offence,"
says Annesley, "he was mulcted no less than four Years, a most
unreasonable time."

With this latest punishment, Annesley succumbs to despair: "a
Melancholy which is not to be expressed hung upon his Heart."
As upon the discovery of his uncle's treachery aboard the ship
that transported him, Annesley begins to waste away physically
to the point where his master grows apprehensive of losing him.
The master instructs his wife to bring James into the house and
feed him from the family's table, but he instructs her to do this
as if on the sly, as leniency in violation of the master's austere
rule. "He imagined," explained Annesley, "that to shew the
least Kindness to a Slave himself, would be derogating from his
Authority."

Subjected to yet another of the quirks encouraged by arbitrary
power, Annesley accepts house-servant food and status, but fails
to regain his spirits. Indeed his closeness to his master's family
only produces a quandary of a different sort.

According to Annesley, the master's daughter, a blond maiden of fifteen, develops, completely unencouraged, an infatuation for the young household servant. At the same time, an Indian girl from a neighboring tribe, who has watched James in the woods felling timber, conceives an equally intense affection for him. "And as the Women of that Country have either less Modesty or more Simplicity than those born and bred up in Europe, she made no effort to conceal the Tenderness he had inspired her with."

In practically no time, the two girls, one a "Brown Beauty, born and bred in Paganism," the other "extremely fair, but a little vain and inclined to Coquetry." are squaring off in a woodland meadow. Torquois, the Indian maid, springs "like an incensed Lioness at her rival's throat; while the fair Maria, less strong than her opponent but with vigor "redoubled by the Pain and Fear of Death, at length unloosed herself and flew with the utmost Speed" to tell Annesley. Torquois, in despair at the prospect of Maria's "Complaint to the dear Object of her Wishes," runs to the river and plunges headlong in, "putting an End at once to her unhappy Love and Life."

Maria, who has witnessed the death scene, is flung by the experience into a coma, continually repeating Torquois's name, and in her delirium also James's.

The master and his wife, determined to get to the bottom of these tragic events, arrange to have Annesley ordered to bring some firewood to their sick daughter's bedchamber. The father and mother when they hear him approach "Concealed themselves in a Closet, where they could easily hear everything that passed."

As the parents conveniently eavesdrop, their daughter's infatuation with Annesley and Annesley's innocence of trifling with her affections are both revealed. The parents agree that "in order to restore the Tranquility of their Daughter, it was necessary this dangerous Slave should be removed." The woman, who had first proposed taking Annesley into the family home and feeding him from the table, suggests that he be freed and permitted to return to his own country, as only fair recompense for the "Honor and Integrity of his Behavior." The husband promises to send him away "by the first Ship that sailed for Europe."

When the day of his departure at last arrives, James sets off with his master for the port of Dover, "with a cheerful Heart" as every step brings him "nearer to the Place where he should receive his Liberty." But as they enter and then pass through the busy port it begins to dawn on Annesley that the master might have plans of his own in mind.

"Tho' the Awe in which Slaves in America are kept prevents them from scarce speaking to their Masters," still James is driven as they bypass a harbor busy with shipping to ask what is to be their destination.

" 'What Concern is that of yours?' replied the other surlily. 'Your Business is Obedience.' "

The avaricious proprietor, possessing a piece of property with the value of five years' owed servitude, has privately decided to sell it.

Unaccompanied by any of his other slaves, "for Fear they should speak of it at their Return," he leads Annesley into the County of Sussex, where they stop at a house "about seven Miles short of the City of Chichester." James follows his master into the house, where he is kept waiting in an outer room, then finally introduced to the owner of the house and plantation, to whom, according to the papers he is for the first time shown, his ownership has just been transferred.

"Thus cruelly deceived, thus raised to Hopes of Freedom only to make slavery more insupportable," Annesley springs upon his former master, seizing him "with so strong a Gripe as, had they not been separated . . . the Father of Maria might never have been able to return to Newcastle."

Forced out of the room, lied against by his former master, who explains to James's new owner that his wife has flattered the servant into groundless hopes of freedom, Annesley is now at the bottom of his hopes and fully prepared for the worst. To his surprise, his new master proves to be "of a more humane Nature than either Drumon or the Father of Maria"; James finds that he now has "a milder Servitude than any he had known since his Slavery." The master, a man of some learning, even lends him books to read, and James becomes something of a family favorite. This gentle treatment, combined with the harsh fact of the added time prescribed by the magistrates after his last escape attempt, leads Annesley to set aside all thoughts of running away for three more years.

As an indentured servant, however, Annesley is still subject to the rule of men and not laws. When after three years his gentle master dies, James is without equity in his work and has no control over his future. The person who succeeds the master, "not being a Lover of Business," sells off a great part of the plantation, including a number of the slaves, and among them James. He is led back by his new owner to Newcastle County, "almost in sight of that very House where he had suffered so many Troubles on the Score of his rival Mistresses."

His new master treats him with less kindness than his last, yet more gently than the two previous ones. His life, though not easy, is "supportable." The fair Maria, he learns, has been made pregnant by one of her father's slaves and "was afterwards obliged to marry him." The story of Torquois, meanwhile, her love for him, her jealousy, her unhappy end, has become a local legend, of which Torquois's two brothers have vowed to write the final chapter.

One morning, "after having lain in wait for many Months," the brothers catch Annesley in a forest on his way to work in a field and fall upon him. With his back against a tree, Annesley holds his own for a time against the two Indians, but eventually they throw him to the ground and are about to cut his throat when a party of slave hunters searching for a fugitive comes to the rescue. Annesley, wounded, weak from loss of blood, is returned to his master.

As he is recuperating, James overhears the master's wife conspiring with a slave against her husband. Confronting the woman with what he has heard, Annesley urges her to abandon her intrigue. Stunned at the extent of what Annesley has discovered, the master's wife attempts first to seduce, then poison him. When the master at last catches his wife and the slave in bed together and expels her from his house, it is the loyal servant James he turns to for a true account of what has happened.

Decently treated and appreciated now, with his health and strength recovered, James goes "cheerfully to his accustom'd Work, in which he continued till the full Expiration of his Time of Servitude."

Much of this is romantic embroidery. Yet the facts of Annesley's return from servitude are also cluttered with coincidence and sudden turns of fortune. In 1740, two Irishmen, John and William Broders, were traveling the Lancaster Road in Pennsylvania when they stopped at the house where James was in service for an old German. Annesley, who had been claiming to be the lost son of Lord Altham and had been ignored, found his story suddenly confirmed. He was brought to Philadelphia, where local figures took an interest in him, recommending him to British Admiral Edward Vernon, who returned Annesley to England by way of the West Indies. On his arrival, Annesley found other friends who advanced funds so he could press the suit for his rights.

Annesley's *Memoirs of an Unfortunate Young Nobleman* were written to encourage interest in his claims, with the elements of his story recast in a more appealingly romantic form. Yet for all the loosely related episodes, plot switches, and laying-on of romance (not a woman in the book is less than "attractive"), the book retains its core of reality: a seething fury at the abuse of arbitrary power. We are, we realize, being presented with not only an individual but a mass injustice. The instances of authority misused are so widespread and convincing that they become the theme of the book.

The story is also a dramatization of the growing fear of the consequences of corruption within the English upper classes. According to this belief, gaining currency in both Britain and the colonies as the time of the Revolution drew nearer, the flow of an expanding empire's wealth had produced among the ministers and favorites of the king "an overruling arbitrary power, which absolutely controls King, Lords and Commons."

The power and interest of these "court-locusts," these "whisperers-into-the-King's-ear," was believed, especially in America, to have grown so great "that the rights of the people are ruined and destroyed by tyrannical authority and thereby . . . become a kind of slaves to the ministers of state."

By appointing well-connected men to colonial office and fabricating webs of influence between colonial rulers and the court, this royal and ministerial manipulation appeared to the indignant colonists to be "sporting with our persons and estates, by filling the highest seats of justice with bankrupts, bullies and block-heads."

The Revolutionary leaders were convinced that they were faced with a deliberate conspiracy to destroy the balance of the English constitution and eliminate their freedom; that, as James Annesley had been reduced to servitude by a scheming British peer, the British, in the words of George Mason of Virginia, were "endeavoring by every piece of art and despotism to fix the shackles of slavery upon us."

It was while he was in London awaiting the opening of his suit against his uncle that James Annesley found himself on trial for murder. While accompanying a man named Joseph Redding in the countryside at Staines west of London, Annesley had shot and killed a man named Thomas Eggleson in the presence of Eggleson's son.

Seizing on the opportunity, Annesley's Uncle Richard involved himself in the prosecution, making free use of his dependent associates to bribe witnesses and offer perjured testimony in hope of convicting and eliminating the threat of his nephew. In the course of the trial, however, it was established that Eggleson and his son were trespassers who had been poaching fish on property where Annesley's companion Redding served as game-keeper, and that Eggleson had been shot accidentally when he attempted to seize Annesley's gun. James was acquitted; behind the trial testimony there lurked the presence of his Uncle Richard, who had gone to such lengths to incriminate his nephew that the presiding judge had difficulty believing that such conduct was attributable to a nobleman.

The jury at "Uncle Dick's" trial that same year in Dublin had no such problem. After hearing fourteen days of evidence and testimony, the panel returned with a verdict against the earl in one hour. Yet James Annesley never secured his estate. The case was appealed to the House of Lords, where the earl was upheld. Indeed there was and is reasonable doubt if James Annesley actually was the legitimate son of Lord Altham, with so much perjured testimony on both sides that the truth will probably never be known. Had Richard simply stood his ground or offered the boy a cash settlement instead of kidnapping him and then trying to frame him for murder, the entire issue would never have arisen; but discretion and intelligence were not among the earl's virtues. During the course of his trial, the earl encountered a key witness from the earlier murder trial at the Curragh, the racetrack near Dublin. The two men engaged in a confrontation which ended with Richard fleeing a fight and having the witness beaten and part of his ear bitten off by his flunkeys. Richard was a hard man to root for, even by the members of his class.

With a recurring history of incidents like this, it is little wonder that colonial apologists such as John Adams were able to point so effectively to social developments in late-eighteenth-century Britain—land enclosures and industrialization, growing debt, rising prices and taxes, a growing thirst for distinction—as evidence of Britain's "present degeneracy and impending destruction." And to give to Revolution a moral as well as political justification.

For many years, James Annesley, lacking money, was unable to press his claim. At last, in 1760, after interest in the case had been revived and funds raised by subscription, James Annesley died on the eve of a new prosecution. With the death of the romantically wronged party, interest in the case, as had the truth, gradually trickled away, leaving behind what Charles Reade, who based a novel, *Wandering Heir,* on James Annesley's life, summarized as "the greatest mass of perjury ever delivered in Great Britain."

Voices

At a time when our dearest privileges are torn from us, and the foundation of all our liberty subverted, every one who has the least spark of love to his country, must feel the deepest anxiety about our approaching fate. The hearts of all who have a just value for freedom, must burn within them when they see the chains of abject slavery just ready to be riveted about our necks.

—WILLIAM GODDARD
The Constitutional Courant, 1765

19

PETER WILLIAMSON

IN 1743, a boy named Peter Williamson, playing on the quay at the port of Aberdeen, Scotland, was approached by two men who enticed him aboard a ship lying in the harbor. Taken below, Williamson found the 'tween decks occupied by a number of boys much like himself. Here the boys were entertained with music, cards, and other diversions but were not permitted to return topside. They remained confined on board the docked vessel, the *Planter,* while the ship was loaded with seventy boys in all, in addition to provisions and cargo. After nearly a month had passed, the *Planter* set sail, bound for the plantations in Virginia.

Sanctioned by the official decrees intended to encourage the resettlement of vagrant children, subsidized unintentionally by bodies like the London Town Council with its clothing allowances, welcomed by planters who could own the labor of a child not just for the customary four-year indenture but until the child was twenty-one, the gathering and shipment of children had in Aberdeen developed into a public branch of trade "carried on in the market-places, in the high streets and in the avenues of the town." Press gangs of men in the hire of local merchants roamed the streets, seizing "by force such boys as seemed proper subjects for the slave trade." Children were driven in flocks through the town and confined for shipment in local barns, and even in the public workhouse, with a town officer serving as their keeper. So flagrant was the practice that people in the countryside about Aberdeen avoided bringing children into the city for fear they might be stolen; and so widespread was the collusion of merchants, shippers, suppliers, and even magistrates that the man who exposed it was forced to recant and run out of town. The stealing of children became so notorious in Scotland that the Scottish term for the practice entered the English language: "kidnabbing."

Although public outcries over kidnapping, spiriting, and other abuses periodically arose in Britain, Parliament made no attempt to regulate the trade in servants. The reason was that mercantilist opinion had turned against emigration while the Crown, devoted to colonization, was doing everything possible to encourage it. Pressured by conflicting interests, the members did nothing, producing the shadowy jurisdictional vagueness that presents maximum opportunity to the unscrupulous. Testifying before a court in 1765, the town clerk of Aberdeen said that he never knew of any indentured servants going abroad without having their contracts attested to by a magistrate. At the same time he admitted that he kept no record of the servants and that the indentures when signed were immediately carried off by the owners.

In the case of Peter Williamson, the ship carrying him and the other kidnapped boys arrived after some eleven weeks at sea off Cape May, at the mouth of the Delaware River. Here the *Planter* ran aground, apparently on a sandbar, and began to take on water. A boat was lowered, into which the captain and crew promptly scrambled and sailed off, leaving Williamson "and my deluded companions, to perish." The ship remained afloat, however, at least until the following morning, when the captain sent some of his crewmen out in a boat, which took the boys ashore to a makeshift camp. They remained several weeks while the abandoned *Planter* broke up; the boys were then taken up by a vessel bound for Philadelphia.

On their arrival, the merchant, or supercargo, sold the boys off in bunches to soul-drivers. "Thus," Williamson recalled, "we were driven through the country like cattle to a Smithfield market, and exposed to sale in public fairs, as so many brute beasts."

It was Williamson's great good fortune to be purchased for seven years by Hugh Wilson, a man with no children of his own, who had as a boy been kidnapped himself from St. Johnstown in Scotland. Whatever revulsion Wilson felt at his own kidnapping had evidently been put aside in the name of necessity. He had not snatched the boy; he could not abolish the practice; but he could offer compensation of another sort.

"Commiserating my condition," Williamson reminisced, "he took care of me, indulged me in going to school, where I went every winter for five years, and made a tolerable proficiency."

This was the unusual quality of servitude, one that dramatically set it apart from slavery. Master and servant were of the same race, usually of the same nationality, often from the same circumstances. They often worked side by side on the same modest farm. Thus the great number of colonists who had risen from servitude could easily imagine the resumption of their own or their parents' former condition and the loss of the rights they had so arduously earned. Tyranny and enshacklement were as observably real as the voices of masters and overseers in the town squares, the cattle-call sales of the soul-drivers, and the ads for runaways that filled the colonial newspapers.

Peter Williamson remained with his good master until Wilson's death, and he inherited as his reward 150 pounds sterling, his master's best horse, his saddle, and all his apparel. At the age of seventeen, the kidnapped boy Peter Williamson was his own master, "having money in my pocket, and all other necessaries." For the next seven years he employed himself in "jobbing," hiring out to anyone who would employ him. Williamson appears to have been the kind of man—mercurial, impulsive, naturally keen but not scholarly, energetic, and inventive—to whom many things, good and bad, seem to happen. He was soon to have his full share of both.

After seven years of hiring out, Williamson married the daughter of a prosperous Pennsylvania planter. His father-in-law set-

tled upon the newly married couple an estate "on the frontiers of
the province of Pennsylvania, near the forks of the Delaware,
containing about two hundred acres," thirty of which were fully
cleared with a good house and barn. Peter Williamson would
seem to have become a man who in just a few years had fulfilled
the rosiest prophecies of the ship captains, merchants, agents,
and crimps.

Among the peculiarities of life in the New World that went
unmentioned by its various sales representatives were the horrors of Indian border warfare. In the series of conflicts that was
climaxed by the French and Indian War, France and Britain contended for domination of the eastern part of the American continent, using rival Indian tribes as surrogate warriors, and the land
of frontier settlers as a battleground. It was a war of sudden
attack and gruesome reprisal, which spared no one and accen-
tuated the worst in all concerned. And its most crucial phase
began in the Pennsylvania backcountry where Peter Williamson
had settled.

The French, "who were sent to dispossess us in that part of
the world . . . using all manner of ways and means to win the
Indians to their interest," had offered a bounty of sixteen pounds
sterling for every English scalp.

"Terrible and shocking to human nature were the barbarities
daily committed by these savages. Scarce did a day pass but
some unhappy family or other fell victims to savage cruelty."
For Williamson and his family, that day came in October of 1754.

Alone in his farmhouse, Williamson was waiting up for his
wife, who had gone out earlier that day to visit relatives. At about
eleven o'clock at night he heard "to my great surprise and terror
. . . the dismal warwhoop of the savages, and found that my
house was beset by them."

Grabbing his loaded gun, Williamson flew to his chamber window, where he counted a dozen Indians surrounding the house.
Threatening them with the rifle, he was threatened in return with
a fiery death if he didn't come out before they burned the house
down. "If I would come out and surrender myself prisoner," the
Indians promised, "they would not kill me."

Williamson chose to go out of the house still carrying his gun,

apparently without realizing it. "Immediately on my approach
they rushed on me like tigers, and instantly disarmed me." After
binding Williamson to a tree, the Indians entered the house,
looted it, then set fire to it. While Williamson helplessly watched,
they then lit his barn, stable, and outbuildings, all of which, including the animals sheltered there, were reduced to ashes.

"Having thus finished the execrable business about which they
had come, one of the monsters came to me with a tomahawk and
threatened me with the worst of deaths if I did not go with them."
Fearful of his wife's falling into the Indians' hands, Williamson
consented. Untied, he was given a load of plunder to carry, under
which he staggered all night. At daybreak, near exhaustion, he
was allowed to put down his load, after which he was bound to a
tree and tortured with burning coals.

For the second time in his young life, Williamson had been
abducted, cruelly mistreated in the sight of his own home, and
thrust into a strange and different culture. "How I underwent
these tortures," he admitted, "has been a matter of wonder to
me."

At the same fire where they had tortured Williamson, the Indians cooked the meat they had stolen from his house. Though
he had little appetite, he ate what he was offered, fearing further
torture if he refused. When night fell, the Indians put out the fire,
covering the ashes with leaves "that the white people might not
discover any traces of their having been there."

With Williamson as pack animal, the Indians followed along
the Susquehanna River for some miles until they arrived at a spot
near the Appalachian Mountains, "where they hid their plunder
under logs." From these "Blue Hills," they proceeded to a
neighboring house, where a man named Jacob Snider lived with
his wife, five children, and "a young man his servant."

"They soon got admittance into the unfortunate man's house,
where they immediately, without the least remorse, scalped both
parents and children: nor could the tears, the shrieks, or cries of
poor innocent children prevent their horrid massacre: having
thus scalped them, and plundered the house of everything that
was movable, they set fire to it, and left the distressed victims
amidst the flames."

There was only one survivor, the Sniders' young indentured

servant, whom the Indians put to work, like Williamson, packing their loot. On the march back to the hiding place in the Blue Hills, the boy faltered. "I endeavoured to animate him, but all in vain, for he still continued his moans and tears . . . which one of the savages perceiving as we travelled along, came up to us, and with his tomahawk gave him a blow on the head." The boy was knocked to the ground, scalped, and left. Shocked at the suddenness of the murder, Williamson was equally stunned at his own survival. Sensing that emotion of any sort was a provocation to the Indians, the concealed his anguish as best he could "but still, such was my terror, that for some time, I scarce knew the days of the week or what I did."

After five days of "skulking" at their redoubt near the mountains, the Indians again made their way toward the Susquehanna. Passing near an isolated house inhabited by an old man named John Adams, his wife, and four small children, the Indians, meeting no resistance, scalped the mother and the four children before the old man's eyes. "Inhuman and horrid as this was, it did not satisfy them; for when they had murdered the poor woman, they acted with her in such a brutal manner as decency will not permit me to mention." The old man pleaded for death rather than being forced to watch. Instead, he was taken captive and, after his house, barn, corn, and cattle were destroyed by fire, forced to march off burdened with stolen goods "toward the Great Swamp."

"Here they lay for eight or nine days diverting themselves, at times, in barbarous cruelties on the old man." Another group of Indians arrived, with three more captives who described to Williamson further humiliation, suffering, and torture. The three new prisoners, "constantly repining at their lot, and almost dead with their excessive hard treatment," attempted to escape, only to be recaptured by other war parties in the area. Two of the captives were tied to trees, burned, and disemboweled; the third was buried up to his neck, "after which they made a small fire near his head" which roasted the head alive.

It was left to Williamson to dig the graves, "which, feeble and terrified as I was, the dread of suffering the same fate enabled me to do." Yet despite his physical and mental terror, Williamson was able to look beyond the Indians to the source of his suffering, "for, had these savages been never tempted with the alluring bait of all-powerful gold, myself as well as hundreds of others, might still have lived most happily in our stations."

With the coming of snow, the Indians, fearful of being tracked by whites, headed into the wilderness, some two hundred miles from the remotest plantations, to their winter quarters. Here there were wigwams, women, and children. "Dancing, singing and shouting were their general amusements." Stripped of his clothing for the Indians' use, Williamson was forced to weather the winter dressed "such as they usually wore themselves, being a piece of blanket, and a pair of mockasons, or shoes, with a yard of coarse cloth, to put round me instead of breeches."

In the spring, with Williamson again as pack mule, the Indian men, about 150 strong, set out on another war party, this time headed toward the Irish settlements near the Blue Hills. A war council was held and the group segmented into companies of twenty men. As they neared the plantations, Williamson was left behind at the Indians' nightly camp; in familiar country now, he began to plan an escape.

One day while Williamson was left bound at camp, the Indians traversed the countryside in search of game. At night, exhausted, they gorged themselves and promptly fell asleep. Williamson attempted to see if any were awake, "but after making a noise and walking about, sometimes touching them with my feet, I found there was no fallacy." He tried to steal one of the Indians' guns, but was unable to get one from under their sleeping heads. "Disappointed in this, I began to despair of carrying my design into execution: yet, after a little recollection, and trusting myself to the Divine protection, I set forwards, naked and defenceless as I was."

Terrified, unarmed, Williamson moved gingerly at first, pausing every four or five yards and looking back toward the Indian camp, waiting for someone to waken and sound the alarm. At two hundred yards, he began to stretch out: "I mended my pace, and made as much haste as I possibly could . . . when on a sudden, I was struck with the greatest terror at hearing the wood-cry, as it is called, which the savages I had left were making, upon missing their charge: *Jo hau! Jo hau!*"

He plunged into the woods, sometimes falling and bruising himself, cutting his feet and legs on rocks. On and on he fled until at daybreak he crawled into a hollow tree to rest. "But my repose was in a few hours destroyed at hearing the voices of the savages near the place where I was hid, threatening and talking how they would use me, if they got me again." He remained undiscovered, however, and stayed hidden "in my apartment all that day without further molestation."

At night Williamson set out again, "frightened; thinking each twig that touched me a savage." The next day he concealed himself again, then headed out again at night, keeping as much as possible off the main paths. Alert as he was, it was impossible to be too careful. On the fourth night, after he had traveled many miles, an inadvertent rustling of leaves flushed out a party of Indians from around a fire in the woods, grabbing up their weapons as they ran. Williamson was frozen in his tracks when "to my great surprize and joy I was relieved by a parcel of swine that made towards the place where I had guessed the savages to be; who on seeing them, imagined that they had caused the alarm."

Bruised, crippled, terrified, he forged on until dawn, "when, thinking myself safe, I lay down under a great log, and slept till about noon." By evening, Williamson had reached the summit of a hill where, "looking out if I could spy any habitations of white people, to my inexpressible joy, I saw some which I guessed to be about ten miles distant."

At about four o'clock in the afternoon of the following day, a figure "in such a frightful condition [that it] alarmed the whole family" knocked at the door of a farmer named John Bell. His wife, who opened the door, fled screaming into the house. Accosted by the master, gun in hand, the wild creature revealed himself to be the same Peter Williamson who had been reported murdered by Indians some months before. Embracing him, the Bells took him in, "affectionately supplied me with all necessaries, and carefully attended me till my spirits and limbs were pretty well recovered."

When he was able to ride, Williamson set out on a borrowed

horse for his father-in-law's house in Chester County, where he arrived on January 4, 1755. "Scarce one of the family could credit their eyes, believing with the people I had lately left, that I had fallen a prey to the Indians."

Received and embraced by his family with great affection, Williamson inquired for his wife and was told that she had died two months before.

"This fatal news greatly lessened the joy I otherwise should have felt at my deliverance from the dreadful state and company I had been in."

As a returned captive, Williamson now found himself an authority on conditions among the Indians. He was sent for and interviewed by the governor, and gave two days of testimony before the Assembly. The Indians, he assured the colonial officials, were friends of the French, who supplied them "with arms and ammunition, and greatly encouraged them in their continual excursions and barbarities," rewarding them not only with bounties for scalps but with presents of all kinds, including rum.

Widowed, with his farm destroyed and his lands laid waste, the accidental Indian expert was invited to join the army being raised by General William Shirley, the governor of Massachusetts, to wage a campaign against the French and Indians. Williamson enlisted "with the greatest alacrity . . . to exert the utmost of my power in being revenged on the hellish authors of my ruin."

Sent to Boston, Williamson drilled with other troops, amid a growing anxiety for retaliation against the tribes now committing "great outrages and devastations in the back parts of the provinces." When a family was butchered within thirty miles of the city, Williamson joined a volunteer party, intent on vengeance. Overtaking a band of Indians within a mile of the ruined plantation, the volunteers rushed in with bayonets fixed "and killed every man of them." While a young woman, a survivor of the slaughtered family, was recovered from captivity, "our men were busily employed in cutting, hacking and scalping the dead Indians . . . so desirous was every man to have a share in wreaking his revenge on them."

The scope of the war was increasing, as well as its intensity. In July, along with his regiment, Williamson marched to Oswego in upstate New York to help garrison the forts along Lake Ontario against the French, Indians, and Canadians. Though the forts had been rebuilt and others added, they were both undergunned and undermanned, nor were the British vessels on the lake of sufficient size or armament to withstand the French. In addition, the British Crown was proving slow with both rations and pay. The result was that by winter there were some eleven hundred men "living in perpetual terror, on the brink of famine, and become mutinous for want of their pay."

The defending forces had been earlier demoralized by the failure of the British general Edward Braddock in his expedition against Fort Duquesne in July. Braddock, who had arrived with a considerable force, ignored the advice of the colonials "and could not conceive that such a people could instruct him." Worse yet, he underestimated his enemy, regarding it "an absurdity to suppose that Indians would ever attack regulars," and he made no effort to instruct his men to resist "their peculiar manner of fighting." This swanking of the locals, yet another preview of British attitudes toward colonials during the Revolution, cost Braddock the battle, the expedition, and his life.

Combined with the unsuccessful attempts on the French forts at Niagara and Crown Point, Braddock's defeat had badly jarred support, organization, and confidence in the British behalf. The French, meanwhile, instead of being satisfied with their victories, grew more aggressive, and the Indian depredations, now often led by French officers, were more flagrant.

At Oswego, the forts were the scene of repeated skirmishes, in one of which Peter Williamson was shot through the left hand, "which entirely disabled my third and fourth fingers." After a brief trip to Albany, he was sent back to the line. Rumors of reinforcements of men and arms tantalized the defenders of the forts; additional men arrived; a new brigantine and sloop were fitted out to patrol the lake; but the British forces were dilatory, while the French, under Montcalm, were able to take advantage of the Indians' experience at backcountry movement and fighting. Traveling in columns, often at night, drawing cannon along wooded paths, wading and swimming rivers to invest and attack their targets, the French forces surrounded the still undersupplied British forts. "About ten o'clock, the enemy's battery was ready to play; at which time, all our places of defence were either enfiladed or ruined by the constant fire of their cannon." A council of war was held, and the engineers concluded that the works could no longer be held.

"The chamade was accordingly ordered to be beat, and the firing ceased on both sides." The French presented their terms, meanwhile bringing up more troops and cannon to enforce them. The forts capitulated and the defenders were taken prisoner, to be shipped off to Montreal. And the French turned loose the Indians, "who scalped and killed all the sick and wounded in the hospitals."

For the third time in his life, Peter Williamson was taken off a captive.

The French, now masters of the lake, carried the prisoners by boat across Lake Ontario and down the St. Lawrence to Montreal, where they were lodged in the fort. Here the French "used various means to win some of our troops over to their interest, or at least do their work in the fields." Williamson, among others, refused. They were then taken aboard ship to Quebec, where they were put in jail.

Here again the French offered to let the prisoners out to help bring in the harvest "they having scarce any people left in that country but old men, women and children." Those men who did go out found themselves worked so hard on starvation rations that they "chose confinement again rather than liberty on such terms."

The presence of some fifteen hundred war prisoners, guarded only by eighteen overworked soldiers, alarmed the townspeople of Quebec. As did the prospect of trying to feed them in a time of local famine. To ensure the health and well-being of the inhabitants and to keep the prisoners from going back to war against them, it was decided to ship them all back to England.

With five hundred other prisoners, Williamson was put aboard a French packet, sailing under a flag of truce. In November of 1756, after six weeks on short rations, the ship arrived at Plymouth. For the first time since his kidnapping, Peter Williamson was about to set foot in Britain.

After a recuperative furlough of four months, the men were ordered back to Plymouth for reassignment. Williamson, on inspection, was declared incapable of service because of the disability of his hand. Mustered out of the army, he was allowed six shillings to carry him home to Aberdeen, "but finding that sum insufficient to subsist me half the way, I was obliged to make my application to the honorable gentlemen of the city of York." Williamson had prepared a manuscript, a memoir of his kidnapping and adventures among the Indians, and the York merchants agreed to subscribe to a printing. "And after disposing of several of my books thro' the shire, I took the first opportunity of going in quest of my relations at Aberdeen."

Returned from another world, loaded with copies of a book recounting his adventures, Peter Williamson headed back to what he anticipated would be a hero's homecoming.

Williamson hoped to support himself by selling his book among his friends and relatives in Aberdeen. No sooner had he offered his work for sale, however, than he found himself arraigned before the town's court of judicature. The complaint against him charged that "I had been guilty of causing print, publishing and dispersing this scurrilous and infamous libel, reflecting greatly upon the characters and reputations of the merchants of Aberdeen, and on the town in general." It was recommended that Williamson be made an example of and that copies of his book be seized and publicly burned.

Denied both counsel and time to prepare a defense, Williamson was threatened by the magistrates with imprisonment unless he signed a recantation of his book, dictated by themselves, which declared that "I had no ground for advancing and uttering the calumnies mentioned in my book against the merchants of Aberdeen."

When he had submitted to their declaration, the magistrates ordered Williamson to remain available "to stand trial on the said complaint at any time when called for, and imprisoned until performance." All copies of his book were seized, he was committed to the custody of the town officers, and taken to jail. Bailed out by his landlord the following day, Williamson heard the magistrates pass sentence on their own complaint. The offensive pages of all copies of his book were to be cut out and "burnt at the market cross by the hands of the common hangman"; Williamson was ordered to hand in a signed declaration begging pardon of the magistrates and merchants, and to consent to have this recantation published "in the York newspapers, or any other newspapers they think proper." To ensure his providing this declaration, he was to be incarcerated in the town tollbooth until he did. After which he was to be fined ten shillings and run out of town.

This flagrant railroading caused Williamson to look back almost nostalgically upon his treatment by the Indians: "I could not help considering myself in a more wretched state, to be reduced to submit to such barbarities in a civilized country, and the place of my nativity, than when a captive among the savage Indians."

Banished from the city to which he had so painstakingly returned, stripped of what little he owned, Williamson pondered how he might redress himself against the magistrates, as he had against his American captors. He made his way to Edinburgh, where "ignorant of the law and unacquainted with any of its members, equally destitute of money and friends, I was utterly at a loss to whom, or in what manner, I should apply for direction." He was every bit as much at rope's end as he had been when he arrived a kidnapped boy bound to servitude in America. Once again he was rescued by a stranger.

It was Providence, according to Williamson, "who threw me in the way of a Gentleman versant in the law," a man of "knowledge, character, and integrity, by whose advice I was conducted and by whose interest I was supported."

When Williamson had finished describing to this unnamed lawyer the circumstances of his arraignment and sentencing, with the magistrates doubling as accusers and judges, the absence of a formal complaint, the lack of legal counsel or time to prepare an adequate defense, the sympathetic attorney announced "that I was not only entitled to ample damages from my persecutors, but that the Court of Session would find no difficulty toward these, with full costs of suit.''

At the lawyer's suggestion, a process of oppression and damages was initiated on Williamson's behalf against the magistrates of Aberdeen. Aware, either from his own experience or from Williamson's description of the extent to which kidnapping was openly practiced in Aberdeen, the lawyer began taking depositions in September of 1760 from people familiar with the trade.

Peter Williamson helped collect them. "And though I had not the least knowledge of or connection with any single evidence I might bring, yet the trade of Kidnaping was so flagrant in that country, and had left such an impression on the minds of the people, that I was under no difficulty to bring a complete proof of the practice.''

The depositions, even today, make infuriatingly convincing reading. Alexander King, a friend of Peter Williamson's father, said that James Williamson went to Aberdeen in search of his son, only to be told that Peter was in custody in a barn "and they would not let him speak to him; and afterwards . . . that the merchants of Aberdeen had carried away his son to Philadelphia and sold him for a slave.'' Robert Reid, who lived near the Williamsons in this country, was visiting in Aberdeen when his sister "proposed to go to a barn to see the country boys who were going over to Philadelphia.'' When they got to the barn, Reid heard "music and a great noise'' from inside, but refused to enter "because it occurred to him, that he had heard in his own country that many boys had been decoyed . . . to go over to America.'' He was told there were between thirty and forty boys in the barn. After this, Reid's mother refused to allow him to go to Aberdeen again, as "the son of one Williamson . . . who lived within two miles of her, was amissing.''

Isabel Wilson, who testified she had heard James Williamson frequently complaining that his son was missing, recalled visiting a malt barn to see one Peter Ley, who had engaged to go to America and who was a man of about thirty and "that upon that occasion, she saw the barn full of boys and men, to the number of fifty and upwards . . . and they had a piper amongst them.'' A man named George Johnston said that as a boy he had been sent over by an uncle to Virginia to be put under the care of a friend there. On his ship, the *Indian Queen,* were more than sixty boys indentured to serve in Virginia. "Many of these boys," Johnston testified, "were engaged by different artifices to enter into the said indentures, without the consent of their parents." An Alexander Grigerson recalled that he and another boy, returned from hunting in a nearby wood, were come upon by "three countrymen on horseback" who asked the boys "if they would go with them, and they would clothe them like gentlemen, and said very kind things to them." When the boys refused the invitation, the three men said they would take them by force "and thereupon alighted from their horses: and while the said three men were tying their horses to growing trees, [the boys] ran away into the wood and hid themselves in a thick bush."

A woman named Margaret Ross testified that some seventeen years before, her son, James Ingram, then about twelve years of age, whom she had sent on an errand of Aberdeen, "was taken up by Alexander Gray, merchant in Aberdeen, in order to be carried to the plantations." Young Ingram was detained in Aberdeen for eight days, but had liberty to go through the town, where he was employed by Gray as a shill, going "through the town with other boys, in companies, beating the drum." Going to church on Sunday at Gallowgate, Mrs. Ross spotted her son, grabbed him, and carried him home with her to Loanhead, about half a mile from Aberdeen. Here she kept him for some time "until four men came out of Aberdeen for him, in the night time, while she and her husband were in bed and their son at their feet." The four men said they had come from Alexander Gray and wanted to carry James Ingram to Aberdeen. "When her son heard them saying so, he wept and shed tears; and they insisting, caused him to rise out of bed and go along with them to Aberdeen."

Her husband, the boy's father, followed the men to Alexander Gray's house, where the following day he met with Gray. The merchant said that if the father paid seven Scottish pounds for the expense of maintaining the boy, Gray would give him back his son. Margaret Ross then went to the provost of the town, who ordered Gray and the Rosses to appear before him. Gray appeared, demanded charges, and claimed that the boy had complained that his mother was cruel to him. When the provost

ordered the boy's return, Gray said "he had given off the boy to
one Mr. Copland at the Gallowgate." Sending an officer for Copland, the provost ordered him to return Mrs. Ross's son to her.
Copland "went along with her to a barn at the back side of the
town, where her son and several other boys were." Several boys
came out of the barn calling to Copland "for shoes and other
necessaries." James Ingram came to the door, where Copland
claimed a striped waistcoat the boy was wearing, "which was
taken from him accordingly." Mrs. Ross "put a plaid about her
son . . . and carried him home with her."

What must have been the most telling testimony of all was
given by William Jamieson, for some years a resident of the town
of Oldmeldrum, about twelve miles from Aberdeen. In the spring
of 1741, Jamieson's son John, then between ten and eleven years
of age, was missing from home. Inquiring among his neighbors,
Jamieson was told that his son had been seen in the company of
a man who was a servant to John Burnet, an Aberdeen merchant
also known as Bonny John, and that Jamieson's son, along with
two other boys of about the same age, were traveling with the
man toward Aberdeen, "and that his son would be sent to the
Plantations." Within days, Jamieson went to Aberdeen and
sought out Burnet, who told him that he had several boys but
didn't know if Jamieson's son was one of them, and that even if
he was, Jamieson "would not get him back, because he was
engaged with him."

Jamieson then left Burnet "and went down about the shore,
where he had been informed the boys were out getting the air."
Here he came upon a crowd of boys, about sixty in number,
"diverting themselves" while under the guard of a man with a
horsewhip. According to Jamieson, when the boys ventured out
of the crowd, the man struck them with the whip. Spotting his
son John among the boys, Jamieson called to him; the boy "came
up to him and told him that he would willingly go home with him
if he was allowed." As they were talking, Burnet's overseer
"came up and gave the boy a lash with his whip, and took him
by the shoulders, and carried him among the rest, and immediately drove them off."

Jamieson followed the crowd of boys as they were marched
through town, keeping pace with the overseer, whom he en-

treated to be allowed to speak to his son. The overseer promised
him they could converse when they came to the barn where the
boys were kept, "but when they came there, the overseer locked
the barn door and refused Jamieson access."

Walking back through Aberdeen, the despondent Jamieson related his story to several trades people, who told him "that it
would be in vain for him to apply to the magistrates to get his son
liberate; because some of the magistrates had a hand in those
doings, as well as the said John Burnet."

Unable to retrieve his son personally or through the Aberdeen
authorities, Jamieson returned to Oldmeldrum. That summer, he
traveled to Edinburgh to seek recourse beyond Aberdeen. There
Jamieson was told that the ship his son was on had sailed for
Maryland "about a fortnight or so" after the father had last seen
him. He was recommended to the clerk of the Duke of Edinburgh, who gave Jamieson a summons against John Burnet,
before the Lords of Council and Sessions, for restitution of his
son.

Returning to Aberdeen, Jamieson was unable to get his summons served on Burnet, since "none of the messengers in Aberdeen would disoblige him." Persisting, Jamieson had the
summons served by a messenger from Oldmeldrum. Burnet, flex-
ing his political muscle, applied to the Earl of Aberdeen, who
also happened to be Jamieson's landlord, to settle the issue. The
three men met at the earl's house, Haddo, where it was agreed
"that the said John Burnet should give his bond to restore [Ja-
mieson's] son to him within the space of a twelvemonth, under
the penalty of fifty pounds sterling."

Jamieson didn't get the bond. Instead, the earl promised that
he would secure it from Burnet. Shortly afterward, at the end of
summer in 1742, Lord Aberdeen died. Jamieson, meanwhile, had
enlisted as a soldier and been sent to Flanders, "where he served
some years, and upon his return John Burnet was become bankrupt and had left the country." Jamieson was left not knowing
whether his son was dead or alive, "having never heard of him
since he was carried away from Aberdeen."

The breadth and depth of these depositions, the willingness of
so many unacquainted people to declare such things under oath,

and the variety and convergence of their experiences suggest that kidnapping in Aberdeen had become an industry, with routines that had become institutionalized through decades of official tolerance and unconcealed practice. And that such exploitation was ingrained in the whole process of recruiting, shipping and selling children for labor, since it rested on a foundation of unequal contracts.

In their testimony in behalf of the magistrates, the Aberdeen merchants, ship captains, and suppliers unwittingly confirmed the same conclusions. A merchant who claimed to have been questioned about passage to America by a volunteering Peter Williamson insisted that "so far as he knows or remembers" under-age children who had been indented could always be returned to their parents or relatives "upon paying up what money the merchant had disbursed on their account." A shipmaster described himself as shipping children to the plantations from Aberdeen, beginning in 1735 up until 1753. A woman who had "provided diet" to boys awaiting passage, including one "Peter McWilliams," had been retained by no fewer than half a dozen different Aberdeen merchant firms for this purpose, beginning in 1740. The town clerk of Aberdeen presented an account book as evidence of Peter Williamson's indebtedness, showing charges of "sixpence for a pair of stockings . . . fivepence for a woollen cap . . . and one shilling and three pence for board," thereby confirming the city of Aberdeen's participation in the practice.

To have supported so extensive a trade over a period of so many years, based entirely on the voluntary shipment of otherwise unwanted boys, Aberdeen would have had to represent the greatest concentration of foundlings, runaways, and vagrants in human history. If, as Peter Williamson pointed out, enlistment was always voluntary, then why was confinement of the boys, aboard ship, in local homes or barns, necessary at all? The very vehemence of the attack on Williamson by the magistrates, who "begrudged me my liberty, and the freedom I took to relate my misfortunes," suggests the suppression of a disagreeable truth. It also raises issues beyond kidnapping that were to reappear in the final rupture between Britain and her colonies.

"Authority improperly used," Williamson, who had certainly

seen his share of it, observed, "may become the most dreadful instrument of oppression."

It was a conclusion in which the judges of the court of sessions concurred. In February of 1762, the lords found for Peter Williamson "to the sum of one hundred pounds sterling . . . and find the Defenders, conjunctly and severally, liable in the expenses of this process." It was a decision that the magistrates protested, only to be overruled.

"Happy is that nation," exulted Peter Williamson, "wherein is justice dispensed with an equal hand to the poor and rich . . . whose judges . . . become the guardians of the liberties and properties of the people . . . and the terrors of the tyrant and the oppressor."

Within fifteen years, the people in the country of his captivity —where the indentured servant "by foolishly listening to the deceitful promises of these recruiters for slaves, at once stakes his happiness, his liberty and perhaps his life"—would, in the name of these same rights, make war.

Voices

If I were sure the colonists had, at their leaving this country, sealed a regular compact of servitude; that they had solemnly abjured all the rights of citizens; that they had made a vow to renounce all ideas of liberty for them and their posterity to all generations, yet I should hold myself obliged in my own day, and to govern two millions of men, impatient of servitude, on the principles of freedom.

—EDMUND BURKE
Conciliation with America, 1775

PART FOUR
STIRRED

Here and there, individual people had begun to question their grievances, examine causes, consider alternative courses. This world was new. Must it be subjected to the old necessities? Were the rights gradually earned in Europe part of a process that must be repeated or, like the vast woods and fields of America, the foundation for something beyond, perhaps something entirely new? Was the voice of authority, based on a king and Parliament an ocean away, still to be heeded here? Or was it like an indenture, a term that, once served, must now be shrugged off, before the freedoms promised might be claimed in full?

Alone at first, or in pockets, they disputed what they had been officially told. Challenged the accepted wisdom of the ages. And found, one senses to their gratified surprise, not the isolation they had risked and perhaps anticipated, but contact with a surprising number of fellow colonials whose experience duplicated or paralleled their own.

20

DANIEL DULANY

IN 1728, Daniel Dulany, a wealthy Maryland lawyer, former Assembly delegate and provincial attorney general, published a pamphlet entitled *The Rights of the Inhabitants of Maryland to the Benefit of English Laws*. The work is considered the prototype of the pamphlets that were to constitute the main body of political discourse up to and including the Revolution. Based on the political philosophy of John Locke, the paper was one of the earliest and most influential colonial arguments in favor of guaranteeing the rule of law and not men in America. The colonists, Dulany argued, were Englishmen, and therefore entitled to the enjoyment of English liberties and the benefits of English law.

"Tis by virtue of this Law," Dulany wrote, "that a British Subject may with Courage and Freedom, tell the most daring and powerful Oppressor that he must not injure him with Impunity."

This argument, with its colonial claim to the legal rights of Englishmen and its invoking of natural law, was half a century ahead of its time. More remarkable is the fact that the man advancing it had, as chief prosecutor of a colony under the propri-

etorship of Lord Baltimore, been the officer responsible for the
enforcement of laws denying those same rights.

Addressed to the people of a colony more dependent on indentured labor than any other, the pamphlet was written by a man
who had entered Maryland as a servant himself.

Born in Queen's County, Ireland, in 1685, Daniel Dulany was
one of three emigrant sons of a shabby-genteel Irish squire,
Thomas Dulany, who proudly traced his family back to a twelfth-
century Irish bishop. Though not a man of means, Thomas Dulany believed in educating his sons, and Daniel Dulany was attending the University of Dublin when the family money ran out.

His father had recently remarried, and his brothers, intrigued
by the recruitment promotion of the Lords Baltimore, members
of the Irish peerage and hereditary proprietors of the province of
Maryland, had decided to emigrate. Daniel chose to join them,
and in 1703 took ship for America as a redemptioner.

Maryland in these years was a plantation colony so committed
to the growing of tobacco that the cured leaf was legally acceptable as cash and was used for paying fines and settling debts.
Tobacco grew down to the shores of the Chesapeake, where
oceangoing vessels anchored to unload their cargoes of servants
and, after the holds were cleansed of pestilence with burned tobacco, set sail for England with a golden load of smokable nego-
tiable currency. This settled, prosperous area of Maryland was
known as the Tobacco Coast, and the inlet where the Dulany
brothers were landed had been christened Port Tobacco.

To be a university-trained (even though not graduated) young
man in this settled, yet expanding community was to find oneself
as immediately employable as a carpenter or a stonemason.
There was to be no stint as a malaria-ridden field hand for Daniel
Dulany. Purchased by Colonel George Plater, an attorney with a
booming practice in a profession as yet hardly known in the
colonies, Dulany was put to work immediately as a law clerk, at
the same time serving the kind of legal apprenticeship which
would soon be reserved for planters' sons.

While his brothers disappeared into the shifting tide of men
along the Chesapeake coast, Daniel Dulany was developing increasingly potent legal muscles in the rough and tumble Maryland

courtrooms. He befriended Thomas Macnemara, a tempestuous, insolent courtroom bully, a lawyer who was also a former Irish redemptioner. A coarse, earthy man who had impregnated and married his master's niece, bitten off another man's ear, and been caught in the act of forcing his attentions on an eleven-year-old girl, Macnemara remained a popular and even admired figure in the courts, and became the unofficial partner of the observant, pondering Dulany. Their friendship was further tested in 1710 by Macnemara's conviction for manslaughter, for which he was branded in the hand with the letter "M." Astonishingly, Dulany remained loyal to Macnemara and seemed to profit from the association, playing the calm, professional Dr. Jekyll to Macnemara's rampaging Mr. Hyde. When Macnemara, who had meanwhile been disbarred by a specific act of the Maryland Colonial Assembly, died suddenly, Dulany was named guardian for his son.

Profiting from the contrast between himself and the mercurial Macnemara, Dulany acquired a reputation for principle and probity and enjoyed the trust of public office. After a series of minor local appointments. Dulany moved to the provincial capital, Annapolis, where he was elected to a seat in the lower house of the Assembly and was appointed attorney general.

The colony during these years was pulled to and fro politically between the planters, with their increasing wealth and urge for corresponding power and autonomy, and the reasserted authority of the office of the lord proprietor. Beginning in 1715, Charles, the new and fifth Lord Baltimore, attempted to rule his palatinate in fact as well as in name as absolute lord proprietor. Appointment to public office, the authority to summon the Assembly, and the dispensation of justice reverted to the proprietor instead of the English Crown. The colony's traditionally broad religious tolerance began to narrow.

Men in public life within the colony now tended to divide on all issues into two blocs—the court party favoring the lord proprietor and his appointed governor, and the country party supporting the interests of the resident planters and freeholders. In 1722, Dulany, in company with Charles Bordley, the colony's other leading attorney, introduced resolutions in the lower house of the Assembly, an elective body responsive to the residents, which would have established its authority over the upper house, which was appointive and effectively controlled by the lord proprietor. Composed by two skillful lawyers, guided by the example of the growing strength of Parliament at the expense of the English Crown, the resolutions actually passed both houses but were vetoed by the proprietor on the recommendation of his legal counselors.

In defense of the resolutions, Dulany became head of a committee which searched the records of the province for instances of the extension of English law to Maryland. In 1724, as attorney general, he prepared a draft oath for judges which would have pledged them to ignore instructions from both proprietor and Crown in dispensing justice. In thus attempting to extend the English tradition of an independent judiciary, Dulany had become the champion of the country party cause.

Lord Baltimore, bristling at this resistance to his reassertion of proprietary powers, disapproved Dulany's judges' oath. Meanwhile, the Annapolis voters, many of whom held or depended upon proprietary office, voted Dulany out of the Assembly. A few weeks later, Dulany found himself dismissed as attorney general by Governor Calvert. He was suddenly out of politics.

Dulany now withdrew into private practice and became a country squire. At the same time, he applied the materials he'd researched on the tradition of English law to the composition of his political testament, *The Rights of the Inhabitants*. Basing his argument on a combination of statute and common law, he wrote in the language of republicanism which members of the country party would quote for years to come.

Like the colonial pamphleteers of the Revolutionary era, Dulany reached back to the republics of antiquity to cite examples of the ideal relationship between ruler and ruled. His theme was as old as the Magna Carta: Which was to govern, laws or men? In phrases that anticipated and may have inspired the writings of Jefferson and Paine, Dulany argued that by the law of nature "All men were equal," and that by the law of reason and the revealed laws of God "Men are enjoyned to treat One Another with Humanity, Justice and Integrity." As Englishmen, the inhabitants of Maryland were entitled to the full protection of English law: "If we may be deprived of any Part of that Right without our Consent . . . We may by the same Reason and Authority be deprived of some other Part; and our Lives, Liberties and Properties rendered Precarious."

Out of office, Dulany grew rich. He drew fat fees from defending the property rights of the prosperous. In a famous case that continued for ten years in the Maryland courts and included five appeals to the King in Council, Dulany successfully represented the merchant firm of Jonathan Forward and Company, owned by the friend and protector of Henry Justice. The merchandise involved was 131 English convicts, "His Majesty's Seven-Year Passengers," transported to Maryland as indentured servants and seized by the Admiralty for the captain's non-payment of debt. As his reward for representing such interests, Dulany acquired absentee property, rent holdings, tobacco land, servants, and slaves. And in a few years he underwent a change in conviction as drastic in its effect on his family's fortunes as one of the tragic turnabouts in Greek drama.

Dulany was now at about the age his father had been when the three Dulany brothers took ship for the New World. Like his father, Dulany had recently remarried. He had five children of his own, as well as Macnemara's son to support. His old friends and occasional legal adversaries, Macnemara and Bordley, who'd spurred him on and kept him honest, were both dead. The thought must have occurred to him that, like his father, he might lose his sons to some remote opportunity if he was unable to provide for them financially.

During these years, Dulany languished politically. He wrote to friends of being depressed and in "despair of a cure" for the colony's ills. Then in 1731 things began to change for the ex–attorney general. Samuel Ogle, a shrewd and self-confident administrator, was dispatched by Lord Baltimore to govern the family fiefdom for which Baltimore paid the English Crown the token rent of two Indian arrows per year. Dulany instantly found himself on better footing with this new governor, who seemed to take a great personal interest in him. What he didn't realize was that Ogle was deliberately cultivating him.

"I find," Ogle confided in a secret report to Lord Baltimore, "that nothing in the world has hurt your interest more than your Governors declaring open enmity to such men as Bodeley [Bordley] and Dulany, who were capable of doing you either a great deal of good or harm."

At Ogle's suggestion, Lord Baltimore came to Maryland to set matters in the colony in order with his own hands. As part of his itinerary he had several private meetings and an exchange of views with Dulany. We can imagine what heady stuff this must have been for a man who had left Ireland an impoverished eighteen-year-old indentured servant. He now was a man of such wealth and influence that he was being confided in by an Irish peer, the proprietor of a great and prosperous colony, who had crossed the ocean to seek Dulany's advice. We do know that an understanding of some kind was reached and that Baltimore, a man who had charmed as sophisticated a judge of men as Frederick the Great, succeeded in winning over the colonial lawyer completely.

The newly converted Dulany found himself rapidly restored to political power. He was given his say in the major share of appointments made by the lord proprietor and was himself offered three different offices: attorney general (his old job), judge of the court of vice admiralty, and chief agent, or collector of Lord Baltimore's quit rents. Dulany eventually accepted, and simultaneously held, all three positions.

As agent, Dulany became directly responsible for overseeing Baltimore's property rights in Maryland, a position that put him constantly in conflict with the interests of the country party. Within a few years, the man who had issued from the depths of his political and legal experience a stirring call against the arbitrary power of any man, was professing the belief that the interests of the country and the lord proprietor were one and the same.

This complete philosophical reverse of field was not simply a matter of opportunism. Dulany was already a wealthy man, and his new course was to leave him increasingly isolated as relations between proprietor and country inhabitants deteriorated. Once chosen, it was adhered to faithfully. The bond between the Dulany family and the proprietor's office was to last beyond the

Revolution, to the Dulany family's immense disadvantage. In Dulany's own eyes, he had not changed positions at all but merely matured, refining his advocacy of the rights of life, liberty, and property to the realizable pre-eminent right of property. It focused the mind with beautiful simplicity, and imbued everything with purpose. In defending property, he was defending everything he had gained in America—land, position, family, wealth, influence—while at the same time separating himself from everything he had been before. His lands, his buildings, his law practice, his sons' careers, all now spoke through him. Property had become his principle.

It now drove him, with a logic of its own, toward a strange new destiny. Beyond being a man of wealth and influence, Dulany was now amassing one of the great estates of the American colonial era. He invested in iron mills and bought and developed great tracts of Western land. He began grooming his sons for the administration of his own private proprietorship. He sent his oldest son, Daniel, Jr., to England to be educated at Eton. His younger son, Walter, he attempted to establish in business in the colonies, buying him into a number of partnerships, including one with the infamous Dutch shipping merchants who carried redemptioners to Philadelphia. As a former servant himself, Dulany could have had few illusions about the nature of the business he was getting into; to his credit, he insisted that "the masters who have the Command of these ships, ought to be very careful of the Provisions, to be kind and humane to the People and to see that everything is kept clean." Yet when the redemptioners continued to sicken and die, he shirked responsibility for this by concluding that the Germans "are naturally very nasty, and that nastiness to which they are accustomed in their own country is destructive in a long sea voyage."

Fancying himself a political realist, Dulany confined his interests to the futures of his sons, the Western settlements, the tobacco trade, and the encouragement of German settlement of the Maryland backcountry. As the general mood of the colonies moved closer to that expressed by Dulany in his *Rights of the Inhabitants,* the sentiments of Dulany and the Dulany family identified not only with the interests of the proprietor but also those of the Crown. In the name of defending the rights of property, they would miss participating in the greatest establishment of rights of all kinds in history. In remaining faithful to Daniel Dulany's understanding with his proprietor, they would shatter and lose the great estate he had built. It is the stuff of Greek tragedy, transported by bound souls to America.

When Daniel Dulany died in 1753, his estate extended over six counties on both sides of Chesapeake Bay and included 190 slaves parceled out among ten plantations. There were, as well, thousands of undivided acres and thousands of pounds of money out on loan. His son, Daniel, Jr., who assumed the administration of the estate in addition to maintaining the family law practice and holding the proprietary office of commissary general, had by 1757 driven himself to a mental breakdown.

Restored after a recuperative stay in England, Daniel, Jr., returned to assume and serve with distinction in the post of provincial secretary. When the Stamp Act and other disputed legislation of the 1760s and '70s widened the chasm between England and the colonies, Dulany as a man of property instinctively adopted a moderate position, which he clung to despite increasing pressure on both sides. Devoted to the principle of law, he withheld nominal recognition of the actual government even when the proprietorship had been scuttled. The Declaration of Independence, based on the same sources as his father's *The Rights of the Inhabitants* and incorporating some of the same phrases, rendered Daniel, Jr., a passive loyalist. His later attempt to declare personal neutrality succeeded only in isolating him further. Dulany Junior's eldest son remained in England throughout the war. Walter Dulany, Daniel Senior's second son, became an active loyalist and entered into an intrigue in which he hinted he could persuade General Washington, "his bosom friend," to bring the colonies back into the empire. Two of Dulany's nephews accepted commissions in the loyalist volunteers and were sent to Florida to fight the Spanish.

Throughout the war, Daniel, Jr., struggled to look after the family's interests, assisting relatives in need and resisting as long as possible confiscation of the Dulanys' holdings. Yet as if the house of Dulany's fall had been ordained by Daniel the elder's fatal choice, the story now ran its full tragic course. Walter Dulany was killed in a duel. One of the Dulany nephews went insane; the other left the state and settled in Delaware. Dulany's eldest son and heir, Daniel III, became a permanent resident of the England of his allegiance.

The Dulany properties, reduced by half during the confiscations of the war, were now subjected to a triple tax. Denied public office, Daniel Dulany, Jr., remained in the family home, the heir to a shattered estate that, but for the consequence of a choice of conscience, might have achieved the enduring family eminence of the Adamses. He died alone, the last direct descendant in the land where the impoverished servant Daniel Dulany had arrived less than a century before.

Voices

It is certainly of the greatest importance to know whether a People are to be governed by Laws . . . or Whether They are to be governed by the Discretion (as some People softly term the Caprice and Arbitrary Pleasure) of any Set of Men.

—DANIEL DULANY
*The Rights of the Inhabitants
of Maryland to the Benefit
of English Laws*

21

ALEXANDER STEWART

IN JULY of 1747, a ship owned by Samuel Smith of London and Richard Gildart of Liverpool arrived off the Virginia capes, bound for Maryland with a cargo of eighty-eight men in chains. Transported to be indentured servants, the men were not convicts but Scottish soldiers taken prisoner at the Battle of Culloden.

Throughout the first half ot the eighteenth century, the royal rule of Protestantism in England was threatened by the continuing claims of the heirs and followers of the last Catholic king in Britain, James II, to the English and Scottish thrones. From time to time, these supporters of the Stuart, or Jacobite cause as it was called, aided by sympathetic governments in France and Spain, mounted political and occasionally military offensives against the Prostestants who had ruled England since the Revolution of 1688.

After the succession of the Hanoverian George I, there was in 1715 a Jacobite uprising, followed in 1719 by a Spanish-backed invasion of Scotland. Though both these attempts failed, Stuart sentiment remained widespread among British Catholics, as well as among certain High churchmen and extreme Tories.

To reduce the threat of another armed, organized uprising, George I pardoned the rebels of 1715 on condition they be transported to the colonies, hiring out the job of shipping them to private contractors. The rebel soldiers, while accepting transportation as a condition of their pardon, balked at signing indentures requiring seven years' colonial servitude. Unlike convict servants, the military prisoners were insistent upon their rights, petitioning both the king and the royal governor in Maryland under the habeas corpus law. Although these attempts to reduce sentence were to no avail, the soldiers who had served out their term returned to the British Isles in such numbers as to keep the Stuart threat constantly alive. And to help mount in 1745 the most serious Jacobite adventure of all.

Led by the Pretender, Charles Edward Stuart or Bonnie Prince Charlie, the Jacobite forces, after an initial victory at Prestonpans, began an advance into England which was halted at Derby. While retreating, the Jacobites were overtaken at Culloden Moor in Scotland, where the largely Scottish army was so thoroughly crushed that the defeat ended both the attempts to re-establish the Stuart monarchy and Scottish resistance to English dominance.

Once again the cry for transportation was raised in England, but this time with an insistence upon harsher terms. It was prosposed that this time each prisoner should be branded in the face, so that the mark of his disloyalty would be on him even if he returned to Scotland. In February of 1747, a pardon was issued to more than seven hundred persons implicated in the rebellion, under the condition that they be transported "to serve . . . in our Colonies in America during the term of their natural lives." In this sentence of transportation for life a loophole was left in a subsequent clause which suggested that the exact period was to be fixed by the custom of the country.

The six hundred or so persons who were finally transported were carried over in ships under the charter of Gildart and Smith. A group of three of these prison vessels sailed for Barbados, but the ships were scattered by storms. One ship, aiming for the

Leeward Islands, was captured by the French, who freed the prisoners at Martinique. The other two ships, with 153 prisoners in all, headed for Maryland.

"On Munday, about twelve o'clock, we weied our ancors and sait sail and away for sea," recalled Alexander Stewart, a young Scottish soldier who was one of the captives from Culloden. "And all the ships for four days kept together till a most violent storm seperat us." Driven apart by the storm, the convoy of prison ships never re-formed, and when Stewart's ship approached the Virginia capes it was alone. Here the prison ship was almost caught when a Spanish vessel "appeared in purshout of us, but could not come within the Capes after us." To the prisoners' regret, the English ship eluded that of the Spanish captain, presumably sympathetic to the Stuart cause. "So this was our misfortune, for if we hade but two hours more play at sea, we had all been his own."

Safe inside the capes, the ship dropped anchor in the Potomac River, after which the captain, a Marylander named Holmes—who, sailing under contract and not at all unsympathetic to these men who were, after all, soldiers in a war that had ended—came between decks and asked them what they intended to do.

"So we told him we was to depend on God's providence and him," to which the captain replied that he would do whatever was in his power for the captured men. At the customs inspection, before his charges had even been put ashore, the captain had the ship's carpenter strike all their chains. "I was the first that got them on," Steward recalled, "and the last that got them off."

On Sunday evening, July 19, 1747, the ship anchored at "Wecomica"—probably the mouth of Wycomico Creek, on the Maryland Western Shore, where the prisoners were to be disembarked. "And as soon as the ship came to an ancor, we was all ordered below dake, for Robert Horner, the supercargo, wanted to speak a queet word to us." The men, gathered below, listened while Horner discoursed on the beauty and goodness of the Maryland countryside and the rich opportunities that awaited them if they would merely sign indentures for a service of seven years. The generosity of the planters was such, said Horner, that "if we pleased them weel," the men's owners would probably release them two years ahead of time and outfit each of them with "a gun, a pick and a mattock, and a soot of cloths." They would then be free to go to any part of the land they pleased.

At this point Stewart—who seems to have been not so much a firebrand as a patient, long-suffering common soldier who at the end of a war had had his fill of taking orders—suggested to Horner that instead of trying to indenture the men in a body, he should go and get the list of the prisoners' names and read it aloud and ask the men individually, "and them that was willing, to answer yes; and them that was not willing, to answer no." Horner agreed and went above to get the list. Upon which the men below crowded around Stewart and asked him what he intended to do.

"I told them they might doe as they pleased, but for mee I would sign non for no man that ever was born, though they should hang me over the yard arms." The stand being taken, the other prisoners then agreed: They would not sign either. "So I told them, Gentlemen, stand by that, then. So they said they would."

It was starting at about this time that British administrators in the colonies and in London began to view the various colonial stirrings of independence as a conspiracy against the Crown. In 1760, Governor Francis Bernard of Massachusetts was convinced that a "faction" had organized a conspiracy against the customs administration; and in 1768, the calling of the Massachusetts Convention so alarmed elements in England that the House of Lords resolved that "wicked and designing men" in the colonies were "evidently manifesting a design . . . to set up a new and unconstitutional authority independent of the crown of England." These feelings intensified as the crisis deepened and became official in October of 1775, when George III declared to Parliament that "the authors and promoters of this desperate conspiracy . . . meant only to amuse by protestations of loyalty to me . . . whilst they were preparing for a general revolt."

When supercargo Horner returned from topside with his list, he began calling roll. One by one the prisoners answered no.

Realizing he'd been had, Horner turned to Stewart and thanked him facetiously, adding, "If you would not doe yourself, you needed not hindred others to have done."

Horner then produced letters from the English king to the Duke of Newcastle, and from Newcastle to Gildart, the merchant who had contracted to transport the prisoners. The letters empowered Gildart, if the prisoners refused to sign the indentures, to go to the colonial governor, where he would get a sufficient guard to keep all the men in prison until they capitulated and signed.

Stewart answered back that Horner might call out whatever guards he pleased, "for we hade the misfortune to be under better guards the time past then that the country was capabile to put upon us." Faced with more than eighty aroused and unchained soldiers, Horner withdrew and went ashore.

The ship's captain, meanwhile, had gone to visit his wife, who lived about a mile and a half from the ship. While Horner headed for Annapolis to enlist support from the governor and from among the local loyalists or "buckskins," the captain wrote letters to the Roman Catholics, Scots, and other Stuart sympathizers he knew in Maryland.

Within a few days Horner had returned, "and all the buckskins in the countrie with him," including Cornel Lee, "a monstrous big fellow, in order to bulle us to assign."

Lee told the prisoners he would make them sign. "And we told him God Almighty had made us once, and he neither could nor should make us again." While buckskin colonials and Jacobite soldiers glowered at one another, Holmes struggled to resolve the situation without bloodshed. On July 22, a sale was announced of freshly transported Scottish servants, to be held on board ship, anchored at "Wecomica," in St. Mary's County, Maryland.

In attendance on the day the sale was held, were "all the gentlemen of three or four counties of Maryland," who had in addition brought their friends, the whole operation orchestrated by the sympathetic Captain Holmes. These men proceeded to buy the indentures of all the eighty-eight prisoners "except three or four that went with the common buckskins . . . and would not take advice to go along with the gentlemen."

Stewart was purchased by a "Mr. Benedict Callvert in Annapolis, who had . . . my being set at libertie at heart as much as any man in the province." Along with the other purchased prisoners, Stewart was promptly set free.

He was then sent along a kind of overground railway from the home of one sympathetic Maryland planter to another, most of whom refused to accept payment of any sort from the money that had been sent to Stewart by his family. At the same time, other Maryland Jacobites were on the lookout for a like-minded sea captain who could be trusted to take Stewart back to Britain.

In this conspiracy of noncompliance with an order of the English Crown can be seen cracks that were to widen into the Revolutionary chasm between colonies and Mother Country. Already there was the realization that royal and parliamentary acts were unenforceable in America without widespread colonial support; the implicit belief that the colonists understood better than the British what was best for their own interests; the spreading sense of shared grievance that politically united men of different classes and economic interests; the willingness to risk individual defiance of the law in the conviction that others would rally to one's side; the overall unspoken understanding that the word of the king was no longer law in America. In all these things we can see the spirit of resistance to British authority that was to reappear again and again during the years of the Stamp Act, the Intolerable Acts, the colonial boycott, the declarations in the colonial assemblies, and the acts of the Continental Congress. As well as the sources of the suspicions of conspiracy, which increased and intensified on both sides.

That this intrigue originated over the issue of indentured servitude in a colony where an estimated two-thirds of the settlers had originally arrived as servants was no coincidence. There were no illusions about what seven years servitude working for a "buckskin"—a marginal frontier planter or tenant farmer—could actually mean in terms of hard work, disease, and short rations. Nor was there any romanticized view of the kind of convict servants the Jacobite prisoners were being lumped with. In 1751, the magistrates of Baltimore and Anne Arundel counties ordered a security of fifty pounds posted as a guarantee of good behavior for every imported felon, only to be overruled by the provincial court. There was hardly a man in Maryland who didn't know the feel of at least one of the manacles—servant's or owner's—that handcuffed men to each other in indentured servitude.

In what seems a remarkable consensus that it was the king who had in fact overstepped the law, the colonists had successfully gutted his order. What was decreed as transportation for life became for many of the Scottish soldiers a round-trip voyage of less than a year.

Alexander Stewart was one of them. "On the 11th of January 1748, I took my live of all my friends and went aboard." The ship was the *Peggie,* bound for Dumfries in Scotland, under the command of Captain David Blair, "ane honest man" and a fellow Scot. The ship was anchored only seven miles away from the home of another Jacobite sympathizer, where Stewart had been staying. The *Peggie* lay in the river a full two weeks before setting sail, and anchored for another twelve days at Hampton Roads, just inside the capes where Stewart's American adventure had begun.

"On the 13th of February 1748, about two in the morning, we got clear of the Capes and put to sea," Stewart concluded, "and befor daylight we got out of the sight of land, and in 27 days we saw the Irish land."

Voices

Warmed with a sense of the injuries which we suffered, neither our gratitude nor our fear could prevent our asserting those rights, the possession of which can alone determine us freemen.

—WILLIAM HICKS
The Nature and Consent of Parliamentary Power Considered, 1768

22

GOTTLIEB MITTELBERGER

IN 1754, Gottlieb Mittelberger, a teacher and organist by trade, returned to the town of Enzweihingen in the Duchy of Württemberg, in what is today West Germany. He set about writing his first and only book, *Journey to Pennsylvania,* a work he had taken "a solemn oath to write . . . even in the name of God."

Four years earlier, in 1750, Mittelberger had left his wife and family and, like thousands of other Palatine Germans during this period, set out down the Rhine River on the uncertain passage to the New World.

The German emigration into Pennsylvania had its origins in a voyage to New York. In 1709, Governor Robert Hunter of New York, then visiting in London, arranged that a contingent of Germans would be recruited to settle in his province for the purpose of providing the British with naval stores: timber, pitch, and oakum. The colonists, called "Servants to the Crown," were contracted to repay the British government for the expense of sending them over. After the Germans had fulfilled their obligations, they were to receive five pounds each, and every family forty acres of land.

In January of 1710, more than three thousand German settlers —the largest single body of colonists ever to leave for America —embarked in ten small ships. It was a long and dreary voyage. The last ship did not arrive until near the end of July, and one vessel was wrecked on Long Island. The deaths en route were officially admitted to be "above 470," and privately estimated at more than 850. Eighty Germans were said to have died aboard a single ship, and most of the survivors were ill. On arrival, the colonists learned that by order of the governor all children were to be apprenticed among the colonists. This exploitive treatment, though it had the effect of turning subsequent settlers away from New York, toward Pennsylvania, nevertheless set the tone for the migration of Germans for the rest of the century.

By 1750, the recruitment and shipment of German settlers had fallen into the hands of Dutch shipping merchants, middlemen with little personal interest in the well-being or prosperity of people in either Germany or Pennsylvania. Locked into the Pennsylvania trade since William Penn (who was half Dutch) had arranged for the importation of English Quakers, the Dutch merchants had refined the redemption system into a cruel and skillful racket.

Certain Germans who had settled in Pennsylvania were hired to return to Germany for the purpose of persuading their countrymen to emigrate to America. Known as Neulanders, these men were paid a commission by the Dutch shipping merchants on every German they talked into taking passage.

With no responsibility beyond furnishing bodies to the shipowners, the Neulanders defrauded rustic Germans by the thousands. Dressed in fine clothing, displaying watches, distributing flyers and pamphlets that depicted America in the most glowing terms, they spoke to country people in the dialect of their own provinces of "Elysian fields abounding in projects which require no labor; [of] mountains . . . full of gold and silver and wells and springs [that] gush forth milk and honey." Pennsylvania was a land, the Neulanders assured their listeners, brimming with opportunity, so rich and varied that "he that goes there as a ser-

vant, becomes a lord; as a maid, a gracious lady; as a peasant, a
nobleman; as a commoner or a craftsman, a baron.''

Law and authority, they reported, were totally controlled by
the people and could be abrogated at their wish. Who, desiring
to better his condition, would not yearn to go to such a country?

And so, "Families break up, they convert their possessions
into money, pay their debts, and the money that remains, they
give for safekeeping to the Neulander.''

More often than not, the money was never seen again.

On the journey down the Rhine, the emigrants had to pass
through as many as thirty-six different customs stations, a procedure which further enriched the shippers by dragging out the
journey into weeks, for which the passengers had to pay by the
day for their keep. Once they had arrived at Rotterdam or Amsterdam, the emigrants were detained another five or six weeks.
After another journey which sometimes took two more weeks,
the vessels arrived at one of the ports in England, where the
passengers encountered yet another delay, while customs duties
were again collected and the ships supplied with full cargo for the
ocean voyage.

"During this time," Mittelberger advised his fellow Germans,
"every one is compelled to spend his last remaining money and
consume his little stock of provisions which had been reserved
for the sea; so that most passengers, finding themselves on the
ocean where they would be in greater need of them, must suffer
greatly from hunger and want.''

Around the docks and wharves and on the embarking ships,
confusion and disorder prevailed. Sometimes one vessel was
loaded with the baggage and chests carrying essential provisions
of people who were assigned to another. No effort was made to
prevent fraud or protect the rights of the emigrants. Many people
who had owned property and converted it into cash were now
swindled out of the last of it by the shipowners, importers, captains, and the Neulanders.

Since the profit in passengers was much greater than in freight,
the ships were so jammed that some people were kept on the
upper deck, exposed to the weather. As a result, the majority of
these died "so that in less than one year, two thousand were

buried in the sea." It didn't matter to the merchants, who collected their fare anyway; the relatives of the deceased were held
responsible for payment of the passage.

Given the most favorable winds, the Atlantic voyage took
seven weeks; often it took eight, ten, or even twelve, under conditions arranged by hardhearted merchants determined to gouge
every last cent of profit out of their passengers: cramped accommodations, cheap meat, bad water, lice. Worst of all were the
storms.

"The waves often seem to rise up like high mountains, sometimes sweeping over the ship," Mittelberger reported. Tossed by
storm and waves, the ship rolls constantly "so that nobody
aboard can either walk, sit or lie down, and the tightly packed
people on their cots, the sick as well as the healthy, are thrown
every which way."

Illness is varied and rampant: seasickness, fever, dysentery,
scurvy, mouth rot. Among the healthy, impatience and resentment grow to murderous levels. People begin blaming each other
for undertaking the voyage, but most of all they cry out against
the Neulanders, "the thieves of human beings." "Many groan
and exclaim: 'Oh!, If only I were back at home, even lying in my
pig-sty!' " Homesick, endangered, physically distressed, people
sink into depression. "Groaning, crying and lamentation go on
aboard day and night; so that even the hearts of the most
hardened, hearing all this, begin to bleed."

Pregnant women and small children seldom survive. A woman
on Mittelberger's ship who died in childbirth during a storm was
pushed through a porthole into the sea when her body could not
be carried to the deck of the cramped, rolling vessel. "I myself,
alas, saw such a pitiful fate overtake thirty-two children on board
our vessel, all of whom were finally thrown into the sea."

Contagious diseases—measles, smallpox—sweep the ship.
There are crippling falls. People are swept overboard.

When at last the new mainland is sighted, the passengers are
physically and emotionally at rope's end. "Then everyone crawls
from below to the deck, in order to look at the land from afar.
And people cry for joy, pray and sing praises and thanks to God.
The glimpse of land revives the passengers, especially those who

are half-dead of illness. Their spirits, however weak they had become, leap up, triumph and rejoice within them. Such people are now willing to bear all ills patiently, if only they can disembark soon and step on land."

Now, with their suffering passed, the goal of it all so tantalizingly near, their resistance at its lowest ebb, the German emigrants are approached by shrewd entrepreneurs, seeking to bargain away their last possession: their personal freedom. Unlike British servants who were indentured to contractors who paid for their transportation and were reimbursed when the servants were sold, the German immigrants were the property of the shipowners, who could keep their passengers on board until they or somebody else paid their sea freight. Only those are let off who can pay for their transportation or give good security. The others must remain on board until they are purchased.

Every day Englishmen, Dutchmen, and High Germans come to the ship from Philadelphia, where the vessel has docked, "and other places, some of them . . . twenty, or thirty or forty hours' journey." From among the healthy people they pick out those who look like promising workers. "Then they negotiate with them as to the length of the period for which they will go into service."

It is a game in which one side holds all the cards. Thousands of miles from home, weakened by illness, generally owing the full amount of their passage, the immigrants must either come to terms or remain aboard ship in sight of the city for another two or three weeks, which means further impoverishment, or in the case of those who are ill, death.

When an agreement was reached, adult persons would bind themselves by written contract to serve three, four, five, or six years, according to their health and age. Children between the ages of ten and fifteen, however, were bound to serve until they were twenty-one.

"Many parents," says Mittelberger, "in order to pay their fares in this way and get off the ship must barter and sell their children as if they were cattle. Since the fathers and mothers often do not know where or to what masters their children are to be sent, it frequently happens that after leaving the vessel, parents and children do not see each other for years on end, or even for the rest of their lives."

Children under the age of five could not be sold. People without the means to pay their way were required to give these children away to be brought up by strangers. In return, the children had to stay in service until they were twenty-one. A person with a sick spouse was held responsible for the fare of the sick partner and was required to serve not only five or six years for himself but also for the spouse. Survivors whose husband or wife had died at sea had also to pay for or serve out the fare of the deceased. Children orphaned by the death of both parents at sea were responsible for their parents' fares as well as their own, and had to serve until the age of twenty-one. "Once free of service, they receive a suit of clothing as a parting gift, and if it has been so stipulated, the men get a horse and the women a cow."

Though Mittelberger observed this ugly practice intimately, he himself was lucky enough to have a paid passage and a job. As organist and schoolteacher at the German St. Augustine's Church in Providence, he supplemented his income by giving private music and German lessons. He made inquiries about the country, he watched, he waited, he listened. And he drew his own conclusions.

"Work is strenuous in this new land," Mittelberger observed, "and many who have just come into the country at an advanced age must labor hard for their bread until they die." Most jobs involved clearing land, great tracts of forest, roots and all. Since new fields were constantly being laid out, Europeans who had been purchased were required to work hard all the time, often in oppressive heat. "Let him who wants to earn his piece of bread honestly," warns Mittelberger, "and who can only do this by manual labor in his own country, stay there rather than come to America."

Running away was useless. Handsome rewards were offered for fugitive servants, and the law was on the masters' side. Terms of service were multiplied upon recapture: for every day of absence an extra week, for every week an extra month, for every month half a year. If the master chose not to take the recaptured runaway back, he could sell him to someone else for the full added punishment term.

Seduced by the Neulanders, people who "believe that in America or Pennsylvania roasted pigeons are going to fly into their mouths without their having to work for them" continue to flood the colony, 22,000 souls in one year, according to Mittelberger. The influx of people reached such a scale that it produced the class of dealers called "soul-drivers," who found it profitable to retail servants among the farmers. Buying the servants from the captains in lots of fifty or more, they would drive them through the backcountry and dispose of them at whatever price they could.

Rank, skill, and learning mean nothing; what is required are workmen and artisans. People not used to manual work "are beaten like cattle until they learn hard labor."

The schoolmaster was offended by the coarseness of life in Pennsylvania. The schools are poorly supported, the education of the young neglected, and teachers are engaged by the season, like cowherds in Germany. Preachers, especially those in rural districts, "are often reviled, laughed at and mocked by young and old." Underpaid, embroiled in quarrels with neighbors, Mittelberger grew increasingly disillusioned with America.

Part of the problem seems to be that he was somewhat misinformed about America to begin with. While he is convincing and seemingly accurate about the things he has seen himself, Mittelberger seems all too eager to suspend disbelief when it comes to what others have told him.

The weather in the colony, in the view of the Indians, has declined since the arrival of the Europeans. The natives suffer heavy snow, cold, torrential rains, as well as severe and terrible thunderstorms, all of which were allegedly unknown to them before the strangers arrived. They blame the Europeans for this "because they, and especially the Germans among them, are for the most part people who use vile and terrible oaths."

In the unfathomed interior of America, Mittelberger assures us, there are, in addition to buffalo, polar bears, monkeys, and "an animal that has a smooth and pointed horn . . . pointing straight out of its head": the unicorn. There are snakes ten, twelve, fifteen, and even eighteen feet long, including an amazing "black snake (twelve to fifteen feet long and thick as an arm)" that has "a marvelous power to charm through their steady glance which, once fixed upon it, forces any creature crossing their path, be it hare, bird or squirrel down from the trees and toward them. Then they pounce on it and devour it."

The black snakes can climb the tallest oaks as well as other trees. "They are also able to charm little children, who are compelled to stand stock-still in front of them. The children then begin to cry pitifully. And so it happens that one can still save them, while the large snakes are still coiled in front of them."

What the Neulanders are to the villages of Württemberg, it would seem, the black snakes are to the wilds of Pennsylvania.

Though there were many things Mittelberger liked about the new country—the variety of plants and wildlife, the plentifulness of food, the opportunity in most trades and professions to make good money—he never got over the horror of the voyage and the cruel exploitation of the Neulanders, "the irresponsible and merciless proceedings of the Dutch traders in human beings and their man-stealing emissaries." These practices he seems to have associated more with the New World than the old. In Württemberg, where there was an established order and everyone knew his place, such barbaric practices could be resisted.

When his desire to return to Germany became known, Mittelberger found himself approached by his former countrymen—Württembergers, Durlachers, Palatines—imploring him "with tears and uplifted hands . . . to publicize their misery and sorrow in Germany. So that not only the common people but even princes and lords might be able to hear about what happened to them; and so that innocent souls would no longer leave their native country, persuaded to do so by the Neulanders, and dragged by them into a similar kind of slavery."

He would, Mittelberger decided, beat the Neulanders at their own game. Returning to Germany, writing in his Palatine dialect, wearing not fancy clothes but his schoolmaster's homespun, he would circulate among his landsmen spreading not seductive exaggerations but the harsh and simple truth.

"And so I vowed to the great God, and promised those people

to reveal the entire truth to the people in Germany, according to the best of my knowledge and ability."

He almost didn't make it.

There was the matter of his voyage home, which could not be made without the knowledge of the Dutch shipping merchants, their agents, the captains, and the hated Neulanders. To these people, who controlled the means of transportation across the Atlantic from Pennsylvania, Mittelberger represented not only the risk of exposure, but was also potentially resalable merchandise, as well as bait that could be used to lure additional catch from among his friends and relatives in Germany. They employed desperate and elaborate forms of trickery to keep him from leaving.

From the shipping merchants in Amsterdam, Mittelberger received word that his wife and child, as well as his sister-in-law and many of his countrymen, had embarked for Philadelphia the previous summer with the year's final transport. If he left now, they would pass one another en route and be separated for at least another year. The merchants knew not only the names of Mittelberger's wife and child, but their ages and heights. Mittelberger's wife, they reported, had stated that her husband had been employed as an organist in Pennsylvania for four years. They showed him a letter to this effect, with his wife's name in it, with the name of the ship and captain that she and their child had sailed with; they even assured him that his wife "had been accomodated in berth Number Twenty-Two with four other women."

"All of this," says Mittelberger, "made me extraordinarily confused and irresolute." He showed the merchants' agents his wife's letters. She would never, she had written, go to America without her husband. On the contrary, she had received word of his planned return and was expecting him with longing. The agents in turn assured him their documents were genuine.

"At last, after mature deliberation, and without a doubt of the intent of Divine direction, I decided to complete my journey."

Yet even now the shipping merchants, alarmed about the consequences of exposure of their practices, were busily trying to keep Mittelberger from reaching Württemberg. They went to his wife and once again tried to wheedle her into going to America. Meanwhile, en route to England, Mittelberger's ship encountered two "dangerous and terrible gales" which the shipping merchants no doubt dearly hoped Mittelberger would not survive.

At last, in October of 1754, Mittelberger's ship anchored in the Thames. He kissed the soil of Europe, and offered a prayer for his deliverance:

> *To God in Three Persons for this great*
> *mercy and preservation be praise and*
> *Thanksgiving rendered now and forevermore.*

Mittelberger's narrative, published in 1756, did little to staunch the flow of German immigrants into Pennsylvania. Though acts were passed to counter the abuses of the merchants and the Neulanders, the lack of any sort of international cooperation made enforcement all but impossible. Repeated military conflict in the Palatine states, followed by famine in 1770, made the New World fields inevitably seem greener to some. Between 1770 and 1791, redemptioners continued to arrive at Philadelphia at an average of twenty-four shiploads a year. Those German redemptioners who emigrated and survived usually lacked Mittelberger's options: a quittable job and a wife waiting in Germany. Through philosophical resignation, doggedness, desperation, or maybe even a degree of personal preference, they made the best of things.

These experiences, common in Pennsylvania, were successfully summoned up by Revolutionary pamphleteers to confirm colonial fears of a British conspiracy to deprive Americans of their rights. John Dickinson, whose *Letters from a Farmer in Pennsylvania* were published in some thirty Pennsylvania newspapers, warned in 1768 that the British ministry threatened to deprive the colonists not only of their liberty and property but even of their understanding: "that, unconscious of what we have been or are, and ungoaded by tormenting reflections, we may bow down our necks, with all the stupid serenity of servitude, to any drudgery which our lords and masters shall please to command."

The German emigrants, moreover, became an increasingly strong force within the colony of Pennsylvania, political make-weights with no allegiance to the British Crown. During the French and Indian War, the Pennsylvania Germans remained neutral. And when the call came for independence, they responded in substantial numbers.

On a more personal level, the Germans of Pennsylvania, most of whom had arrived as redemptioners, became people of a certain shrewd, skeptical, hard-earned autonomy. Privately generous, they were publicly watchful. They grasped the fact that the survival of the religious and moral values of each depended on the tolerance of all. Born into and then torn from an established social order, they understood that in its absence their only true protection was under law.

Voices

Another ship reached Philadelphia with 400 Germans and it is said not many over 50 remain alive . . . A certain man whose wife was nearly famished bought every day meal and wine for her and their children, thus kept them alive: another man who had eaten all his week's bread asked the captain for a little bread, but in vain. He then came to the captain and requested the latter to throw them overboard at once rather than allow them to die by inches. He brought his meal sack to the captain and asked him to put a small quantity into it: the captain took the bag, put in some sand and stones and returned it to the man. The latter shed some tears, laid down and died, together with his wife . . .

Should Cain return to earth in our time and interview a good lawyer, with gold enough, he would be able to prove he had not even seen Abel.

—FROM *The Pennsylvania Berichte,* quoted by Frank Dieffenderfer in *The Redemptioners*

23

ALEXANDER TURNBULL AND CARLO FORNI

ALEXANDER TURNBULL was a Scottish physician, enamored, as only a Northerner can be, of the Mediterranean: its climate, culture, and peoples. He had traveled extensively in the Mediterranean lands and had married a woman from Smyrna, in the Levant, now the Turkish city of Izmir. When in 1766 Dr. Turnbull arrived with his family in the newly acquired British territory of Florida, he was a man with the means and the will to give living form to his fondest vision.

Here in the warm latitudes, on the great vacant tracts of the land that so reminded him of the blue-and-white Mediterranean, he would build not just a settlement but a city, sun-blest and radiant, with roots to the best the ancient world had to offer. Called New Smyrna, after his wife's birthplace, Turnbull's city would be settled not by dour, driven North European emigrants, but by the people of the sunny South: Italians, Greeks, Minorcans, living among groves of olive and citrus, transplanting culture along with agriculture, carrying the seeds of civilization as the Trojans had carried them to Rome, and the Phoenicians to Carthage.

Turnbull managed to combine this Mediterranean romanticism with the hardest sort of Scottish canniness in putting together something new under the sun: the first of the great Florida land schemes.

With the Treaty of Paris in 1763, the British had acquired Florida as part of the Spanish settlement after the Seven Years' War. By the time of Turnbull's arrival, the evacuation of Spanish people to Havana had been completed. The territory was vacant, settlement was encouraged, and vast tracts of land were available to men of appropriate standing, with the right sort of capital and connections.

Like most men of ideas, Turnbull found capital difficult to come by, a situation he compensated for by shrewdly enlisting rich and/or influential partners: Sir William Duncan, Sir Richard Temple, and British Prime Minister George Grenville.

In this linking of ministerial and private interest, Turnbull and Grenville seemed to be realizing the threat of "Robinarchal" government feared by colonists as well as by opposition circles in Britain. Coined by Henry St. John, Viscount Bolingbroke, a Tory opponent of Robert Walpole, the term "Robinacracy" was used as a catchword for the age-old English danger of ministerial usurpation and political corruption.

The Robinarch, maintained Bolingbroke, was not merely prime minister but in reality a shadow sovereign, "as despotic, arbitrary a sovereign as this part of the world affords." Admitting no one to important office who was not "a relation, a creature, or a thorough-placed tool," the Robinarch and his accomplices intended to load the people with taxes and debt, and eventually to create, on the pretext of insuring public safety, a mercenary army to perfect their dominance.

These arguments, popular among radical and nonconformist elements, had relatively little political influence in England at large. In America, however, they proved immensely popular and served as a source of colonial thought and rhetoric growing in influence after 1763 when the hated Stamp Act Prime Minister George Grenville, eventually Alexander Turnbull's partner, seemed the embodiment of all the dangers to life and liberty suggested by the darkest Robinarchal fears.

By January of 1767, Turnbull had presented to James Grant, British governor of Florida, orders from the King in Council for two tracts of twenty thousand acres each for himself and for Duncan. The property south of the Ponce de Leon inlet was to be administered solely by Turnbull. Once granted his colony, the doctor immediately bought black slaves to work a cotton plantation under the eye of an overseer, ordered cattle driven down from Georgia and Carolina, and set some of his blacks to clearing land and other workmen to building houses for settlers. He then embarked for Europe to recruit his colonists.

Before a single settler had been enlisted, Turnbull had already expanded his holdings. In April of 1767, he obtained a second order from the Crown, for five thousand acres in the names of each of his four children. At this point, Grenville and Temple also decided to join formally in the enterprise, and acquired grants for twenty thousand acres each. This brought the total holdings to be administered by Turnbull to just over a hundred thousand acres.

The spiraling expansionist view that Dr. Turnbull took toward land he also applied to people. Since a certain sum had been guaranteed him by the British government for each settler he imported, it was in Turnbull's interests to fill his colony with as many recruits as possible. Through the fall and winter of 1767 and the spring of 1768, the single ship intended for Turnbull's recruited indentured servants was expanded into a fleet, and the hundreds of settlers into more than a thousand.

From Greece, from southern Italy, from Minorca—then under British rule—Turnbull recruited his colonists, people enraptured by the idea of working their own land in a congenial climate in a settlement of people from their own country who spoke their language, planting the New World with seeds they had brought from the Old. They would serve for a term of years, owning half the produce that they raised and ultimately plots of land. The people, some of whom were near starving, responded in enormous numbers. In Livorno, Italy, the mayor protested to the British over the departure of so many of his citizens. Asked to intervene, the British minister to Tuscany, through his consul, simply overruled the local authorities. The single ship grew to a fleet of eight, with a Royal Navy frigate as an armed escort, and the number of settlers grew from the original five hundred to almost fifteen hundred. Turnbull, thinking expansively, was relying on resigned acceptance to a fait accompli.

"My numbers increase daily," Turnbull boasted to the Earl of Shelbourne in a letter from the island of Minorca, "from the marriages between the Italians I brought here and the young women of this Island, which I encourage."

Gradually, Turnbull found himself drawn into the quandary of the overambitious and undercapitalized promoter. His reach had exceeded his grasp, and the humane and considerate part of his personality began to give way to the shrewd bargainer made insecure by his own ambitions, unwilling to concede the slightest possible advantage. Overwhelmed and gratified by the response to his promotion, haunted by the thought that he might be impoverishing himself and his family by a gigantic giveaway, Turnbull desperately insisted upon his own interests. The settlers were required to sign indentures for ten years. Worried that in the pleasant Florida climate people might grow lazy and refuse to work, Turnbull arranged to have them prohibited from fishing. The plans to grow olives and citrus were put aside in favor of a market-dictated plantation economy based on indigo, a plant none of the imported Mediterranean farmers had ever seen. He hired as overseer of his colony a no-nonsense supervisor named Cutter. This wasn't an exercise in philanthropy, after all. As the man with the original idea, the individual who had assumed the greatest risk, Turnbull was entitled to the largest rewards.

Aboard the emigrant ships a number of people had died, but these were mostly older people whose loss was acceptable. Scurvy had also broken out on the voyage, which had now stretched into an ordeal of more than four months. On June 23, 1768, two of the eight vessels in Turnbull's fleet arrived at Savannah, Georgia. Their masters reported that two more ships had reached St. Augustine, in Florida, and that one was making for Charleston, South Carolina.

Turnbull's arriving settlers found "instead of a grateful, fertile soil, a barren arid land, instead of promised fields, a dreary wilderness." The contingent of five hundred blacks who had supposedly already cleared the land was reported as having been "drowned." There was not enough shelter or food. Scurvy and gangrene swept the settlers, killing people by the score. Those able to work were required to clear land of the local scrub and palmetto trees under the midsummer Florida sun.

The cruelest disappointment was the food. Instead of allowing each family to eat as they pleased, the settlers were required to join in a common mess, to which they were summoned by the beating of a giant drum. Here they were served hominy, a sort of coarse gruel, ladled out of a single copper pot. Originally, each settler was allotted a quart of corn a day and two ounces of pork a week, but even this was cut when the rations turned out to have been depleted by the pilferings of a thieving cook.

Turnbull's overseer, Cutter, rather than loosen the rules in the light of circumstances, chose to tighten them instead. To prevent runaways and discourage the reassertion of Spanish influence among their fellow Latins, masters of passing vessels were forewarned against giving any settler bread or meat. People who stole food were beaten or starved.

Turnbull, meanwhile, was apparently so pleased at the progress of his model colony that he brought a group of planters down from the Carolinas for a tour. He had set out with his party on the return trip when he was overtaken on the way to St. Augustine by a messenger who announced that a number of his colonists had risen in revolt.

Of all the dangers that tormented the sleep of the colonial masters, an armed uprising of indentured servants was the most sweeping, threatening, and immediate. There was, first of all, the sheer number of them, more servants during the colonial era than either black slaves or free workingmen. There was the presence among them, increasing as the colonial era wore on, of known criminals; but most of all there was the incitement of stimulated, then frustrated, expectations. Led to expect a better life, bound servants found that they had to undergo yet another ordeal, often living worse than they had in Europe, sustained by the distant prospect of someday living better. It shouldn't have come as a surprise to the colonial authorities that even a class of people who had remained docile and submissive in Europe could be prompted in the New World to organize, flee, and resist.

In Maryland and Virginia particularly, there were constant rumors of servant plots, with enough actual attempts to make the threat alarmingly real. In 1721, a band of convict servants in Maryland was caught while planning to seize the magazine at Annapolis in a bold stroke at freedom. In Virginia, a York County overseer joined with his servants in refusing to work unless their master provided them with decent food. Banding together, the men threatened to lay waste the countryside until they were appeased with satisfactory rations. In Gloucester County, another group of Virginia plotters had planned to march on the governor's mansion and demand release from one year of their indentures. There were numerous attempts to escape by sea, to run away and join up with the Indians, or to flee to the Spanish in Florida, and the situation remained so volatile up through Bacon's Rebellion that planters, especially in the South, eventually elected to replace the restive white servants with the more identifiable and presumably less criminal black slaves. The common sense of injury, the feeling of having been cheated, remained simmering among the men and women who had been or who had come from servants, to be heated up again by men like Paine and Washington when the time came to fight the British.

In Florida, the settlers at Dr. Turnbull's New Smyrna were living in what was in everything but name a penal colony. Dressed in uniforms, worked in gangs under overseers, isolated by scrub and swamp, served vile food in chow lines, granted pitiful portions of land in return for ten years' labor, these emigrants from "the plentiful cornfields and vineyards of Greece and Italy" found themselves dragged back beyond servitude into feudalism. Despairing, enraged, the disgruntled settlers required only a leader to articulate their grievances and direct their fury.

On August 18, 1768, Carlo Forni, one of the Italian overseers at New Smyrna, marched into the town square, where, backed by twenty men, he addressed the settlers, who set aside their work to listen. Forni is one of those men who appear out of nowhere at the forefront of revolts, thrown up out of the crowd by an uncommon ability to speak and act upon the feelings of others. A man of obscure origins, he had joined the Turnbull colonists at Livorno. He has been characterized as everything from a child-rapist to the first militant hero of American labor.

Forni announced to the crowd that he was now in command of the Italians and Greeks at New Smyrna. The Minorcans, as members of a British dependency, would presumably remain loyal to Turnbull. Forni promised to lead his people to Havana, where they would seek protection under the Spanish. They would be freed from unrelenting work, unspeakable food, and cruel masters.

The full fury of the cheated settlers now broke upon Turnbull's community. They took possession of the storehouse, and casks of rum were rolled into the street. Firearms were distributed among Forni's followers. When Cutter, the hated English overseer, tried to intervene, he was attacked with a sword, an ear and part of one of his hands were cut off, and he was locked in a storeroom closet. Forni's Italians and Greeks, now numbering almost three hundred, turned on the Minorcans, looted their quarters, and seized a ship lying in the inlet, which they loaded with provisions. About a hundred people went on board, where they waited for the tide to carry them out of the inlet so they could set sail for Cuba.

Turnbull, notified at midnight of the same day, forwarded the message to Governor Grant, who by August 21 had dispatched two ships, the *Juno* and the *Florida Packet,* with troops, provisions, cannon, and ammunition, to intercept the rebels. Another detachment of troops was sent overland. The two vessels arrived just as the seized ship was warping out of Mosquito Inlet, and they blockaded its entrance. About twenty of the insurgents' ringleaders, including Forni, jumped into a boat, cut the rope, and rowed away. The governor's ships then fired at the mutineers on the remaining vessel; they capitulated and were brought ashore.

Forni and the other leaders escaped, heading in an open boat down the Florida coast, where they were pursued and eventually overtaken, after four months, on the Florida Keys. They were returned to stand trial at St. Augustine.

"The distress of the sufferers touched us so," wrote Captain Bernard Romans, a member of the grand jury which sat fifteen days in judgment of the rebels, "that we almost unanimously

wished for some happy circumstances that might justify our rejecting all the bills, except that against the chief [Carlo Forni],
who was a villain." One of the rebels was convicted of having
"curtailed" Cutter of his ear and two of his fingers. Another was
found guilty of shooting a cow, the only fatality of the uprising,
which "being a capital crime in England, the law . . . was extended to this Province." Forni and three other men were convicted of burglary for having broken into the storehouse and were
sentenced to death. The jury had been under pressure to convict
more. "I had an opportunity to remark by the appearance of
some faces in court, that the grand jury disappointed the expectations of more than one great man."

Governor Grant pardoned two of the convicted men. A third
was offered freedom on condition he agree to be the executioner
at the beheading of the other two. "On this occasion," wrote
Romans, "I saw one of the most moving scenes I ever experienced." The man agonized over the choice: saving his own life
at the price of being his friends' executioner. He repeatedly
called out that he preferred to die rather than put his comrades
to death. Finally, the pleas of the victims themselves put an end
to the conflict. "Now we beheld a man thus compelled to mount
the ladder, take leave of his friends in the most moving manner,
kissing them the moment before he committed them to an igno-
minious death."

The rebellion crushed, Turnbull's New Smyrna juggernaut
wobbled on, shuddering under the impact of mismanagement,
political intrigue, and illness. By 1773, almost nine hundred of
the colonists had died from scurvy and other diseases. A political
feud had developed between Turnbull and the new Florida governor, Patrick Tonyn. When in 1776 Dr. Turnbull went to England to defend himself against charges made by Tonyn, the
governor made his move at New Smyrna. Sending a group of
agents to Turnbull's colony to draft militia, Tonyn had the agents
tell the colonists that when their terms of servitude expired they
would get no land. The settlers, overwhelmingly Catholics, could
not get title, as Protestant landowners were specified in the
grants. Infuriated, a group of settlers went to St. Augustine in

May of 1777 and preferred charges against Dr. Turnbull; they alleged that he had held some of them in bondage beyond expiration of term and that he had committed certain crimes of violence. They were imprisoned by the court of sessions until they agreed to return and work out their contracts. Tonyn secured their release and encouraged them to break their indentures. The political feud between the two men produced an odd sort of stalemate, almost like a preview of the governmental separation of powers.

In the autumn of 1777, when Turnbull returned from England, he found his indentured servants had escaped. His colony was deserted, its future in litigation, its settlers huddled in St. Augustine, where sixty-five more died due to lack of food, shelter, and medical attention.

Beset on all sides now, Turnbull stubbornly struggled on. To replace his indentured settlers, he imported black slaves. Some of them were captured by the Spanish; others ran away. New Smyrna declined into a ruin; its survivors founded what became a significant Greek and Italian population in Florida.

Alexander Turnbull was a man accused of trying to live like a Levantine pasha, and praised as a misunderstood humanitarian reformer. He seems rather a man with a single dream that combined his faith and his fortune, whose trajectory he rode with uncommon persistence all the way up and then all the way down, to the end of hundreds of people's lives, and the ruin of his own. In its dramatization of the encroaching nature of power at the expense of liberty, the growing ministerial corruption of the British government, and the justification of rebellion in extreme circumstances, the revolt against Turnbull at New Smyrna was both a capsule preview and a justification of the American Revolution just ahead.

From the wreckage he had caused, Alexander Turnbull staggered heartbroken out of Florida. He moved to Charleston, South Carolina, where he resumed the practice of medicine, his life a kind of monument, weed-grown, cracked, neglected, to the power, and folly, of indomitable will. He died in Charleston in 1792.

Voices

They would get a matter of Forty of them together and get Gunnes and hee would be the first and lead them and cry as they went along, who would be for liberty and freed from bondage, and that there would enough come to them and they would goe through the Countrey and Kill those that made any opposition and that they would either be free or dye for it.

—TESTIMONY IN YORK
COUNTY, VIRGINIA,
SERVANTS' UPRISING, *1659,*
as reported by Richard Morris

PART FIVE
RELEASED

They had become a new people, settled, and at the same time restless. Scattered, largely illiterate men and women whose thoughts and energies were mostly consumed by the daily round of rural chores: tending stock, minding crops, hauling water, toting wood. People who did not speculate about John Locke or debate Rousseau. Yet who clung with an individually-earned touchiness to certain personal rights—the freedom to marry, buy and sell land, work at a trade, change jobs, travel without a pass. Who could easily grasp, from experience—their parents', their neighbors', their own—what it meant to have these fresh-earned freedoms infringed upon. And who responded —with an intensity and resolve difficult for people elsewhere to comprehend—to certain words which suggested the reimposition of the past or the compromise of what had been so arduously won: tyranny, enshacklement, slavery.

24

MATTHEW THORNTON

As THE earliest and closest of British colonial possessions, Ireland had the distinction of being the testing ground for practically every form and technique of servant recruitment. During the seventeenth and eighteenth centuries, the Irish found themselves transported as vagrants, rogues, political and military prisoners, criminals, mercenary troops, breeding stock, and religious exiles. The inveiglement and kidnapping practiced so skillfully elsewhere were first developed in England's neighboring isle. This scattering of the Irish had the unintended effect of spreading antagonism toward the English in the New World, where an instinctive, vehement, and lasting opposition took root.

On August 4, 1718, a fleet of five small ships arrived in Boston harbor carrying nearly 750 emigrants from northern Ireland, intent on settling in New England. Led by Presbyterian pastors—one of whom had charged his congregation to sell their goods and leave their homes in order "1. To avoid oppression and cruel bondage; 2. To shun persecution and designed ruin; 3. To withdraw from the communion of idolators; and 4. To have an opportunity of worshipping God according to the dictates of conscience and the rules of His inspired word"—the passengers represented some 120 families of Scotch-Irish, a people who had already been uprooted and transplanted once.

The importation of Scots into Ireland had begun in the early 1600s, at almost the same time as the introduction of indentured servants into the American colonies. In both instances, the intention was to use an undesirable domestic people to help impose order on undesirable distant tribes, all under the firm guiding hand of the English. Conceived by Francis Bacon, extended and intensified under Cromwell, the settlement of northern Ireland by Scots was to produce a sequence of prosperity, rivalry, repression, and resistance like that which occurred in America. And it would serve as a testing ground for many of the ideas and passions of American independence.

The Scots, settled on lands confiscated from the Irish Earls of Tyrone and Tyrconnel, were regarded as "such as either poverty, scandulous lives or at the best adventurous seeking of a better accomodation had forced thither." Nevertheless, by the beginning of the eighteenth century the Ulster territories had prospered to such a degree that Irish goods and produce were considered a threat to English commerce. The Irish woolen industry centered in Belfast was, through a series of repressive acts of Parliament, shut down. Irish beef was prohibited from the English market; and shipping was so restricted that at one point Irish fishermen were required to go to sea only in English-built vessels.

These heavy-handed economic sanctions were accompanied by equally harsh political measures. Under the Test Acts, any Irishman not a male member of the Church of England was prohibited from holding office above the rank of constable, teaching school, or performing marriages; and everyone was required to tithe 10 percent of his produce to the support of the Anglican Church. Unable to gain redress of grievances, the Scottish Presbyterians in Ireland began to emigrate in droves. "The bad seasons for three years past," reported the Presbytery of Tyrone, "together with the high price of lands and tythes, have all contributed to the general run to America, and to the ruin of many families, who are daily leaving their houses and lands desolate."

Despite vigorous efforts to discourage the emigration, including the requirement of bonds for shipowners and the occasional jailing of masters, the trade continued, and the streets were crowded with passengers ready to sail, even though departing citizens were not allowed to carry as much as their own bedclothes on board with them.

Among the immigrant families arriving at Boston were the Thorntons, James and Elizabeth, and their sons James and Matthew. They were redemptioners whose first step out of bondage had only led them into bondage of another kind. They were sold into service and were taken to Wiscasset in what is now the state of Maine. Here the Thorntons, who had been fortunate enough not to have been sold off individually, served out their years of indenture and when their time was up promptly moved to Worcester, Massachusetts, where a Scotch-Irish settlement had been started.

As in Ulster, the Scotch-Irish found themselves surrounded by a hostile culture and religion. New England had been settled mainly by English Congregationalists, people who chose their own clergy and who looked upon the Scottish Presbyterians, who followed the lead of their pastors, as backsliders, almost as priest-ridden as Irish Catholics. In Londonderry, New Hampshire, named after the Scottish town in northern Ireland, a group of Scotch-Irish attempting to build a settlement on the edge of a wilderness were confronted by an armed force which arrived, to the armed men's embarrassment, during the Scotch-Irish celebration of the Lord's Supper. This was followed by a more subtle attempt to starve the colonists out by cutting and carrying off the surrounding meadows' natural hay.

In Worcester, where the English were already established, opposition to the Scotch-Irish took a more direct form, culminating in the burning of the Presbyterian church in 1740. For the Thorntons, this was enough. Along with most of the Scotch-Irish of Worcester, they moved to Londonderry that same year.

As in Ireland, the Presbyterians made the best of a hostile situation. Pushed to the edge of the frontier, they became the men of the border garrisons, the explorers, the settlers who struck out for the interior. In Maine, in western Massachusetts,

New Hampshire, and Vermont, they were the chief colonizing force. The settlement of Londonderry prospered in its isolation and became the province's second-leading town. Like the freed-men of Virginia pushed west into Kentucky and Tennessee, the Scotch-Irish in New England carried with them a shared sense of grievance against arbitrary power, which they associated with English rule.

Matthew Thornton, his parents' second son, had been four years old when the family emigrated from Ireland. He was edu-cated in Worcester and afterward was apprenticed to a Dr. Grout of Leicester, Massachusetts, for the study of medicine. When the Thornton family moved to Londonderry in 1740, Matthew Thorn-ton moved with them and proceeded to open a medical practice. Tall, black-eyed, "one of the most companionable of men," Thornton prospered as a physician and surgeon and eventually branched out into a civil and military career. In 1745, he was a military surgeon accompanying a New Hampshire regiment against the French at Louisburg and he was later commissioned a colonel in the Londonderry regiment by the royal government. From 1758 to 1762, he was Londonderry's representative in the provincial legislature.

Yet though he involved himself in public affairs, Matthew Thornton remained as unassimilated as the Scotch-Irishmen of Ulster. He continued to live and practice medicine in London-derry, where he met and married Hannah Jack, also of Scotch-Irish descent. His sister married another Scotch-Irishman. Trans-planted across the ocean, holding a royal military commission, Thornton remained part of an organized resistance to English religious and political rule.

When opposition to the Stamp Act began, led by seaboard political radicals like Sam Adams, it was immediately recognized by the frontier Scotch-Irish as the extension of their old quarrel with the English authorities. "Though the body of people seemed disposed to pay obedience to the Stamp Act," reported John Hughes, distributor of stamps for Pennsylvania, "Presbyterians and Proprietary minions spare no pains to engage the Dutch and lower class of people, and render the royal government odious."

In May of 1775, following the battle of Lexington, Matthew Thornton was chosen president of the New Hampshire Provincial Congress. He was also one of a committee which persuaded the congress to raise local troops by pledging the members' honor and estate to pay the troops' expense. On the same day this resolution was adopted, Thornton was appointed to the Committee of Safety, which, during the recess of the congress, was to have full executive and legislative power in the colony.

Thornton, a man with only a fingertip hold on respectability, a physician and minor civil figure, the son of servants risen from servitude himself, had pledged all he had and was in the name of a shaky and none-too-promising cause. Such risks are not taken by sane people in the name of abstractions.

Not surprisingly, it was the Irish statesman Edmund Burke who seems to have had the truest grasp of depth and durability of the colonists' feelings. "Abstract liberty," Burke told Parliament in his address on conciliation with America in 1775, "is not to be found. Liberty inheres in some sensible object, and every nation has formed to itself some favorite point . . . which becomes the criterion of their happiness."

To Matthew Thornton, enshacklement was no more remote than the crowded hold that had brought him and his parents and brother to be sold in America, tyranny no more distant than the gutted Presbyterian church in Gloucester. The act of ordinary men willing to take extraordinary risks, the willingness to become whatever was needed, the sense of grievance multiplied many times over, was the lever of the Revolution—the tiny, then accelerating, budging of an empire.

"They went with hearts burning with indignation," the nineteenth-century Irish historian W. E. H. Lecky wrote of the Scotch-Irish emigrants, "and in the War of Independence they were almost to a man on the side of the insurgents. They supplied some of the best soldiers of Washington."

Things moved rapidly after this. As president of the Provincial Congress, Thornton was in correspondence with officials and public bodies of the other colonies. He chaired the committee which drew up the New Hampshire Constitution, the first adopted by any of the American colonies, and considered in itself an act of insurgency. Thornton was elected speaker of the house.

In June of 1776, Thornton was sworn in as justice of the superior court of judicature for the colony. In September, he was chosen delegate to represent the state in the Continental Congress for the following year. He arrived in Philadelphia on November 3, 1776, and on the following day presented his credentials and signed the Declaration of Independence. His head was now officially in the royal noose.

Operating out of his instinctive opposition to English authority, Thornton threw himself into events with the same intensity with which they were changing. He seems to have assumed new responsibilities almost monthly during this crucial period, to become whatever was needed at the time, yet without being swept away by megalomania or losing sight of the original causes of the revolt and of the goals of independence. He served two terms as delegate to the congress, then returned to New Hampshire, where he resumed his duties as judge. Following the war, he served both as delegate to the New Hampshire Assembly and as a state senator.

He seems not to have been a man hungry for a public career so much as a person animated by a desire to be of use. Political office was neither a stepping-stone nor an onerous chore, but a duty borne with equanimity and a simple civic honor. He was not above taking a lesser office if that was where the need was; it was enough to be considered useful.

By 1788, his voice slightly palsied, his wife dead, he was in semi-retirement yet still a man whose counsel and company were eagerly sought. A town he had founded in 1763 had been named after him, and the river landing near where he lived had become known as Thornton's Ferry. He was like a man from an earlier, more heroic age, a Homeric figure in a Hellenistic New Hampshire, a man of "simple and unaffected tastes," whose table, we are told, "was seldom without guests."

In his life and work, Matthew Thornton embodied two key elements of the later Jacksonian coalition. He was Scotch-Irish, one of a resettled people pushed out to the edge of the wilderness. And like the small farmers and growing class of city workingmen, he was a son of servitude, someone who'd entered America in bondage and who carried within him an instinctive resentment toward the abuse of power.

"I do most solemnly assure those of my constituents who put any sort of confidence in my industry and integrity," Edmund Burke warned Parliament about America in 1775, "that everything that has been done there has arisen from a total misconception of the object: that our means of originally holding America, that our means of reconciling with it after quarrel, of recovering it after separation, of keeping it after victory, did depend, and must depend, upon a total renunciation of that unconditional submission which has taken possession of the minds of violent men."

Matthew Thornton lived on at Thornton's Ferry in the town of Merrimack into the new century. In the early summer of 1803, a neighbor recalled seeing him pass on horseback. He stopped; the two men talked. Thornton was on his way to Newburyport, Massachusetts, to visit his daughter. A few days later his body was carried back, the same way, for his funeral. He was eighty-nine.

Voices

If I were to define the modern colonists, I should say they are the noble discoverers and settlers of a new world, from whence as from an endless source, wealth and plenty, the means of power, grandeur and glory, in a degree unknown to the hungry chiefs of former ages, have been pouring into Europe for 300 years past: in return for which those colonists have received from the several states of Europe, except from Great Britain only since the Revolution, nothing but ill-usage, slavery, and chains, as fast as the riches of their own earning could furnish the means of forging them.

—JAMES OTIS
*The Rights of the British
Colonies Asserted and
Proved, 1764*

25

JOHN HARROWER

HIS NAME was John Harrower, a Scotsman from the village of
Lerwick in the Shetland Islands north of Scotland. From about
the middle of the eighteenth century, conditions in the Shetlands
and throughout the Highlands had steadily worsened for most
Scots. Rents for tenant farmers were raised, and raised again;
there had been bad years for both cattle and crops. The panic of
1772 intensified an economic crisis into a state of desperation.
Like thousands of other Scotsmen of the 1770s, John Harrower
set out to find work in England.

He was forty years old, with a wife and three young children
—two daughters and a son—in Lerwick. He had had some training as a bookkeeper but was willing to accept employment of
almost any sort. He carried with him a supply of the prized Shetland stockings to sell as he needed for capital. Alone and friendless in a country where people spoke what seemed an alien
tongue, he confided his feelings to a journal, and placed his trust
in his Presbyterian God: "And hopes he will for Jesus sake,
Provide for me and soon."

He made his way by fishing boat and sloop down the British east coast, asking at each port—Dundee, Newcastle, Tynemouth —about opportunities for work, or even passage for Holland, without finding so much as a day's employment. From Portsmouth, on the southern English coast, he walked overland to London, a distance of sixty-five miles, arriving in the city "like a blind man without a guide, not knowing where to go, being friendless and having no more money but fifteen shillings and eight pence farthing."

For a while he tried to keep up appearances, breaking out a last hoarded set of clean clothes, rationing his money for minimal meals, answering ads for bookkeepers and clerks, only to find each time that the job had already been filled. Offering himself to shipmasters as a steward and to merchants and tradesmen in any capacity whatsoever produced the same bleak result. "Hundreds are sterving for want of employment," Harrower observed, "and many good people are begging."

On January 26, 1774, reduced to his last shilling, Harrower was "oblidged to engage to go to Virginia for four years as a school-master for Bedd, Board, washing and five pound during the whole time." He wrote to his wife, then went aboard a ship lying at Ratcliffe Cross, where he was issued his hammock and bedding.

The ship, the *Snow Planter,* lay in the Thames accumulating its human cargo for sixteen days: a surgeon, a glassblower, two watch- and clockmakers, ten weavers, a groom, a butcher, a baker, three gardeners, a hatter, a bricklayer, two tailors, a smith and farrier, a farmer, a boatbuilder—seventy-five men in all, indentured each for four years. There were fellow Scots among them, who gravitated toward each other, eating and sleeping in their own "Scottish Mess." The captain, it turned out, was also from Scotland, though he hadn't been back since entering the Virginia trade at the age of fifteen.

On February 6, the ship got under way. At Gravesend, the merchant who had contracted for the shipment of servants came aboard to fill out the indentures for men in the categories most in demand. Indentured as a clerk and bookkeeper, Harrower was guaranteed no such berth. He would have to take his chances in Virginia.

Meanwhile, the men were examined by a doctor, after which "two was turned ashore haveing the clap." There were threats of a mutiny, blamed on a skimpy allowance of bread, but Harrower's mess refused to join the protest and the disturbance was quelled. When, near the Isle of Wight, the captain briefly went ashore, he first took Harrower aside and asked him to stand by the mate in case any disturbance arose among the rest of his servants.

By March 11, the men of the *Snow Planter* had already buried one of their number at sea and were encountering their first taste of the Atlantic's winter weather. "The wind blowing excessive hard and a verry high sea running still from the westward," Harrower noted. The captain was forced to batten both fore and main hatches, confining the indentured servants below and producing what Harrower considered "the odest shene [scene] betwixt decks that ever I heard or seed."

"There was some sleeping, some spewing, some pishing, some shitting, some farting, some flyting, some daming, some Blasting their leggs and thighs, some their Liver, lungs, lights and eyes, And for to make the shene the odder, some curs'd Father, Mother, Sister, and Brother."

The storm raged for two days, and after it subsided the sick and ailing, "the number of which I really cannot now ascertain," were taken up on deck for air. Two servants protesting again about the food were briefly put in irons.

"Fever and ague" now began to rage among the servants and sailors. When the first mate collapsed with fever, the captain asked Harrower, as a man with clerical training and of proven responsibility, to keep the ship's log. So Harrower marked the miles traveled at the change of each watch and at the same time gave the sick what comfort he could. When one of the servants, "a young lad," sick with fever, pleaded for someone to ask the mate for a cure, Harrower obliged him. The mate asked for a slip of paper, on which he wrote the following:

> *When Jesus saw the Cross he trembled,*
> *The Jews said unto him why tremblest thou,*
> *You have neither got an Ague nor a fever.*

Jesus answered and said unto them
I have neither got an Ague nor a fever
But whosoever keepeth my words
Shall neither have an Ague nor a fever.

The incantation, the mate insisted, must be wrapped in a hand-kerchief and worn at the boy's breast, "with strick charge to him not to look at it himself nor let any person see it . . . untill he was got wel."

Eventually, worn down by the weather, the rigors of the voyage, the sense of separation from his family, Harrower fell ill "with an Aching in my bones" and took to his hammock. Within a few days he had recovered, and was standing on deck when the ship came in sight of Cape Henry, at the mouth of Chesapeake Bay.

The ship anchored inside the capes at Hampton Roads, where Harrower was charged with preparing a clean list of the servants' names, trades, and ages. The captain, taking five servants with him, went ashore, hoping to sell their indentures. He returned at midnight, having disposed of only one servant, the boatbuilder, in exchange for "Four Barrells Virginia Pork, one Puncheon of rum, and 3 live hogs."

The *Snow Planter* then worked its way up the Rappahannock River toward the town of Fredericksburg. Tantalizingly close to land, on the verge of being sold to someone else for a minimum of four years on a strange new continent, the men grew anxious, restless, apprehensive. Some of the men were allowed to go ashore. One returned "so drunk that he abused the Capt., Chief Mate and Boatswain to a verry high degree." He was horse-whipped, put in irons, and thumbscrewed. Two days later, when Harrower was permitted his first liberty ashore, the man was still in handcuffs.

Now men began to come aboard to shop among the *Snow Planter's* merchandise. Among them, Harrower observed, were two "Soul drivers": men who "make it their bussiness to go on board all ships who have in either Servants or Convicts and buy sometimes the whole and sometimes a parcell of them as they can agree, and then drive them through the Country like a parcell

of Sheep untill they can sell them to advantage." This time the
soul-drivers went away soulless.

One by one, the servants with the most valued practical skills
were sold or accepted on a trial basis: a cooper, a blacksmith, a
cabinet maker, a shoemaker. The merchant who had contracted
for the shipment of servants assured Harrower that, based on his
assumption of responsibility aboard ship, he would do his utmost
"to get me settled as a Clerk or bookkeeper if not as a schoolmaster."

The servants were then ordered ashore at Fredericksburg,
where they were offered for sale in a tent, where several of their
indentures were sold. That afternoon, Mr. Anderson, the merchant, brought Harrower to meet a friend of his, a Colonel Daingerfield, a Virginia planter who had come to Fredericksburg to
attend the local fair. The colonel, who spoke "nothing but high
english and hade his Education in England," was looking for a
schoolmaster to educate his children, and Anderson had recommended Harrower to him as the man.

"We immediately agreed," Harrower wrote, "and my indenture for four years was then delivered him and he was to send for
me the next day." Harrower was ordered to get his clothes
washed, at the colonel's expense, in town, and given five shillings
pocket money. The following day, sixteen weeks after boarding
the *Snow Planter,* Harrower left the last of his old life behind him
and went off to meet his new owner, who was attending a horse
race.

In Colonel William Daingerfield, John Harrower encountered
his most significant piece of good fortune since he'd set out from
Lerwick. Without a prearranged position, and categorized in a
trade not much in demand in the plantation colonies, Harrower
could easily have been sold off as a field hand and been worked
to death by some struggling tenant farmer in the Virginia frontier
country. Instead, he found himself on a bluff overlooking the
Rappahannock, on a 1,300-acre plantation complete with a mansion house and the amenities of a small village: laundry, dairy,
smokehouse, school, barns, corncribs, stables, slave quarters.
This was at the time in Virginia when among the larger planters

indentured servants had been phased out as field hands and replaced by Negro slaves, with the remaining whites serving as
overseers or skilled tradesmen. Though Daingerfield employed in
addition to Harrower a white housekeeper and overseer, the vast
majority of his plantation hands were black—"how many young
and old the Lord only knows," Harrower reported, at least thirty
in the field plus the servants around the house.

In purchasing John Harrower as his children's teacher, Daingerfield was relying on more than a labor contractor's endorsement. Scots were traditionally the most valued of indentured
servants, looked upon as unusually ambitious and industrious,
enduring servitude faithfully with an eye to setting up afterward
on their own. Daingerfield's confidence in his choice was apparently quickly confirmed. Within eight days of Harrower's arrival
on the job, "the Colonel rode through the neighboring Gentlemen
& Planters in order to procure scollars for me." For these additional recruits, the colonel agreed, Harrower could keep whatever fees he earned.

Harrower slept each night in the schoolhouse where by day he
taught. He was obliged to teach English which he had never
done, and which at first was awkward for him and, one can imagine, also for his students. Soon both were plunging ahead into the
ABC's, syllables, and reading, filtered no doubt through a thick
Scottish burr.

As schoolmaster, he ate at the master's table, with coffee or
chocolate and warmed baked bread for breakfast, and ham, pork,
lamb, duck, or chicken for dinner. A "bonny black bairn" reported every morning to the schoolhouse to clean it out and make
Harrower's "fine feather bed," and the laundry was so efficient
that "I may put on clean linen every day if I please." John
Harrower had, it seems, traveled from penury to privilege in the
space of an ocean crossing.

Yet, comfortable as it was, the situation was neither of his
making nor one he was free to leave. The colonel's plantation
was, in effect, a kind of prison honor farm, where one was always
subject to the whims of arbitrary power, under a system that
ultimately rested on force. When Mrs. Daingerfield, the master's
wife, overheard Harrower chastising one of her children, she

interrupted, removed the child, and complained to her husband about the schoolmaster. To Harrower's relief, Daingerfield supported his servant, but from then on the mistress of the house bore a grudge against him. And when a "Neiger fellow," a blacksmith from a nearby plantation, rode off on a brood mare from the Daingerfield pasture, the countryside was aroused, and both man and horse were recovered by the following afternoon. The blacksmith was stripped to the skin by the overseer and given thirty-nine lashes with hickory switches, "that being the highest the Law allows at one Wheeping."

Most painful of all to Harrower was his loneliness, his distance even in the comforts of his situation from his wife and children. "It brings tears to my eyes," he wrote his wife, "to think of you and my infants when at same time it is not in my power at present to help you." He estimated he would have to finish his term before beginning to acquire the land or capital to send for them.

In addition, there were the deepening differences between the North American colonies and Britain. There was, Harrower observed, no tea in America, "none drunk by any in this Government, nor will they buy any kind of East India goods" in protest against the tax. With his family in Britain, Harrower took no side in the dispute, yet he urged his wife not to underestimate the colonists' resolve: "If the Parliment do not give it over, it will cause a total revolt as all the North Americans are determined to stand by one another.

To hasten the time when he could pay for his family's passage, Harrower took on extra pupils. At night and on Sunday, he tutored a young carpenter, often by candlelight, while for ten shillings per quarter, he included among his "scollars" a deaf mute, a boy of fourteen, "and I have brought him tolerably well . . . he can write mostly for anything he wants . . . understands the value of every figure, and can work single addition a little." It is one of the first instances of the instruction of the deaf recorded in America.

When his pupils' parents were slow in paying him, Harrower tactfully but firmly dunned them.

"I yet hope (please God)," he wrote his wife, "if I am spared, some time to make you a Virginian Lady among the woods of

America which is by far more pleasent than the roaring of the raging seas round about Zetland.''

The sights and sounds of war grew closer and louder. There were reports of the shooting of townsmen in Boston by British troops. ''General Washington's lady'' came to dine at the plantation. A camp for a battalion of five hundred private men was marked out, in tents, just back of Harrower's school. After a few weeks, the troops decamped, leaving Harrower out of pocket for borrowed money.

His life was further complicated by the discovery of an affair between Miss Lucy Gaines, a housekeeper of the plantation, and Anthony Frazer, the overseer who roomed with Harrower at the schoolhouse. As Harrower either playfully or guardedly recorded, using nautical metaphor, in his journal, he accidentally walked in on them one morning: ''This morning before day light I found the Anthony, Man of War & the Lucy Friggat of this Place both Moor'd head & stern along side of each other in Blanket Bay within school cape, this being the second time they have been Moored in the same harbour.''

Alone, an ocean apart from his family, with any communication with them increasingly threatened by war, at risk no doubt in the stern eye of Mrs. Daingerfield for countenancing fornication in his schoolhouse, bound by law to stay put where he was, with only an occasional visiting Scot to confide in, John Harrower occasionally sought a traditional Celtic refuge: He got drunk. ''Monday, Dec. 25: At night, Drunk. . . . Tuesday, 26th: Sick all day, at night, Ditto.''

Hung over, remorseful, lonely, confined, facing the turn of the year with two years of servitude yet ahead of him, Harrower confided his feelings, in verse, in his journal:

> *Both the last nights quite drunk was I,*
> *Pray God forgive me of the sin;*
> *But had I been in good company,*
> *Me in that case No man had seen.*
>
> *Plac'd by myself, without the camp,*
> *As if I were unclean;*

No freendly soul does my floor tramp,
  My greiff to ease, or hear my moan.

For in a prison at large I'm plac't,
  Bound to it, day and night;
O, grant me patience, God of grace,
  And in thy paths make me walk right.

His patience already under great strain, Harrower was now burdened with the confidences of both the plantation lovers, each of whom looked to him for advice.

At night, lying in the dark in their bunks in the schoolhouse, Anthony, the young overseer, turned to the older schoolmaster. "He asked me if I thought that it [his marriage to Miss Lucy] would be a match, I told him I did; And asked him if he did not think so himself. He answered me that he had a great many thoughts. That he was young & cou'd hardly maintain himself, That it was a Daingerous situation & ought to be well considered of, That he had a fickle Master to do with & was uncertain of his time here." Harrower, sensing a young man in the throes of altar fright, tried to paint an encouraging picture of marriage. "I told him that one in his Bussiness could afford to live better married" . . . that everyone who saw Lucy thought well of her and that she would make "an extream good wife." Still, sensing the bridegroom's skittishness, Harrower did "not think it prudent to aquant Miss Lucy with this conversation at least for some time."

A few days later, after Lucy had again spent the night in the schoolhouse, obliging the testy Mrs. Daingerfield to sleep in the nursery with her children, the Lucy Friggatt signaled the harbormaster about her Man of War. "When she told me she had a mind never to come more nigh the School, I told her she ought to not breack off coming all at once, But to confine herself to the houre of 10 or 11 at farthest, and if he insisted on her staying longer to desire him to Marrie at once." At the same time, Harrower cautioned her "not to build too strongly on him as the time proposed to finish the Bargain was far distant, and he seemingly determined not to shorten it."

Returning to the school one evening, Harrower found the door "Barrocaded on the inside. But after pushing, rapping with my foot & hollowing, I recd. no anser from within nor would Anthy. Frazer oppen the door." At the same time, the schoolmaster could see Frazer and Lucy Gaines covered up in bed together. A romance based on such lack of consideration for others was, in the schoolmaster's view, doomed: "My opinion of this courtship is in short this, That he never intends to marrie her."

The affair had now become the talk of the plantation, with the colonel complaining that the work, thanks to his overseer's distraction, had got greatly behind hand, while Mrs. Daingerfield had so argued with Lucy over Anthony that the housekeeper proposed to leave. The lovers had spats, which grew more intense and increasingly involved John Harrower.

"Miss Lucy . . . returned to school a little after sun sett, in order to Wait Mr. Frazer . . . She staid chatting with me untill about ten o'clock . . . She laid herself down in Mr. Frazers bedd with her cloaths on, was verry uneasy & fell a crying, thinking then, he used her extreamly ill in not keeping his word. I soathed & comforted her all I could as there was none in the school but her & me. I soon got her to talk pretty cheerfully; & we continued so until one or two Clock as I supposed when I fell asleep & continued so much until they came for corn to feed the horses in the morning."

For all his spoofing of the "Lucy Friggat and the Anthony, Man of War," Harrower was torn by his conflicting loyalties. Frazer was his roommate and a fellow Scot. Lucy was one of his pupils; he had taught her to read and write. Gradually the weight of Harrower's sympathies swung toward Lucy: "She is a tender hearted, agreeable, good girle and one that is strictly virtuos, honest and modest, without making any vain show of it . . . nothing but her excessive love for Anthy. Frazer . . . has created her all the trouble that oppresses her. . . . Her over fondness of him," he sadly concluded, "was her loseing of him."

In the daily drama of estrangement and reconciliation between Lucy and Anthony there were echoes of Harrower's own troubled relationship with his wife. He was a man who saw his family receding from him, even as he attempted to draw it to him. The brewing storm between the colonies and Britain had come to overshadow relations between Harrower and his wife and children. Correspondence between the two countries took four to six months, and was subject to official seizures as well as piracy. There was no secure way for Harrower to remit his slowly accumulating capital from teaching fees. It was his hope to pay his family's passage over and establish them in Virginia. This was something, he realized, that would require the winning-over of his wife. When Harrower had left Lerwick he was, as far as they both were concerned, going away temporarily to work in England or, at most, Holland. Now, relocated across the ocean, separated by thousands of miles and years of absence, he was asking her to leave home and friends and with their children risk a dangerous voyage in a time of growing hostility between their two countries.

When she responded favorably to the suggestion, Harrower's spirits soared. "I cou'd not be certain if you wou'd come to this Country or not until I recd. your last letter. But as I find by it you are satisfied to come here, you may believe me nothing in this world can give me equall satisfaction."

"I will," Harrower vowed, "how soon I am able, point out the way to you how you may get here." He promised to make what remittance he could in order to assist his wife on her way. "But you must consider that as I hade not a shilling in my pocket when I left you It must take me some time befor I can be able to make you a remittance." The time, he assured her, was just as long to him as it was to her, and the "National disputes and stopage of trade" between colonies and Mother Country promised, unless settled, to make the agonizing delay even longer. "Therefore," Harrower urged his wife, "have patience and keep up your heart and by no means let that fail you."

It was counsel he was offering himself, in the process of advising her. By early 1776, conflict between the colonies and Britain had widened into open, if undeclared, warfare. In January, Norfolk, the largest town in Virginia, was reduced to ashes by "the Men of War & British Troops under Command of Lord Dunmore." Direct communication of almost any kind with Britain was cut off. Harrower had no way to contact his family or of arranging to bring them over if and when he could afford it.

He turned to his work, visiting other plantations to tutor additional pupils, and settling accounts in Fredericksburg on behalf of the colonel, who was entering upon difficult times himself, financially.

On July 10, 1776, Harrower spent the day at the neighboring plantation, teaching until sunset. On his return home to the schoolhouse he heard the sounds of guns firing, toward the town of Fredericksburg. At about midnight, the colonel sent Anthony Frazer to investigate what was happening.

Frazer "returned and informed him that there was great rejoicings in Toun on Accott. of the Congress having declared the 13 United Colonys of North America Independent of the Crown of great Britain."

After this, the entries in John Harrower's journal grow briefer; by the end of July they have ceased altogether. It is as though this indefinite postponement of reunion with his wife and family, after the years of separation, were too painful for him to contemplate. In April of 1777, Colonel Dangerfield wrote to Harrower's wife, in a correspondence that was carried on through merchant houses in Hamburg and Rotterdam, that her husband had died. His death was attributed to "fever," which in that time and place probably meant typhus. Daingerfield also sent the widow some seventy pounds sterling which, he said, her husband had saved toward the family's passage. Harrower's widow regarded the remittance "as an act of your generosity as I know my late husband had not anything but what came from you."

In a footnote testifying to the precariousness of any communication at the time, she added: "If this letter Comes to the hands of any British Officer it is humbly hoped that in Compation to a poor Widdow He will forward it as directed."

John Harrower was a man who had chosen, out of desperation, a life whose odds were overwhelmingly against him. Yet he had reason to believe his luck had changed. He had been indentured to a kind master, not a cruel one; he was well clothed, well housed, well fed. There was land available in Virginia; it was possible to become a freedman and achieve autonomy. He liked the country and became convinced, as did so many other immigrants, that hard as it sometimes was to get to America, once you did, it was easier to get lucky here. In accepting bondage, a man might actually be taking a step toward an independence impossible for him in the Old World. In this struggle for earned independence, for which men were willing to forfeit rights granted them in Britain by birth, Harrower personifies the power and durability of revolutionary resistance itself, the energy with which men were willing to defend what they had earned, and could so easily envision losing.

Yet the odds caught up with him.

He was but one man among thousands of indentured men and women, unusual only in that he left a record, which will have to stand, in part, for many others, as a solitary voice against what V. S. Naipaul has called "the silence of all serfdom."

It was, on balance, not an easy time for masters either, including as estimable a man as Colonel Daingerfield. By the end of 1782, his financial affairs had reached what he considered a crisis. He had sold off portions of his plantation and was deeply in debt. Prominent as he was, the colonel had not outrun the possibility of penury, even debt servitude for himself. In January of 1783, according to a Fredericksburg lawyer, James Mercer, Daingerfield was found at New Castle, with his throat cut.

"Can you believe it?" wrote the lawyer. "I really shall be afraid of a . . . Knife for a month to come."

Voices

GENTLEMEN: We the Freeholders and other Inhabitants of Boston in Town Meeting duly Assembled, according to Law, apprehending there is abundant to be alarmed at the plan of *Despotism* which the enemies of our invaluable rights have concerted, is rapidly hastening to a completion, can no longer conceal our impatience under a constant, unremitted, uniform aim to enslave us.

—SAMUEL ADAMS
*A letter of correspondence
to the other towns, Boston,
November 20, 1772*

26

JOHN LAMB

ON DECEMBER 31, 1775, a colonial captain of artillery named John Lamb was leading his men in an assault on an overwhelmed British position outside the city of Quebec. The defenders, after strong resistance, had broken from their guns, abandoning the battery, when a lone gunner returned "linstock in hand" to light off a final round. Lamb, spotting the returning gunner, attempted to fire his pistol twice at the man, but the cold, wet weather had dampened his fuses. While priming his pistol for a third try, Lamb was hit when the gunner's cannon went off, sending grapeshot into Lamb's left cheek, near the eye, carrying away part of the bone and knocking him senseless back into the snow. Carried into a cooper's shop by his men, Lamb was laid upon a pile of shavings, where he was captured, still unconscious, by the British after the overextended colonial troops were forced to withdraw.

As a British surgeon worked to revive the wounded captain, a Scottish commissary who had been a servant in New York and knew Captain Lamb by reputation suggested that it would be more humane to let the prisoner die. Lamb was one of the founders of the Sons of Liberty, the most radical of colonial Revolutionary organizations, an inflammatory speechmaker and pamphleteer, who would certainly be tried and hanged for his offenses. The more charitable course would be to save him from the gallows. The surgeon revived him nevertheless, and Lamb was dispatched to the convent of the Sisters of Mercy. In the course of this journey, he suffered the loss of his shoes and buckles, in addition to losing the sight of his left eye.

While in this injured state, complicated by a severe case of gout, Lamb was visited by the commissary, who told him that the accepted procedure for dealing with rebels was that they would be sent home in irons to be tried. If His Majesty should wreak such vengeance on him, the weakened Lamb replied, General Washington would retaliate "by awarding the same fate to as good a man" as he was.

The abortive expedition against Quebec, part of a Continental campaign to protect the northern frontier and to persuade the Canadians to join the revolt against England, had been hastily conceived by the Continental Congress. John Lamb's actions in its behalf, however, sprang from origins of a different order, based on personal conviction two generations deep.

By the conventional order of descent, John Lamb should have been a Tory. The son of a self-made man who had reached eminence in his field, a successful merchant himself, Lamb was a man with a certain stake in the existing order of things; but he had never forgotten or forgiven his father's New World origins, the odds against his rise, and the influence of luck upon his life.

John Lamb's father, Anthony Lamb, had left England a convict, transported from Newgate prison as a thief. On October 10, 1724, along with ninety-six other convicted felons, he was shipped aboard the *Forward Frigate,* Daniel Russell captain, bound for Maryland. Anthony Lamb was twenty-one.

Somewhere—either in Maryland, where he landed and served out his indenture, or in Philadelphia, where he lived for a time, or in New York, where he eventually settled—Anthony Lamb acquired an advanced skilled trade. He became an optician, a maker first of spectacles and then instruments: telescopes, spyglasses, sextants. He taught mathematics, surveying, and navigation; and he became prominent in these disciplines in the America of his day. He trained his son in his skills to a degree that qualified him for a direct commission as an artillery officer in the Continental army. And he remained, to the end of his long life, an enthusiastic supporter of the Continental cause and a vehement anti-Tory.

Anthony Lamb was settled in New York when his son John was born, in 1735. For a time, the young man followed his father's trade, but by 1760 John Lamb had entered business for himself as a wine merchant. It was while engaged in the endless negotiations of merchandising that Lamb encountered the ruinous impediments of the Stamp Act. In October of 1765, he was among the leaders at a meeting of New York merchants where it was proposed that a committee be formed to organize a boycott of British goods, to open correspondence with the other colonies, and to propose articles of confederacy. This was the beginning of the Sons of Liberty in New York, and Lamb was one of its most ardent associates.

He was a touchy man—proud, rash, impulsive, sensitive to slights—a legacy of his father's humble beginnings in America. He was in considerable pain throughout most of his life, yet capable of enduring great hardship, a man, as his British captors discovered, of unshakable physical and moral courage.

Transformations such as Anthony Lamb's had bred an unexpected iron into the American soul, and caused the colonies' rebellion to be something more than an uprising to be suppressed with a few mercenary troops. "America is not subdued," Edmund Burke pointed out to Parliament in 1777. "Not one unattacked village which was originally adverse throughout that vast continent has yet submitted from love or terror. You have the ground you encamp on, and you have no more. The cantonments of your troops and your dominions are exactly of the same extent. You spread devastation, but you do not enlarge the sphere of authority."

Among John Lamb's detachment captured at Quebec had been some soldiers of British birth who found themselves under pressure to enlist in the king's regiments. Lamb, still ill with gout and missing an eye, was so vituperative in denouncing those men who did go over that the British commander reprimanded him and ordered his silence.

It was perhaps for this reason, combined with the fact that the British at this early date regarded the Continental troops as incapable of sustained military action, that the annoying Lamb, in June of 1776, found himself paroled along with several of his brother officers back to the colonies. The men were returned but forbidden to take up arms unless exchanged for captured British officers of comparable rank.

On arriving in New Jersey, Lamb, never a man to luxuriate in benevolence, reported immediately to Washington, professed his readiness for service, and urged, in his behalf, the earliest possible exchange.

Now a major, Lamb was offered command of a group of volunteers engaged against the British in Connecticut. He rode his horse sixty miles to assume charge of the detachment that was now attempting to dislodge a complement of British soldiers, sailors, and marines dug in on Compo Hill near Saugatuck Bay. Here Lamb led a charge against an entrenched artillery position, and while scaling a wall he was wounded again by grapeshot, which pierced his side and back and only narrowly missed his spine.

Following his recuperation, Lamb was ordered to take command of Fort Montgomery, overlooking the Hudson River in New York. The idea of a garrison post was frustrating to the restless Lamb, who yearned for a field command; but he soon found himself with more than enough of the action he craved as the British attempted to storm the fort, which was incompletely fortified and undermanned. With Lamb directing the artillery, the British, who attacked with "an invincible resolution in no instance exceeded during the American war," suffered severe losses but succeeded in overcoming the American positions. Lamb, at the head of his men, was forced to cut his way out through the enemy.

Promoted to colonel, Lamb was given command of the American artillery along the Hudson River, where he found himself caught between the political maneuverings of General Horatio

Gates, Washington's rival, and Lamb's friend and old commanding officer at Quebec, Benedict Arnold. Twice, incensed over
issues of rank and precedence, the testy Lamb resigned his commission, only to be persuaded by Washington to retain his responsibilities.

In June of 1780, Lamb was given command of West Point, the
major American fortification on the Hudson, under the overall
authority of General Benedict Arnold. While certain differences
developed between Lamb and Arnold over the severity of
Lamb's treatment of a prisoner he regarded as a spy, and Lamb's
opposition to Arnold's depletion of the fort's detachment of
troops, the two men, both wounded at Quebec, remained friends.
While staying at the Highlands, near Stony Point, Arnold frequently visited the house of Joshua Hett Smith, whose wife was
related to Lamb's wife, and who was known to Lamb to be a
Tory. Invited by Arnold to join him at Smith's house on several
occasions, Lamb repeatedly declined, adding that "he would not
visit his own father, were he of a similar political stripe."

Once, while dining at Arnold's headquarters, Lamb discovered
to his embarrassment that Smith was also an invited guest. During the course of the meal, Arnold mentioned that certain messages, amounting to peace feelers, had been received from a Tory
colonel named Robinson. Anxious to make terms for the restoration of his confiscated estates, Robinson had offered to propose
some preliminary grounds for a settlement between Britain and
America. Lamb heatedly responded that any proposition of that
kind ought to be made to Congress rather than to a general commanding a district. Arnold soothingly insisted that communications had to be opened through some channel, and that was all
that this represented. The subject was thereupon dropped.

In the late summer and early fall of 1780, Arnold continued to
requisition troops and ammunition from West Point, orders
which Lamb complied with, but only under protest. The garrison
grew so depleted that Lamb could not turn out more than enough
men to do fatigue duty and stand guard.

On September 24, Lamb was informed by Washington that
Arnold and Smith had been part of a plot to surrender West Point
and the other forts in the Highlands of the Hudson to the British,

thus guaranteeing the ruin of Washington's army. Smith, who had been prevailed upon by Arnold to accompany a British major, John André, through the American lines, had been caught, along with André, carrying papers which revealed the plot.

Lamb, first thunderstruck then angry, was placed briefly in command of the crucial artillery batteries at Stony Point and Verplanck's Point, then put once again in charge of West Point. By constant activity under his direction these posts were put in an effective condition for defense.

Lamb neither forgave nor apologized for his old friend's treason. When a messenger bringing news of André's capture conveyed to Lamb General Arnold's regards, Lamb instructed the man to reply to Arnold "that the acquaintance between us is forgotten; and that if he were hanged tomorrow I would go barefooted to witness his execution."

Yet he would not allow anyone to disparage Arnold's courage or conduct in the field. Years after the conspiracy, while dining at General Israel Putnam's headquarters, Lamb, who had joined in an anti-Arnold toast of "confusion to the traitor," lashed out at one of Putnam's generals who had questioned Arnold's personal bravery.

"Sir," Lamb is reported to have said, "let me tell you that, drunk or sober, you will never be an Arnold, or fit to compare with him in any military capacity."

For the British army in the field, the two big surprises of the Revolutinary War were the adaptability of American troops and their resolve. In John Lamb's military career, we can see demonstrations of both.

The British army had *invented* military drill. It originated in the introduction of firearms and the necessity to impose some sort of discipline to prevent large groups of men from inflicting massive accidental wounds. By the late eighteenth century, techniques had been developed that were so successful—firing by ranks, the defensive square, fields of fire—that the British were able to rule history's largest empire with an astonishingly small number of regular troops. It was discipline rather than hardware alone that made insurgents against the British so many times wear themselves out in human-wave assaults or, more often, to break and run.

The American colonials broke and ran too, especially in the early going. At the Battle of New York, Washington had to draw his sword on a brigadier general to prevent him from fleeing with his men; but the Americans, officers and men, learned from their mistakes to a degree uncommon among traditional armies. Men rose to responsibility; they were more amenable to change.

Like Washington, John Lamb represented this new kind of soldier, unawed by things as they had always been, convinced from his father's example that a man freed from the constraints of arbitrary power was capable of accomplishing more than was conventionally considered possible by the strict rules of inherited rank. Lamb's skills at the employment of ordnance and his acquisitiveness of learning—grown from the mathematical training given him by his father—helped bring the artillery under his command, like that of the colonial forces generally, to impressive levels of proficiency.

At Yorktown, we are told "the skill of the American batteries astonished their more experienced allies." The field commander of artillery on the day of Cornwallis's defeat was John Lamb.

Beyond this was the individual conviction, the belief in oneself and one's cause, that sustained men like Lamb throughout a seven-year (in Lamb's case, an eight-year) war. It was always clear to him exactly what he was against. Whenever John Lamb had to decide what was right—not right for the captured troops who joined the king's regiments at Quebec, or right for Benedict Arnold, anxious to restore his lost personal holdings—he could look inside himself and it was there.

His father had remained active in his trade throughout the war, relocating his business twice, once in New York and then again in Connecticut, to avoid being forced to live or serve under the British. It was only after the war ended that Anthony Lamb died, at the age of eighty-one.

For John Lamb, the Revolutionary army had given his life a focus and provided an application for his talents and energies that he was never to find again. He emerged from it a one-eyed brigadier general, something of a minor military hero. He was

elected to the New York Assembly, where he vehemently opposed the restoration of property or extension of the ballot to
returning Tory sympathizers. He opposed the adoption of the
Constitution, which he regarded as an unwarranted Hamiltonian
centralization of powers. A leading anti-Federalist, he stood
guard outside his own house when it was threatened by political
rivals. He supported the Revolutionary government in France
and was a charter member of the Order of the Cincinnati, an
organization considered an elitist conspiracy by some, but regarded by Lamb with a harmless fraternal fondness.

Though his circumstances had changed, his conscience remained active. It played him false but once.

As a reward for extraordinary services rendered during the
Revolution, General Lamb had been appointed collector of customs for the port of New York. In this capacity, Lamb had tried
to assist a certain Englishman who had been imprisoned for debt.
The amount was so large that the man seemed excluded forever
from any hope of redemption, yet the man was represented to
Lamb as a person of integrity and ability. Here, it seemed, was
his father, Anthony Lamb, all over again.

Lamb not only shouldered the debt, using his own property as
guarantee, he gave the freed man a job as a clerk at the customs
house. The man displayed industry and skill and was promoted
to a position of confidence. Left in charge of the fiscal concerns
of his department, the clerk began "a system of peculation and
embezzlement." He bought a coach and entered into a "luxuri-
ous and expensive style of living." A shortage of funds was soon
discovered, and Lamb and his pledge of security were held accountable for both the debt and the amount of the embezzlement.
His lands were sold at sacrifice prices, and his family was ruined.
Even political rivals like Hamilton protested against the rigorous-
ness of the course pursued against the old soldier. Thrown into
poverty despite the best efforts of his friends, Lamb was now
ravaged by the gout that had continually plagued him, and was
"seldom free from paroxysms of an alarming nature."

He died on May 31, 1800, a man who incorporated within
himself much of what the country itself had become. He was the
son of a transported convict, and he became a Revolutionary

agitator, soldier, legislator, and the father of an American general-to-be—Anthony Lamb, named after his convict grandfather. John Lamb remained a Son of Liberty in more than one sense of the term.

Voices

There are but two sorts of men in the world, freemen and slaves. The very definition of a freeman is one who is bound by no law to which he has not consented. Americans would have no way of giving or withholding their consent to the acts of this parliament, therefore they would not be freemen. But, when luxury, effeminacy and venality are arrived at such a shocking pitch in England, when both electors and elected, are become one mass of corruption, when the nation is oppressed to death with debts and taxes, owing to their own extravagance, and want of wisdom, what would be your condition under such an absolute subjection to Parliament? You would not only be slaves. But the most abject sort of slaves to the worst sort of masters!

—"Novanglus"
John Adams, 1775

27
MATTHEW LYON: 1

IN 1765, Matthew Lyon, a fourteen-year-old Irish boy whose father had been put to death by the British, struck a deal with a ship captain to be transported to America. In return for passage, Lyon was to be sold as a redemptioner until he reached the age of twenty-one. The precocious Lyon, who had received some formal education, including Latin and Greek, and had learned the trades of printer and bookbinder at a Dublin publishing house, was already planning to improve upon the terms of his bargain. While still aboard ship, he ingratiated himself with the captain, whom he served as cabin boy. Capitalizing on this intimacy, Lyon used the last of his money, a golden guinea, to bribe the skipper to lie about his age. The captain agreed to represent the big-boned, mature-looking young man at auction as already eighteen, thus cutting Lyon's term of service to three years. In addition to keeping the guinea, the captain paid Lyon nothing for his services as cabin boy.

In New York, Matthew Lyon was purchased for a term of three years by Jabez Bacon, a wealthy, impetuous Connecticut merchant and trader. Bacon, who cleared as much as forty thousand dollars in a single day speculating in New York pork cargoes, was a man of fascinating entrepreneurial skills and, to Matthew Lyon, odious politics: He was an enthusiastic Tory.

The boy, whose father had been executed along with the other leaders of the White Boys, an association of Irish farmers organized to resist rack-rent evictions, and who had himself worked as a printer on the anti-British Irish *Freeman's Journal,* had arrived in America already a convinced anti-Tory. Now, to secure his own freedom, he began applying the enterprise he admired to escaping the politics he despised.

From a neighboring farmer, Hugh Hannah, the cunning cub Lyon arranged to buy a pair of bulls on credit. The full purchase price was to be paid after Lyon terminated his servitude with Bacon. The boy then traded the bulls to Bacon for the remainder of his three-year indenture. Then he went to work for Hannah to work off the purchase price of the bulls—but as a freeman, not an indentured servant.

By two shrewd pieces of trading, Matthew Lyon had cut a required servitude of seven years to one. As a clerk in Hannah's store, he had free time enough to resume his studies. At last he had found room to maneuver. It was the turning point of his life, an event he memorialized until the day of his death with his idiosyncratic oath: "by the bulls that redeemed me!"

Lyon's combination of Irish romantic desperation and studied Yankee shrewdness was to carry him both far and fast in the somewhat cloistered New England colonial society, while at the same time maintaining in him a stubborn adherence to first principles.

When he had paid his debt to Hannah, Lyon went to work in Connecticut's first ironworks, where he learned the smelting and fabricating business. He also married the owner's niece, and in time moved to a valley in the New Hampshire Grants (later to become Vermont) that his boss was developing for settlement. When Lyon's employer organized his neighbors for a military force pledged to resist the threat of eviction, it was the reincarnation of Lyon's father's adventures with the White Boys in

Ireland. Lyon joined as a private, and thus became one of Ethan Allen's Green Mountain Boys.

In the spring of 1775, Lyon was among an irregular band which appeared out of nowhere at Fort Ticonderoga in upstate New York, where Ethan Allen demanded, according to legend, that the British commandant surrender the fort, its guns and ammunition "in the name of the Great Jehovah and the Continental Congress." Here was one of life's rare opportunities to avenge family, self, and country with the same blow. Lyon enthusiastically embraced it.

Here again we see at work the remarkable dynamic of Revolutionary resistance and colonial independence. An orphaned Irish boy, an impoverished runaway, is transformed into a colonial infantryman with a personal, tangible sense of earned freedom, the will and the means to defend it, and the ambition to expand upon it. And the mechanism of change was servitude.

"In this character of the Americans," Edmund Burke warned Parliament that same year, "a love of freedom is the predominating feature . . . what they think the only advantage worth living for."

"Eighty-five of us," recalled Lyon, years later, still exhilarated by the victory, "took from one hundred and forty British veterans the Fort Ticonderoga. That fort contained when we took it more cannon, mortar-pieces and other military stores than could be found in all the revolted colonies."

It was the first spring flood of American independence, and Lyon, swept up in it, undertook the conversion of the capitulated British troopers. "I persuaded many of the Royal Irish company taken there to join us, who afterwards distinguished themselves in our cause."

The ordnance captured at Ticonderoga was used against the British throughout the war, at battles ranging from Boston to Yorktown. Meanwhile, Lyon advanced rapidly to the rank of colonel, and commanded a regiment of Green Mountain Boys at Saratoga and Bennington. When a general convention was called in 1776 of delegates from towns in the New Hampshire Grants, Lyon represented his community. Part of the body that formed the state of Vermont, he served in its Assembly during its first four years.

It was the beginning of a long and influential political career, which was to be a lifetime extension of the freed-servant mandate to act on one's beliefs.

"We cannot falsify the pedigree of this fierce people," Edmund Burke warned his fellow Britons about the uprisen American colonists. "We never seem to gain a paltry advantage over them in debate, without attacking some of those principles, or deriding some of those feelings, for which our ancestors have shed their blood."

"An Englishman," he concluded, "is the unfittest person in the world to argue an other Englishman into slavery."

Voices

But enslave your country! entail vassalage, that worst of all human miseries, that sum of all wretchedness on millions! This, this is guilt, this calls for heaven's fiercest vengeance.

—WILLIAM GODDARD
The Constitutional Courant

28

CHARLES THOMSON: 1

IT WAS in 1739 that John Thomson, an Irish widower, took ship for America with four of his six children. One of thousands of Ulstermen forced to leave his home country because of the destruction of the linen trade, Thomson apparently had paid for all or part of his sons' passage. He intended to settle in Pennsylvania. On board the ship, however, which appears to have resembled one of the floating pesthouses described by Gottlieb Mittelberger, John Thomson took ill. Attacked by "a violent sickness," he died within sight of the American shore.

"I stood by the bedside of my expiring and much-loved father," his youngest son, Charles Thomson, then ten years old, wrote later, "closed his eyes and performed the last filial duties to him."

The father had left his orphan children with little else but a sum of money entrusted to the captain, and a deathbed plea: "God take them up."

They were to begin learning the hard lessons of immigrant children almost immediately.

John Thomson was buried at sea, off the capes of the Delaware. The ship landed at New Castle, Delaware, where the four surviving sons were put ashore. Here the captain presented them with a small amount of cash—all, he said, that was due them from their father's estate. The sons, who lived into their eighties, were to maintain throughout their lives that they had been cheated, but being young and without proof in a strange country, they were unable to protest. Instead, stranded without means on a foreign shore, they would have to scramble for survival instead of exploring available opportunities.

The three oldest boys found work, with the idea in mind of acquiring money to buy land. The youngest boy, Charles, was sent to live with a New Castle blacksmith. Here the young boy's alertness and acquisitiveness suggested that he be apprenticed to learn to work at the forge. By law, he would be required to serve his master for seven years. Overhearing the family's plans for him one night, the boy, "determining from the vigor of his mind that he should devote himself to better business," sneaked from his bed and, with what little he owned packed upon his back, made his escape.

Walking the road, aimed anywhere but New Castle, the young Charles Thomson chanced "to be overtaken by a traveling lady of the neighborhood." The woman began a conversation with Thomson and eventually drew him into a discussion of his ambitions. He would like to be a scholar, he confided to her, "or to gain his support by his mind and pen." This woman, whose name is lost to us, was so taken with the breadth of the runaway boy's vision of his future, "that she took him home and placed him at school."

The school that Charles Thomson attended, after a brief period of preparation, was the academy of the extraordinary Dr. Francis Alison at New London in Chester County, Pennsylvania. A classical scholar, educated at the University of Glasgow, Dr. Alison instructed at least four governors, eight congressmen, and four signers of the Declaration of Independence, and was considered by the president of Yale "the greatest classical scholar in America." A dour man, who Thomson, who lived for five years in the Alison house, described as never having been seen smiling, Alison not only instructed his students in Latin and Greek but drilled them in science and mathematics, as well as having them abstract articles from the respected English periodicals of the day. His curriculum produced a reverence for classical learning, combined with exposure to the scientific rationality of the Enlightenment that was to characterize the intellectual spirit of the Revolution.

Thomson bloomed in this atmosphere, developing the deep love of classical learning, if not the strict Presbyterian convictions of Dr. Alison. It was this relationship that led Thomson, on leaving New London, to find work as a teacher and, in 1750, for Dr. Alison, now rector of the new Academy of Philadelphia, to appoint Thomson to the academy's faculty.

In Philadelphia, Thomson sought out a new mentor, Benjamin Franklin. As a former runaway apprentice come to Philadelphia hungry for knowledge, experience, and success. Thomson must have reminded Franklin of himself as a young man. The two formed a friendship that lasted until Franklin's death in 1790. And when Thomson married in 1758, he and his wife moved into a house across the street from Franklin's.

In admitted imitation of the older man, Thomson and some of his new friends formed a mutual improvement society patterned after Franklin's "Junto." Once a week the members would gather to discuss books, ideas, and ways and means of improving their personal state and that of the society around them. Under Franklin's guidance, and in the stimulating surroundings of other young, ambitious men, Thomson was developing a set of convictions which seemed to require political expression.

These were heady times for a young man in Philadelphia, especially for one such as Charles Thomson, whose desires for advancement, autonomy, and recognition must have seemed at one with those of the colonies. The possibilities of both seemed limited only by the lingering presence of an imposed and largely unnecessary outside authority.

The colony of Pennsylvania was divided politically between the proprietary interests, representing the heirs of William Penn and most of the large landholders, and that of the Quaker party, representing mostly businessmen. The key issue was the defense of the colony's western settlements against attack by the Indians, with the militant landholders lining up on one side and the mostly pacifist Quakers on the other. Thomson, who in 1755 was employed as master of the Friends Public School of Philadelphia, found himself a de facto propagandist on the Quaker side.

In 1756, Thomson was among a group of Quaker leaders who proposed to negotiate peace with a group of tribes united under the chieftan Teddyuscung. During the negotiations, the Pennsylvania governor asked the Indians the cause of their grievances. Teddyuscung complained about unfair land purchases made by the proprietors. When the governor's secretary refused to record these claims, saying that the Quakers had already encouraged them, Thomson read back Teddyuscung's entire speech, which he had taken down in his own variety of shorthand. At the next session of the negotiations, Thomson was appointed secretary to the meetings, at Teddyuscung's insistence. The Indians were so pleased that Thomson's notes supported their claims that they resolved to adopt him into their tribe. Thomson's Indian name was "the man who talks the truth."

In 1759, through the efforts of Franklin, Thomson's account of the proprietary mistreatment of the Indians was published as *An Enquiry into the Causes of the Alienation of the Delaware and Shawanese Indians from the British Interests*. An attack on the Penn proprietors, which accused them of land fraud, coercion, and bad faith in dealing with the Indians, Thomson's *Enquiry* proved surprisingly popular, and was the authoritative work on the colonists' treatment of the Indians in Pennsylvania for more than a century.

By 1766, Thomson's revived Junto had been renamed "The American Society for Promoting and Propagating Useful Knowledge." At Thomson's urging, the society had added corresponding members from the other colonies, and Thomson clearly intended it to be a propagandizing organization in behalf of intercolonial union. He encountered opposition, however, and the American Society and a competitor were eventually merged into the American Philosophical Society.

Meanwhile, again following the example of the ever-practical Franklin, Thomson had entered business, opening a mercantile shop in Philadelphia specializing in a variety of imported dry goods. Thomson also invested in a linen factory. Thus in 1763 and 1764 Thomson was to have direct experience with American businessmen's frustrations over the Stamp Act. He became to Franklin—now in England as the colony's agent to the Crown—the most reliable authority on the colonists' reaction to the Act.

Gradually, Thomson gravitated to the radical position among the colonists of Pennsylvania. In 1770, his wife died; she had been in declining health since the death, some years earlier, of their newborn twin sons. Thomson was left alone, stripped of family as he had been on his arrival in America. The pain and frustration of that time were now vividly recalled to him.

Thomson's earliest American experiences—the death of his father, being bilked of money by a ship captain, separation from his three brothers, a narrow escape from bondage to a blacksmith —were of the personal intensity that can mark an individual for life. There was, however, powerful compensation. In the process of becoming the man he now was, Thomson had acquired the skills to articulate his resentments to others.

During 1771 and 1772, Thomson directed his appeals against the acts and claims of Parliament increasingly to the tradesmen, mechanics, and small shopkeepers of Philadelphia. As in Boston, these elements were just beginning to become a force in local politics; and Thomson, like them descended from servitude, understood their fears and frustrations. He wrote letters and articles, supported boycotts, and encouraged the formation of patriotic societies and Committees of Correspondence. Promoting resistance at this level, he carried on a more cautious dialogue at the same time with Sam Adams and Ben Franklin.

When the port of Boston was closed in retaliation for the Boston Tea Party, Thomson was part of a corresponding committee that led the city of Philadelphia to pledge itself to Boston's support. Outmaneuvering the governor and the Pennsylvania Assembly, Thomson and his associates called for a provincial convention of representatives chosen by the counties to select delegates to a Continental Congress.

Under the pretense of an excursion, Thomson and his fellow radicals stumped the colony, enjoying particular success among the Germans, just beginning to assert themselves politically.

Pressured by the prospect of a popularly supported rival delegation representing Pennsylvania at the Continental Congress, the
Assembly agreed to send its own delegates. They thus gave official recognition to the Congress on behalf of one of the oldest
and largest colonies. For the first time, representatives of all the
colonies, except Georgia, gathered in Philadelphia to prevent the
enforcement of British acts.

"No longer," concluded the early historian John Adolphus of
this first Continental Congress, "did America exhibit the appearance of rival colonies, piquing themselves on separate rights . . .
the same grievances, although not felt by all, were complained of
by all."

At the time of the Congress's opening, in September of 1774,
Thomson arrived in Philadelphia, accompanied by his new wife,
the niece of his political associate John Dickinson. The new-
lyweds' carriage was stopped by a messenger, who told Thomson
his presence was requested by the president of the Congress; the
radicals had succeeded in getting Thomson appointed secretary.
It was a post he would hold for as long as there *was* a Continental
Congress.

Voices

Can any one reason be assigned why 160,000 electors in the island of Great Britain should give law to four millions in the states of America? . . . Were this to be admitted, instead of being a free people . . . we should suddenly be found the slaves not of one, but of 160,000 tyrants.

—THOMAS JEFFERSON
*A Summary View
of the Rights of British
America, 1774*

29

John Sullivan: 1

In August of 1774, an ambitious young lawyer named John Sullivan arrived in Philadelphia as one of the colony of New Hampshire's two delegates to the first Continental Congress. A man who brought a certain intensity to everything he did, Sullivan, at the age of thirty-four, had already acquired a reputation as, with the possible exception of John Adams, the ablest attorney in New England, a considerable personal fortune, and a resentment on the part of his neighbors so deep that a group of them had once surrounded his house with the intention of killing him.

Sullivan's turbulent early legal career in Durham, New Hampshire, was a product not only of his vehemence, but also his novelty. As the town's first lawyer, he introduced the idea of hired advocacy, pressing suits against his neighbors so vigorously and successfully that a considerable number of them came to regard him as the source of their financial woes. On June 2, 1766, a small mob gathered outside Sullivan's house; shots were fired into it, and members of the mob threatened to burn it down and kill him if need be "to rob him of many Writs and Notes of

hand which he then had in his possession.'' Sullivan, a man
whose ambition never exceeded his courage, refused to yield
either his life or his papers, so his hostile townsmen appealed to
the courts instead. On June 26, they petitioned the general court
against the "Oppressive and Extortive behavior" of John Sullivan. He was accused of gouging "poor harmless people" for
"unreasonable fees" and of selling himself "to the highest bidder
. . . to plead a Case before Justice." The petition carried 113
signatures.

His reputation for relentless pursuit of an interest only enhanced Sullivan's desirability as a counselor in a court of law.
His practice grew, as did the stature of his clients and his personal estate. By the early 1770s, Sullivan owned land in Durham
and elsewhere, as well as six mills and several slaves, and was
on friendly terms with the colonial governor John Wentworth,
who had awarded Sullivan a major's commission in the militia.

Possessing inherent gifts of leadership—energy, vehemence, a
flair for oratory, physical bravery—Sullivan found himself drawn
to the colonial side in the growing dispute with England. He was
of Irish descent, he was ambitious, and he craved the acceptance
that seemed to come with association with a popular cause.
When Governor Wentworth dissolved the New Hampshire Assembly rather than let it send delegates to the proposed congress
in Philadelphia, Sullivan joined a rival provincial congress, where
the combative young lawyer was selected to go instead. He and
his fellow delegate were accompanied to the New Hampshire
border by an escort of "150 Gentlemen." It was Sullivan's first
taste of popular acclaim, and it thrilled him.

Sullivan arrived in Philadelphia confident, self-important, a political moderate, and threw himself with characteristic energy
into the debates and committee work of the Continental Congress, as well as the more congenial task of exploring his first
large city. Philadelphia was America's deep core, drawing on the
thoughts and opinions of the first men of the continent's colonies,
circulating the ideas of nationhood out to the remotest villages
and farms. Here too were the other arrivals, the continuing
stream of immigrants, particularly the redemptioners, the Palatine Germans, and others about to be indentured servants, whose
flow was now at its peak. The Dutch shipowners' vessels were

docked a few short blocks from the Pennsylvania State Assembly House where the delegates met. The notices of arrival, the advertisements of sale, the reward offers for runaways appeared on posters and in newspapers. John Sullivan, curious, energetic, ambitious, had only to look around him to see the beginnings of his own parents' American lives.

His father, Master John Sullivan, had been born in Limerick, Ireland, in 1691, during the siege of Limerick by William III. His father was a major in the Irish army, and following a truce and a peace that didn't last, the major and his family were forced to take refuge in France.

The Sullivan family stayed in France for several years, remaining even after the major himself had died. The son, John, was carefully educated by his mother, a proud, aristocratic woman who gave special attention to languages, particularly French. When peace of a kind settled over Ireland, Mrs. Sullivan was allowed to return with her children to take possession of what seem to have been substantial family estates. The Sullivans apparently held a position of some consequence in Limerick society.

In time, a dispute arose between John Sullivan and his mother. The son wished to marry a girl whom the mother insisted was beneath him. Widowed, only recently restored to her family lands, Madam Sullivan did not wish to see the family social standing in further jeopardy. She forbade her son to have anything more to do with the girl, and gave him two weeks to break the engagement; otherwise he would be disinherited. John Sullivan, of the same stubborn temper, gave his mother two weeks to consent to the marriage; otherwise he would leave Ireland, and neither she nor the girl would ever hear of him again.

The two weeks passed. Neither mother nor son would yield. In the fall of 1723, Master John Sullivan took ship for America. "As my mother had absolutely refused to furnish me means for paying transportation," Sullivan recalled more than half a century later, "and I had no means otherwise, I was obliged to enter into an agreement with the captain to earn the money for my passage." He was a redemptioner, accepting transportation for the price of servitude.

The ship John Sullivan sailed on had been destined for Newburyport, Massachusetts, but "owing to a stress of weather" was forced to land at York Harbor in Maine. Here John Sullivan was sold by the captain to a farmer named McIntire, in Scotland parish, who put the educated thirty-two-year-old Irishman to work as a laborer.

Sullivan hated his situation. "Unaccustomed to farm labor and growing weary of manual occupation," he later recalled, "I applied to Rev. Dr. Moody, pastor of the parish, for assistance." Sullivan represented himself as a scholar whose abilities were being wasted in servitude as a farmhand. As a demonstration of his attainments, he composed the letter in seven languages. Impressed, the Reverend Moody "became interested in my behalf, and being conversant with my ability to teach, he loaned me the money with which to pay the captain the amount I owed for my passage."

Having rescued Sullivan from the McIntire farm, the Reverend also helped him establish himself as a schoolmaster. In May of 1723, Master "Sullefund" was chosen one of the two teachers in the town of Dover. He kept school at a place called Somersworth, which became a separate parish and in time a village. Here he worked for the next thirty years, "a tall, spare man, very mild and gentle, thoughtful and studious, an excellent scholar, but averse to bodily exercise." He is said to have been unhappy with his own lot in life, but to have never complained about it. As an educator, he probably taught more men who took a significant part in the Revolution than any other teacher in New England.

While on board the ship carrying him to America, Sullivan had made the acquaintance of a nine-year-old girl, also an Irish redemptioner, named Margery Browne. Born in Cork in 1714, she took passage to America under circumstances that remain a mystery. Her parents may have died aboard ship, or the girl may even have been a stowaway. Whatever the cause, she had no money to pay her passage, and the captain had to sell her service at auction to get his fare. Tradition has it that she was so young and small that nobody would bid for her, and that Sullivan himself raised the price of her passage by cutting shingles in the woods and carrying them down to the captain by boat.

For the next twelve years, Margery Browne worked in or near

York, probably as a household servant. Here, in 1735, she and John Sullivan became reacquainted. Margery was short, pretty, energetic, quick-tempered, utterly uncultivated, and something of a scold: a perfect foil for the tall, forbearing, scholarly Sullivan. They fell in love and were married. He was forty-four, she was twenty-one.

Each adopted, not without difficulty, something of the other's traditional role. Margery, vigorous and resolute, worked outdoors in the field so that John Sullivan, bored and unhappy with farm chores, might devote himself entirely to teaching. This reversal of form created a certain stress in their marriage, and eventually open conflict. In the summer of 1743, fleeing his wife's stormy temper, John Sullivan, now the father of several children, walked out and went to Boston. Margery, in a curious mixture of humility and aggression, wrote her husband an abject letter of apology, which she had published as an ad in the Boston *Evening Post*. Unless he returned, she insisted, his wife and eldest son "who take your departure so heavily" would suffer "a lingering though certain death."

Margery Sullivan knew her man. Stirred by compassion, or perhaps simple embarrassment, John Sullivan returned to his wife. The two remained together for the next fifty years.

It must have been a remarkable household to grow up in, especially for the time. A mother and father who had arrived in America in the humblest of circumstances, who were decades apart in age and polar opposites in temperament. The father, a scholar who detested farming, living in an agricultural community and eventually the owner of a farm. The mother, rude and uneducated, a bundle of ambition and masculine energies, assuming most of the practical responsibilities.

It produced remarkable children, who grew up isolated in a small community in a remote rural colony, without formal schooling, yet who were tutored by their father to the highest university level of their day; who were driven by their mother's energy and subject to her fits of temper, in a society where the old ranks were crumbling along with the limits to individual possibilities. From among them were to come two governors, a general, and a naval officer.

For John Sullivan the Younger, delegate to the first Continental Congress at Philadelphia, the time and place in which he was raised, his parents humble beginnings, the rapidity of his rise in a sparsely populated backwoods state, caused him to be both vain and insecure in a way that thrust him into controversy throughout his life. Removed from the usual schoolboy give-and-take, trained by apprenticeship as a lawyer, he remained hypersensitive, given to self-pity and complaint, unwilling to shoulder blame for reverses, yet unquestionably courageous, ardent, and active. To his father's erudition and his mother's energy, he added their combined redemptioners' sense of injury and hatred toward arbitrary power.

He had gone to Philadelphia a moderate, but Sullivan returned to New Hampshire a Revolutionary radical. In December of 1774, he was among the leading instigators of a raid on the British military stores at Fort William and Mary at New Castle, New Hampshire. Ordered arrested by proclamation of Governor Wentworth, who had again dissolved the Assembly, Sullivan lost his major's commission, yet remained at large and was elected a delegate to the second Continental Congress in 1775. Here Sullivan was among the faction led by John Adams urging the Congress to recognize the fact that war with Britain had already begun. When Congress finally agreed to draft rules and regulations for a Continental army, and George Washington was chosen as commander, the energetic John Sullivan was appointed a brigadier general and sent to oppose the British in Boston. The Americans, he announced to John Adams, would "take possession of the town, or perish in the attempt."

Sullivan's military career was a mixture of personal valor, impetuousness, squabbling, bad timing, and bad luck. He never achieved the great victory against the British that won other, and in some cases lesser, generals mention in schoolbooks. His greatest military achievement was an extermination campaign against the Iroquois Confederacy, the Six Nations. He was vain, even for a general, loved pomp and ceremony, and was so given to complaint that Washington, whom Sullivan idolized, rebuked him: "No other officer of rank, in the whole army has so often conceived himself neglected, slighted, and ill-treated as you have done, and none I am sure had less cause than yourself to entertain such Ideas."

Yet Washington endured Sullivan's complaints and defied his critics, appointing him to important commands despite opposition in the Congress and from men of the stature of Jefferson and Adams, valuing his desire to serve and his initiative in a war where generals on both sides tended to dawdle.

At Boston, in Canada, at the Battle of Long Island, where Sullivan was taken prisoner, in the victory at Trenton and the abortive attempt at a joint attack with the French on Newport, and in the war of attrition against the powerful Six Nations, Sullivan performed with valor, industry, and diligence. His personal foibles, however, tended to cancel out his modest successes and to exaggerate the most minor of his failings; his insistence on the pre-eminence of his own abilities guaranteed that those abilities would be called into question.

When, in November of 1779, following his successful campaign against the Indians, Sullivan, not for the first time, submitted his resignation to the Continental Congress, it was in expectation of being granted a temporary leave. Instead, the majority of the Congress, preferring to see Sullivan out of the army, voted to accept the resignation. Sullivan, to his surprise, found himself headed back to New Hampshire, a civilian, carrying as his spoils of war only a vote of thanks from the Congress for his past services to the country. His controversial military career had ended; his stormier political career was about to begin.

Voices

e pluribus unum
novus ordo seclorum
annuit coeptis

—PHRASES FROM *The Aeneid* as
incorporated by Charles
Thomson into the Great Seal of
the United States

30
CHARLES THOMSON: 2

THROUGHOUT THE course of the American Revolution, wherever Charles Thomson was the Continental Congress was. As secretary, the sole unelected custodian of its minutes, records, traditions, and secrets, Thomson became its element of continuity as the Congress moved from session to session and from town to town: Philadelphia, Baltimore, Lancaster, York, Princeton, Trenton, New York. As the most effective executive officer of the Congress, Thomson corresponded with the states to get them to comply with laws and requisitions, issued passports, letters of marque and reprisal, and published proclamations. Through an extensive correspondence with the colonies' overseas representatives, including Franklin, Jefferson, John Jay, and John Adams, Thomson served as what amounted to secretary of state.

Within the Congress, Thomson had and exercised the opportunity to express both his philosophical and political convictions. With his classical background, his identification with the Romans of antiquity, he could help show the colonial delegates how to function as legislators. He let them know how to *be*. And as keeper of its minutes and journals, and the one constant member of the changing committee that set its agenda, he interpreted what the Congress collectively was.

During much of this time, many of the documents he signed put him under automatic sentence of death. When the Declaration of Independence was originally issued, Thomson's name and John Hancock's were the only signatures on it. Only months later were the other signers' names added, in order to spread the risk. Throughout the Revolutionary War, wherever he went, Thomson carried with him evidence that could not only incriminate himself but make practically the entire colonial leadership indictable for treason. He supervised the keeping of the Congress's journals, occasionally editing or deleting passages, and most of the entries were in his handwriting. Many years later, after his retirement from public life, Thomson was urged by Benjamin Rush to write, from his insider's knowledge, a true history of the Revolution. "I ought not," Thomson replied, "for I should contradict all the histories of the great events . . . Let the world admire the supposed wisdom and valor of our great men . . . I shall not undeceive future generations."

As secretary of the Congress, Thomson was also keeper of the Great Seal, the authorizing emblem that was to be applied to official documents. The problem was that during most of the war there was no seal. Three committees chosen by the Congress had been unable to agree on a design. In 1782, the Congress turned the matter over to Thomson. Taking elements from the recommendations of all three committess, Thomson sketched out a rough approximation of the seal used today. On the face was the eagle, holding an olive branch in one claw and a bundle of arrows in the other. Thomson added the motto "e pluribus unum"—one from many—adapted from Virgil, which was put on a banner clutched in the eagle's beak. The reverse side, with its occult-Masonic unfinished pyramid and all-seeing eye, and the inscriptions "novus ordo seclorum" (a new order for the ages) and "annuit coeptis" (He has favored our cause), represents a hybrid of Thomson's deepest personal beliefs: his Enlightenment Freemasonry and his love of the classics and identification with republican Rome. Thomson's work has endured for more than two hundred years, and is the oldest visual representation of the United States.

Like many other Revolutionary radicals, including John Adams, Thomson grew increasingly alarmed at the strength of the passions released by independence, and he became disillusioned with the attempts at government that followed in its wake. Political liberty had produced not the simple triumph of virtue but a continuing, complex, and exhausting conflict of competing interests. As the individual colonies struggled to implement various republican constitutions, and the quality and effectiveness of the Congress declined under the Articles of Confederation, Thomson came to accept the idea that some checks must be applied to direct representation of the people. One-house directly elected legislatures, like Pennsylvania's, led to unbalanced government, which was only another form of tyranny.

Over the years, Thomson also grew disenchanted with the Continental Congress itself, as with his classical standards he was bound to. In his letters he mourned the decline of "wisdom, dignity and prudence" in the Congress, and he wished at the end "that it could be obliterated from the annals of America, and utterly effaced from my memory."

Unlike so many men of Revolutionary prominence, Thomson was not enriched by American independence. His small country estate, Harriton, near Bryn Mawr, became a battlefield and was mostly destroyed; his business interests languished; and his pay as secretary to the Congress was sporadic and in chimerical Continental dollars. None of this seemed to trouble Thomson greatly; his was a mind capable of inhabiting more than one era at a time, and he seemed to derive fulfillment from his love of learning and books. In a perspective of thousands of years, the loss of personal property or of business opportunities was insignificant.

The one reward he would have liked—formal recognition of his services from the new Constitutional government he helped implement—was denied him.

With the enactment of the Constitution of 1789, the Continental Congress, with Thomson as secretary, was out of business. Thomson negotiated with several members of the new Senate, hoping to establish himself in a new, largely ceremonial post as

"Secretary of the Senate and the United States Congress," but it was not to be. In his fifteen years of service, Thomson had become associated too closely with the Continental Congress, and such a combination of ceremonial and de facto power would not be welcome in the new government.

In April of 1789, as his last official act as secretary, Thomson traveled to Mount Vernon, where he notified George Washington of his election by the Senate to the new office of President of the United States. To triumphant rejoicing, Thomson escorted the President-elect to New York, where, as Washington took the oath of office, Thomson bade farewell to public life.

In retirement, Thomson found release for the full range of his intellectual energies. He restored Harriton, his country estate, became an enthusiastic natural scientist, and engaged in a lively correspondence with, among others, Jefferson and Franklin. He involved himself in Indian affairs, and was one of the earliest and most effective supporters of fair treatment for people still considered dangerous and hostile adversaries.

For the great work of his life, Thomson returned to the classical studies which had formed and guided him since his days as an ex-indentured orphan with Dr. Alison. Beginning in 1789, he set to work translating the *Septuagint,* the Greek Bible, into English. Working alone, in a remote city with limited source materials and hardly even any books, Thomson produced in 1808 the first American translation of the Bible, a work which some seventy-five years later was considered by Dr. Francis Bacon of Harvard to "challenge comparison with the best results of the united labors, during the last ten years, of two companies containing thirty or forty of the best scholars in America and England."

Thomson was fulfilled by and grateful for the work. "It had kept my mind employed so that I can say that I have not during the last 19 years found one hour hang heavy on me."

In the breadth of his interests and abilities—classical scholarship, education, Indian affairs, politics, philosophy, government administration, business, science, polemics, foreign affairs, translation—Charles Thomson was very much a man of his time. In the distance of his journey from his American origins as an impoverished castaway orphan, he embodied the phenomenon of his new nation. Like some windblown spore drifted west from one neglected corner of the empire only to flower with amazing rapidity in another, he seems to have contained within him some ingrained element of radical, exponential growth. Like other Ulster emigrants, ex–indentured servants, and runaway apprentices, Thomson "found a home to which England later had to regret that she had allowed them to be driven."

It was Thomson's great gift to be able to articulate the feelings of people who had known similar high hopes and hard usage, and transform those feelings into unifying political convictions. "They seem to me," Edmund Burke wrote of the colonies in 1774, "rather ancient nations grown to perfection . . . than the colonies of yesterday—than a set of miserable outcasts of a few years ago, not so much sent as thrown out on the bleak and barren shore of a desolate wilderness three thousand miles from all civilized intercourse."

Charles Thomson died, rich with honors, at Harriton in August of 1824. The following month his portrait was placed alongside those of Jefferson, Hancock, and Adams at Independence Hall.

Voices

[The opponents of the Constitution are] a motley mixture of Ancient Toreys, friends to paper money, Tender Laws, Insurrection &c; persons in Debt, distress, & poverty, either real or Imaginary; men of blind piety, Hypocrites and Bankrupts; together with Many honest men bound by Instructions to vote against the Constitution at all Events,

—JOHN SULLIVAN,
President of New Hampshire,
1788

31

JOHN SULLIVAN: 2

JOHN SULLIVAN, Revolutionary radical become general, found his attitude toward authority changed by the responsibilities of exercising it. Like Charles Thomson, he grew increasingly disenchanted with the excesses of republican government. Only in Sullivan's case the conflict was more direct.

When he returned to New England, John Sullivan found that the abilities of the Sullivan family were still very much in demand. His father, now in his late eighties, was still teaching school in the community of Berwick. He owned a farm, which was tended by Margery Sullivan. John Sullivan's older brother Daniel, a captain in the Revolutionary forces, was a British prisoner of war. His younger brother James was a Supreme Court justice for the district of Maine. His sister Mary, a teacher like her father, was married and living in Durham. And his youngest brother Ebenezer had enlisted in the Revolutionary army as a private, had risen to be captain of a company, had been taken prisoner, and narrowly escaped being burned at the stake by Indians. The claims of service, and the number of Sullivans willing to fill them, seemed mutually inexhaustible.

By 1780, John Sullivan was back in the Continental Congress, reluctantly, as delegate from New Hampshire. He had hoped to remain home, renew his law practice, and repair the business losses to his mills, but the legislature had appointed him when he was out of state and had adjourned by the time he'd returned.

As in the army, Sullivan's service in the Congress was well intended, of considerable industry, and often undermined by the general's personal quirks. Short of funds, he accepted money from the French which Sullivan insisted was a loan but which the French minister of foreign affairs, at least, considered a bribe. Through his brother Daniel, a British prisoner, Sullivan was approached by the British with an offer to pay him for information on the doings of the Congress, an offer which the financially distressed Sullivan appears to have at least considered. He used his influence to get the members of the Peace Commission to follow the French lead in the negotiations in Paris, and he appealed, with mixed results, for compensation for the depreciated currency of his war pay. He left the Congress in August of 1780, disgruntled and unhappy, poorer after seven years of public service than he had been before, and determined thereafter to confine what talents and energies he had to his home territory of New Hampshire.

He continued to be drawn to the heat and glare of public office. Men of ability and experience were rare indeed in sparsely settled New Hampshire, and as a man who held most of his earnings of the past seven years in Continental paper, it was in Sullivan's interest to help establish a strong and solvent government.

By 1782, he had assumed the duties of attorney general of New Hampshire, in a time and place of extreme civic disturbance. In certain parts of New England, people, mostly debtors, many of whom were descended from servitude, continued to oppose all forms of outside government. Urging the printing of paper money, the repudiation of debts, and the abolition of taxes, they kept the western counties of Massachusetts in a state of revolt for years, and formed the grassroots support for the uprising that became known as Shays' Rebellion.

Sullivan had agreed to serve as attorney general only on condition that he not be required to act in cases where he had a previous interest. By 1785, having joined the Society of the Cincinnati and become a Mason, he was a candidate for president (governor) of the state. He finished third, but was elected on his next try in 1786.

In John Sullivan there had always been two men. One, the son of servitude, the fiery agitator who had defied the legal colonial authorities, could always be overruled by Sullivan the acquisitor, pressing debtors for payment, hungry for acclaim, soothed and gratified by the pomp of public office. With his election as first citizen of his home state, this second Sullivan was now in full ascendancy.

On September 20, in what was a New Hampshire version of Shays' Rebellion, Sullivan led both New Hampshire houses in defying the attempts of a group of men headed by a farmer named French to force the government to print paper money, repudiate debts, abolish taxes, redistribute land, and eliminate courts and lawyers. It was the angry gang of debtors surrounding his house all over again, and Sullivan made the same spirited response he had as a young lawyer. Confronting the mob personally, Sullivan announced that he would tolerate no bloodshed, then led the general court out of the meeting house and summoned the militia. The opposition collapsed, and the following day Sullivan, exercising his taste for pomp, rode between the lines of assembled troops and accepted resolutions of thanks from both houses.

It was popular uprisings of this kind that helped convince men like Jefferson that the concentration of governmental power in any single legislative body would only lead to tyranny. "173 despots," he pointed out, "would surely be as oppressive as one . . . an elective despotism was not the government we fought for."

The following year, capitalizing on his prestige as the "hero of the paper riots," Sullivan took the lead in the fight for ratification of the Constitution in New Hampshire. As Charles Beard has demonstrated, the movement for the Constitution originated among men whose personal financial interests—in money, public securities, manufactures, trade, and shipping—had been adversely affected by the Articles of Confederation. Sullivan, as the owner of several mills and a man who was still trying to collect his depreciated military back pay, was among those who saw the Constitution as the guarantee of his personal possessions. He toured the state, greeted by official proclamations and military salutes, demonstrating that order had been established, and in his message to the New Hampshire Senate and House urged that delegates be sent to the Constitutional Convention at Philadelphia.

When at the state ratifying convention the following February it became apparent that a majority of the New Hampshire delegates were opposed to ratification of a minority document stacked heavily in favor of the propertied classes, Sullivan entered the battle, arguing with his characteristic vigor in behalf of adoption. Instead, the delegates voted by a small majority for postponement. Sullivan predicted ratification at the next session by a three-to-one majority.

In New Hampshire, as elsewhere, the people divided along economic lines over ratification. Conceived to protect and defend property, framed by men most of whom had a strong economic advantage in the establishment of a new system, the Constitution attracted overwhelming support among men who owned significant amounts of land and money. It was opposed by most small farmers and debtors, men who were in large part—like John Sullivan—the descendants of servitude. Some of the framers, like Hamilton, opposed these people on principle—a projection, perhaps, of his misgivings about his own origins—as being unfit to participate in government. Others, like Madison, feared their potential for yielding leadership to demagogues. In both instances, a minority of propertied men, startled at the intensity of passions released by the Revolution, alarmed at the prospect of armed, experienced soldiers contesting the existing owners of property under the leadership of disgruntled trained officers like Captain Daniel Shays, were careful to minimize the popular voice in the adoption of the Constitution. Property qualifications for voting disfranchised most of the adult males, and there never was a direct, popular vote for or against approval.

Even with the overwhelming weight of money, skill, experience, and leadership on the Constitutional, or Federalist, side, the campaign for approval encountered difficulty. In New Hampshire, as in other states where the debtor class was strong, concern for the liberties of the people was appeased by Sullivan and the other Constitutional advocates by offering amendments—the same set of guarantees as incorporated in the Bill of Rights—although the New Hampshire men wouldn't insist on them as a condition of ratification.

At the close of its second session, the New Hampshire Convention approved the Constitution, not by Sullivan's three-to-one margin but with a plurality of ten votes out of a hundred and four. New Hampshire became the ninth, and deciding, state to ratify.

It was to be another generation, during the great leveling of the Jackson era, before the spirit of the amendments, the sop to civil liberties that became the Bill of Rights, was put into effect. And it was only with the elimination of property qualifications for suffrage and the abolition of imprisonment for debt that the long march of American indentured servitude was officially brought to an end.

In 1789, John Sullivan was again elected governor of New Hampshire, but he left office in October of that year when Washington appointed him federal judge for the district of New Hampshire, a political sinecure.

Sullivan's personal fortunes and his physical health now deteriorated rapidly. He got into an ugly local feud in Durham, fell into debt, drank heavily, and indulged in eccentric behavior, exhibiting symptoms of the rampant senility now classified as Alzheimer's disease. "His intellectual powers were broken down . . . he approached a state of idiocy. Early in the year 1794, he could neither feed, dress, or undress himself."

His father, Master John Sullivan, although over a hundred years old, occasionally rode to Durham to see his ailing son. The father had taught school until the age of ninety, wrote a good hand until he was a hundred and two, and continued his reading of the Bible and Horace until the age of a hundred and four.

Arriving in America a humble redemptioner, cast up in a spot where he had no intention of landing, married to a redeemed servant girl, he had inculcated in his children ideas of resistance to arbitrary power he had understood and felt in concrete form through personal experience. One son had organized and commanded a company and been taken prisoner in the colonial cause; another had been a Revolutionary radical, a delegate to the Continental Congress, one of Washington's generals, and a postwar governor; a third was a delegate to the first Continental Congress and later governor of Massachusetts; a fourth, enlisting as a private, was captain of a company and also a prisoner of war.

His best-known son, General John Sullivan, was a complex man, not a simple patriot, but also not the Tory that ambition alone might have made him. Whatever appeals might have been made to him, whatever his weaknesses of character, he remained, from his early advocacy of independence, through his active support of Washington during the Revolution's early and most critical phase, to his postwar service in New Hampshire, one of the young country's most essential citizens.

The Sullivans were part of one of the greatest transformations in history: the emigration and resettlement of people who—but for servitude—would have remained in Europe. As part of a larger American experience, this transformation helped produce the extraordinary release of energy which stimulated and sustained the Revolution, the founding of a republic, and the institutionalization of that Revolution in a Constitution which, because it placed ultimate sovereignty in the people, retained its capacity for change.

Again, Edmund Burke: "Whoever goes about to reason any part of the policy of this country with regard to America, upon the mere abstract principles of government, or even upon those of our own ancient constitution will be misled . . . The object is wholly new in the world. It is singular; it is grown up to this magnitude and importance within the memory of men; nothing in history is parallel to it."

Master John Sullivan died in June of 1796, at the age of a hundred and five, surviving his son John by a year. Margery Sullivan died in 1801; she was buried beside her husband in a field on a hillside opposite the farm they had owned in Berwick, New Hampshire, since 1754.

Voices

But it must be remembered that the rich are *people* as well as the poor . . . they have as clear and as *sacred* a right to their large property as others have to theirs which is smaller. . . . They are, in general, the best men, citizens, magistrates; . . . they are the guardians, ornaments, and glory of the community.

—JOHN ADAMS, *1787*

32

MATTHEW LYON: 2

IT WAS Matthew Lyon who survived the Revolution with his republican principles and democratic zeal intact.

At the end of the war, Lyon was a public figure and a man of property. He built and operated a sawmill and speculated in land; but unlike many other Revolutionary figures, he didn't become part of the new colonial aristocracy. Proud, contentious, Lyon avoided being wounded by mention of his origins by noisily embracing them. As a man who had never forgotten where he'd come from, who swore by the bulls that redeemed him, he felt entitled to call to account those men who had.

As a newly elected member of the House of Representatives in 1797, Lyon was a committed Jeffersonian, a leader of a small but vocal minority opposed to what Lyon viewed as the increasingly aristocratic tendencies of President John Adams's Federalists. A master of invective, Lyon waged tireless guerrilla warfare on Adams's increasing pomposity of public office: street processions, flattering speeches, the deferential waiting of the Congress upon the appearance of the President, references to people of "American blood."

Adams, who had spent five years as American minister to England and admired the stately demeanor of king and Parliament, represented to Lyon the old Tory values, gussied up in a Federal style. Along with Albert Gallatin and the young Andrew Jackson, Lyon assumed the burden of keeping the young American government democratic, in opposition to the style and values of the administration.

For his efforts, Lyon found himself under attack by the British polemicist William Cobbett. Not yet the great reformer of his later English period, Cobbett was at this time the hired mouthpiece of the Crown in America, doing missionary work among the heathen. Under the pen name Peter Porcupine, he charged that during the Revolutionary War Lyon had been dismissed from the American army and made to wear a wooden sword as a badge of cowardice. When the charge was repeated, twice, to Lyon personally by the Federalist Roger Griswold on the floor of Congress, Lyon spat in Griswold's face.

The indignant Federalists attempted to expel Lyon for the insult but failed to secure the required two-thirds vote. The following day, as Lyon sat at his desk on the floor of the House, Griswold approached him from behind and began beating him over the head with a hickory stick. The two men then grappled, Lyon seizing a pair of tongs from a congressional fireplace and using it to knock the stick from Griswold's hands. They then stumbled over a footstool and were fighting on the floor when other congressmen pulled them apart. The following day, a Federalist representative introduced a motion expelling both men, which was defeated following a five-day debate.

For these incidents, but beyond that, for the point of view he represented, for the ex-indentured servant's insistence on taking the freedoms guaranteed in the Bill of Rights at more than face value, John Adams detested Matthew Lyon. To Adams, Lyon, along with the Swiss-born Albert Gallatin, was one of a handful of "foreigners and degraded characters who . . . encouraged by a few ambitious native gentlemen, have discomfited the education, the talents, the virtues and the property of the country."

"We have," Adams concluded, "no Americans in America." It was a situation that, to his own satisfaction, Adams and the Federalists promptly set out to correct. Taking maximum advantage of the Federalist majority in both houses, and the fact of a Federalist President, the party was able to have enacted in 1798 the notorious Alien and Sedition Acts.

The Alien Act authorized the President to expel from the United States any foreign-born person whom the President might judge to be dangerous to the peace and safety of the country. The Sedition Act provided fines and imprisonment for any person publishing any malicious writing against the government or the President. To further serve the Federalists' interests, both laws were limited to the duration of this particular term of the presidency. Once the Federalists were out of office, the same laws couldn't be used against them.

Both laws were eventually found to be unconstitutional. Yet not before they had produced the desired effect of convicting Matthew Lyon, foreign-born, who published a newspaper vehemently critical of Adams and his administration.

Some three weeks before the Sedition Act became law, Lyon had written an anti-Federalist letter to the editor of a rival newspaper, responding to an attack upon himself. The editor, who was a Federalist, held the letter until after the enactment of the law and then published it. Within days, Matthew Lyon had become the first American indicted under the Sedition Act.

Tried and convicted, Lyon was sentenced to four months in jail and fined a thousand dollars. The jail sentence was arranged to coincide with the congressional by-election, so that Lyon would have to campaign for office from a cell.

The Federalist press was elated. The caged Lyon, reported the *Courant* of Connecticut, had cavorted in Congress "like a Monkey . . . where he was taken for an Ass by his braying, for a Cur by his barking, for a Puppy by his Whining, for a Hog for his eating, for a Cat by his spitting, and for a Lion, by nothing but his being the greatest of beasts."

When word got out of Lyon's incarceration in the Vergennes, Vermont, jail, it started a groundswell of anti-Federalist indignation. In Virginia, Senator George Mason, a former Revolutionary general, collected funds to be used to pay Lyon's fine. Among the contributors were Thomas Jefferson, James Madison, and James Monroe. Confined to prison, Lyon ran for re-election anyway and was returned to Congress by a thumping margin. Upon his release from jail, Lyon returned to the State Capitol, followed by a parade. "The train," we are told, "extending a distance of twelve miles."

In 1800, with the election of Jefferson by one congressional vote which Matthew Lyon helped assure, the combative congressman wrote a valedictory letter to the outgoing President, John Adams, whom he addressed as "Fellow Citizen," concluding with these wishes: "I hope and pray that your fate may be a warning to all usurpers and tyrants, and that you may, before you leave this world, become a true and sincere penitent, and be forgiven all your manifold sins in the next."

Out of office himself, with the Alien and Sedition Acts expiring along with the Adams regime, Lyon now left Vermont for the new, developing lands to the west. He moved to property in Kentucky he'd bought some years before at the suggestion of Andrew Jackson.

On the banks of the Cumberland River, Lyon laid out a town that was later called Eddyville, named in honor of one of the builders of the Erie Canal. At Eddyville, Lyon built mills, a brick works, and ultimately a shipyard. Yet his political persecution by the Federalists had made him a national hero. Within six months, Lyon was serving in the state legislature; and by 1803 he was back in Congress as representative from the Western District of Kentucky. He was an elder statesman now, Jefferson's loyal lieutenant who, even old Federalists now admitted, had been unfairly persecuted. Yet he remained true to what he believed to be republican principles, caustic in his criticism even of fellow Jeffersonians for what he considered aristocratic tendencies.

Combined with this was a boomer's urge to remain on the cutting edge of things. To found rather than to settle. A need, regardless of age, to push on rather than remain rooted, propertied, a potential Tory.

In 1811, out of office once again, Lyon accepted the invitation of an old friend and moved to St. Louis, where he became a candidate for Congress from the new Missouri Territory. Defeated in this attempt, he returned to Eddyville in time for the outbreak of the War of 1812.

Working without a government contract, Lyon devoted his shipyard to the building of barges and gunboats for use on the Western rivers against the hated British. A fleet of Lyon-built gunboats was wrecked in a Mississippi storm; the same storm sank his merchant boat, the largest launched to that date on any American river. Lyon, who had put all he owned into the building of the boats, under no authority from the government, had no legal claim for their value. By 1818, his fortune wrecked, Lyon was writing to what few friends of his remained in Washington in hope of a government job in one of the new territories.

In 1820, James Monroe, who had supported Lyon when the congressman had been in jail, appointed Matthew Lyon United States factor to the Cherokee Nation in the Territory of Arkansas. He moved to Arkansas, ran for delegate to Congress, and lost by sixty votes. In 1822, at the age of seventy-one, Lyon ordered a flatboat built, loaded it with furs, peltries, and "Indian commodities," and commanded it down the Arkansas River to the Mississippi and on down to New Orleans, returning with a cargo of storekeeper's goods and utensils after a wintertime journey of some three thousand miles. We are told he insisted upon doing his share of rowing, steering, and towing line, and that he was always the first to jump into the water when it was time to get out of the boat and shove. It was the old Lyon's last prowl. He died on August 1, 1822.

The genius of the American people, remarked George Mason, was in favor of democracy, "and the genius must be consulted." Matthew Lyon helped give that genius voice at a time when the prevailing tone of political life was overwhelmingly against it. He helped keep it alive into a changed society, an era of broadening representation, with its state-by-state elimination of property qualifications for voting and imprisonment for debt and, eventually, the elimination of servitude.

Conviction of this quality cannot spring solely from ideology. It demands the entire person—head, heart, practical experience, energy, emotion. Matthew Lyon was a politician, a practical man who dealt in realities. His redemption from servitude had been the opening of a door to a remarkable American life that paralleled and helped produce an extraordinary era. Like other colonists who came to America in servitude—half of all who arrived —Lyon saw issues like the defense of liberty against the expansion of power not as abstractions but as the very stuff of life, to be struggled with each day.

Servitude did not provide the ideology of the American Revolution. What it did furnish was its constituency, the body of popular support that confirmed the ideas of the Revolutionary thinkers and enabled them to be translated into action.

It was through this interaction of the intellectual with the practical that America was able to put into practice a limited government without first enduring a tyrannical one, a government that was required by the people to guarantee rights at its inception instead of granting them later; and one that institutionalized its Revolution in a Constitution capable of responding to and incorporating change.

Thus, through the experience of servitude, freedoms that had been earned individually stimulated, supported, and sustained the freedoms we now hold in common.

Matthew Lyon was a man whose principles remained fixed, perhaps because Lyon himself kept moving. By changing constituencies, moving on, he was starting over, seeking redemption, perhaps, of another kind. He avoided the moral quandaries of an aristocratic estate by losing his. The town he'd founded became, without his animating energy, a bypassed river backwater. Even the family declined. His son, Chittendon Lyon, served ten years in Congress as a representative from Kentucky. Then, nothing. He had been out of Congress some four years when in 1840 a bill was passed refunding to the heirs of Matthew Lyon the full amount, plus interest, of the fine imposed on him under the Sedition Act. The Irish redemptioner had been redeemed for one last time.

Voices

Whereas the traffic of White People, heretofore countenanced in this state, while under the arbitrary control of the British Government, is contrary to the feelings of a number of respectable Citizens, and to the idea of liberty this country has so happily established: And whereas it is necessary to encourage emigration to this country, upon the most liberal plan, and for that purpose a no. of Citizens of this state have proposed to liberate a cargo of Servants, just arrived, by paying their passage, and repaying themselves by a small rateable deduction out of the wages of such Servants—Such of the Citizens of this state, as wish to encourage so laudable an undertaking, and (if necessary) petition the legislature for a completion of their humane intentions, are requested to meet at Mr. Day's, at the sign of the Hyder Alley, the lower King Street, this evening, at six o'clock.

—New York *Independent
Gazette,
January 24, 1784*

PART SIX
TRANSFORMED

And still the ships continued to arrive.

The crimps in the deadfalls of London and Limerick and the glib Neulanders swaggering through the Rhineland villages kept the captains well supplied; the appetite for cheap labor in Pennsylvania and Maryland continued unabated. The way to amass wealth in America remained the same: get others to work your land at no pay.

It was questionable whether the new nation could endure without servitude. Jefferson, the enunciator of American liberty, author of the Declaration of Independence, believed it couldn't. Servitude, he contended, constituted a salubrious "seasoning" period, wherein European workers could accustom themselves to the American climate before setting up on their own. They might also acquire a hardy resistance to the local diseases like malaria and yellow fever, providing they survived the first year, when as many as half of the New World servants traditionally died.

There were glaring inconsistencies. In Maryland, the British attempted to deliver a load of transported convicts after the Rev-

olutionary War had ended; it wasn't even British territory any-more. Freed black slaves fled north only to become indentured servants because they were without funds. There were Quaker abolitionists, like Elizabeth Drinker's family, who campaigned for black freedom while owning white indentured servants.

The country was undergoing its next great transformation. In the cities a new class of free workingmen, often descended from servitude, was just forming. On the Western frontier, territories with a high percentage of freed-servant settlers—like Kentucky, Tennessee, and Ohio—were pressing for statehood. The base of the country was shifting from Jeffersonian agriculture to the manufacturing foreseen by Hamilton; Jefferson himself had quietly embraced most of the Federalist platform. Private corporations, most conspicuously the Bank of the United States, were developing to a size and power that threatened to exceed the regulatory authority of the federal government.

The war had ended; but the American revolution was still going on.

33

DANIEL KENT

"I MAKE bold to trouble you with these lines," a young man named Daniel Kent gingerly addressed his parents in Ireland in 1786. Some months before, he had set out from the family home in Limerick, hoping to find work as a cutler—a sharpener and repairman of knives—in Dublin or Cork. He was writing to his family now as an indentured servant laboring on a farm in Pennsylvania.

Kent had left Cork and headed for Waterford on foot, where being "much fatigued," and after being told by Thomas Quin, a cutler and family friend, that there was no work, he decided on impulse to leave for America.

"I heard that there was a Vessel there Ready to Sail for this Continent freighted With Passengers On Which I went On Board Being Seventh [day] Afternoon And we weighted Anchor on the first day [Sunday]."

Perhaps Kent was persuaded to take ship by a crimp; he may have embarked while drunk; or simply being young and head-strong, he may have made up his mind to act on his own. What-

ever the circumstances, he was seized with "a Strange notion
Coming In My head of Going On Board that I could not Get Over
it though Thomas Quin used his Endeavors to Persuade me
against going. . . . I hope with the help of God," he added, "it
will be all for the Better."

After a voyage in which the ship's bowsprit had been torn away
and its foremast nearly lost, Kent and his company arrived in
Philadelphia on July 26. Here Kent spent some four weeks as
unsold merchandise.

"My business is of little use here," he observed. "Blacksmiths, Carpenters, Shoemakers, Bricklayers, and taylors are the
Chief trades . . . But there is Enough of Each trade here Already."

Instead, along with some twenty other servants, he was taken
upcountry by the mate of the vessel, acting as soul-driver, who
sold the redemptioners off to planters along the way. At West
Bradford in Chester County, Kent "found Such a man as I
wished for, Whom I am to Serve three years from the time the
Vessel Cast Anchor here. His name is Joseph Hawley, By
Profession a Quaker and Occupation a farmer and has a large
Plantation."

Kent's parents were distraught at the news. "To think that one
of your tender rearing should voluntarily plunge yourself in the
state of a slave," his father wrote the boy, consoling him at the
same time "that you had the luck to fall in the hands of the good
man that you represent him to be. We may easily infer," Kent's
father continued, "that some of those People who sailed with you
have met since their arrival in America with the severest cruelty
and hardship."

The America that young Kent had emigrated to was in these
years a shaky proposition, a loose federation of contentious, financially fragile self-styled republics, still looked upon in Europe
as a dumping ground for outcasts, slaves, and convicts. In his
father's eyes, the son could at best only sink down a class, becoming the equivalent of an Irish peasant. There is in these early
letters a reproving tone, a sense of injury in his words that suggests maturity's pained disapproval of youthful folly.

Though he had to work harder in America than at home, Daniel
Kent assured his parents that he preferred his new country to his

native one, and was satisfied with farm work. Yet he would advise against any more of the Irish emigrating as servants:

"There are but four or five out of twenty and upwards that Came to this part of the Country With me that have Stayed with their Masters. The rest ran away. Some have been taken up and condemned to serve a longer time."

Like the runaway Irish student that Benjamin Franklin mentioned working with in his *Autobiography*, Daniel Kent had injured his parents by emigrating to America without telling them. It was his own private declaration of independence, and they responded to it with the puzzled affront of defied authority. Where had they failed in raising their son? Why had he turned his back on them? How could he possibly make his way in the world without their help?

To justify his own role in the son's life and at the same time to make his way in the New World easier, Kent's father sent him a letter of recommendation, "signed by Persons of Consequence that have known me & the tender Education I gave and brought you up in." The letter describes Kent as an "Indented Servante to Mr. Joseph Hawley," the son of William Kent, a cutler of Limerick who had been "decently and honestly reared by his said Father and Mother in the Love and fear of God & in the Protestant Religion."

This is followed by an irresistible parental dig. Kent, "being bred to his Said Father's Trade by his said Father, & thinking himself too much restrained from the Liberties that the folly of Youth is subject to, or howsoever led by some foolish infatuation —departed from his Father without cause or compulsion." The score is settled. The letter of recommendation, circulating among "Persons of Consequence" in Limerick, explains to the local businessmen, officials, and clergy what has happened in a way that exonerates Kent's father from any blame, all in the name of providing the son with a recommendation necessary and useful to him in his new life.

"My Thanks for the trouble you have taken In obtaining A Certificate for me," Daniel Kent wrote in a somewhat puzzled reply. "I hope it will be of Some Service to me Hereafter." He made no mention, nor apparently any use, of it again.

Kent's Uncle Richard, a surgeon aboard H.M.S. *Cygnet,* calling at Jamaica, joined in the family delegation of blame. Writing to his nephew Daniel, whom he mistakenly addressed as "George," he reminded the young man that "you need never have been a Servant if you had Consulted your Parents, or me, they would have Willingly Payed your Passage."

It was a strange transition, the rank-conscious naval surgeon remarked, "from a Tolerable Cutler to a Farmer, alias Laborer." Yet if the young man was satisfied, then "be those things as they may."

Kent's new life continued to puzzle and disturb his father. "It seems that Dan is a professed Quaker," his father wrote to his uncle, "however I will not say he has changed for the worse. He says he is now free from the gross vices to which he was subject at home . . . I fear he has changed for the worse, tho he seems contented . . . perhaps providence will yet make a way for his return."

Yet Kent himself was proud and defensive of his hard-won American autonomy. He was a freedman now, doing plantation work for a man named Isaac Coats, on a farm about seven miles from his old master. "I keep myself out of bad Company [and] do not spend my earnings foolishly. I have not drank a pint of Spirits this 10 months.

"I am so far from thinking that farming is as Laborious as you Imagine it to be," Kent explained to his parents, "that I think it is the Sweetest Employment in the World, and I know not of Any Trade or Calling Whatsoever that I would change it for." So much for returning to Limerick and a career as a cutler. As for his religious conversion, "as I was Sitting very Pensive And thoughtful in one of these Meetings a Minister Stood up and Spoke So Closely to my State, reaching the Witness of God in my heart that I could not Withstand Any Longer."

In April of 1791, Daniel Kent confirmed his commitment to his new country and new faith by marrying Esther Hawley, the Quaker daughter of his former master.

After his marriage, Kent went back to work on his father-in-law's farm; "but finding I could not make out much I rented a farm about four miles distant. I bought stock and farming utensils & went into debt for most of them."

Daniel Kent was now part of a large and growing body of

Americans with a personal interest in cheap, plentiful money and
the abolition of imprisonment for debt. If he should be unable to
pay his debts, then let the creditors take his implements, his
stock, or even his farm. Let him work for wages for someone
else, only don't deprive him of his freedom. These feelings
among the small farmers coincided with those among the expanding class of city workingmen and shopkeepers. Together, they
heavily outnumbered the planters and land speculators who effectively controlled the government, and it would be in their
interest that property qualifications be eliminated from voting
and the election of presidents be based on the popular vote.
These values, and in many cases the people espousing them,
were descended from servitude. They incorporated the frustration of the Virginia freedmen pushed out into Kentucky and Tennessee, the resentment at religious persecution of the Scotch-
Irish frontiersmen of New Hampshire and Maine, the Pennsylvania redemptioners' sense of injury at the extravagant promises
of the Neulanders, and the anger of the colonial craftsman forced
to give up his tools and report to a factory.

It was the political figures who arose from among these people
—the indentured servant Matthew Lyon, the Scotch-Irish James
K. Polk, the maverick Hudson Valley landholder Martin Van
Buren, the Scotch-Irish Andrew Jackson—who between 1820
and 1850 led the fight for the unfulfilled promises of servitude to
be enacted into law: extension of the vote, popular election of
the President, the breaking of the monetary control of the Bank
of the United States, and the state-by-state abolition of imprisonment for debt.

With the achievement of this last, between 1819 and 1840,
there passed the final required element of legal force from indentured servitude. The practice had served, at great cost, both a
national and individual interest, producing both capital and a
working class where there had been none before. In the process
it also produced a new kind of American—vigorous, contentious,
skeptical, inventive, alert to possibilities, with an instinctive resistance to taking orders and doing things the way they had been
done before. Sometimes simply *because* they had been done before.

Like the young country he'd come to, Daniel Kent was getting along in the New World in the way that challenged certain assumptions on the part of people in the Old. "We make Butter & Cheese which we take to market in Philadelphia With Veal, Pork, Mutton & Whatever else we can spare, all which has sold well," Kent wrote his parents in 1794. "We have now got a pretty Good Stock Eight Cattle four Horses a score Sheep, Pigs &c. All which we got by our own Industry."

The note of apology, the tone of guilt for his abrupt leave-taking, has disappeared from Kent's letters. He has succeeded in establishing a life of his own. His father continues to remind him of how well his brothers and cousins and uncles are doing; but after Daniel Kent begins raising a large family of his own, the balance in their relationship shifts. The headstrong boy has become an autonomous man, with a knowledge of the world that is wider than his father's. His rashness in leaving Ireland has begun to look like prescience in the light of the declining state of affairs in his father's country.

"Nocturnal meetings are still frequent in the country," Kent's father complained in 1803, "as likewise the robbing of Gentlemens Houses of their Arms . . . You may judge then that poor people are sadly put to for to live in any Degree Comfortable as to our part we scarcely have known such hard times."

Time and experience, which were supposed to have endorsed the father's position, have instead justified the son's.

"Seeing this then to be the true state of our affairs," Kent's father admitted, "you may judge that a little of your assistance would be very acceptable & this I think might be done without you being much hardship'd."

The young dependents, boy and country, have become providers.

"I remember him as a stout, heavy-set, medium height man," Daniel Kent's grandson recalled his emigrant grandfather, "who set his feet down as though he had an undisputed right to put all his weight on the earth. He had a face that varied widely with his moods of mind, and it was always uncertain as to what mood we would find him in at any given time . . . open and inviting and wreathed in smiles, or stern and forbidding almost to the point of repulsion.''

Kent and his wife had seven children and dozens of grandchildren. His impetuosity in running off to America was only the beginning of a release of energy that was to transform his own life and help transform his new country. Stirred awake, unbound people made the new nation hum.

''He was always a very industrious man,'' Kent's grandson recalled, ''and when we visited . . . we always found Grandfather busy in the house or at the woodpile . . . when we were notified of his death, we were told he died sitting quietly in his arm chair, and that he had been chopping wood the day before.''

Daniel Kent died at seventy-eight in 1844, a freeman, a landholder, and a voter.

Voices

TEN DOLLARS REWARD

Ran away from the Subscriber, on the night of the 15th instant, two apprentice boys, legally bound, named WILLIAM and ANDREW JOHNSON. The former is of a dark complexion, black hair, eyes and habits. The latter is very fleshy, freckled face, light hair, and fair complexion . . . I will pay the above Reward to any persons who will deliver said apprentices to me in Raleigh, or I will give the above reward for Andrew Johnson alone.

—JAMES J. SELBY, TAILOR
Raleigh *Gazette*
June 24, 1824

34

ANDREW JOHNSON

IN THE end, the legal system of indentured servitude was undone by its children. It was the growing city class of mechanics and artisans; the poor whites from the mountain country of North Carolina and Virginia, Georgia and Tennessee; the frontier Scotch-Irish of Kentucky, Vermont, and Ohio; and the German small farmers of Pennsylvania who removed the force from the forced-labor system. Whatever their differences, they had three desperate interests in common: the elimination of property qualifications for voting and office holding, cheap money, and the abolition of imprisonment for debt.

A workingman had small chance for decent wages when prisoners could be contracted out of jail to replace him; a small farmer imprisoned for owing money would never get back to working only for himself; the lands to the west, once opened to slavery, would be merely a reproduction of the speculation-and-plantation cycle of the Southeast. It was the old story of the powerful few against the powerless many; but this time, encouraged by what had been said in the Declaration of Independence and promised in the Bill of Rights, animated by the passions and energies first released by the Revolution, new voices emerged from "the silence of all serfdom."

The voices were often coarse and vulgar; they sometimes came from mouths that drank and swore, through lips that spat tobacco. They, and the ideas they expressed, were often offensive to gentlemen. And between 1820 and 1850 they claimed what had been promised them and their ancestors, and changed the character of the country. "My pedigree," said Abraham Lincoln, the son of Scotch-Irish Kentucky frontiersmen, "is short and sweet, like the annals of the poor."

Without imprisonment for debt, lack of money alone couldn't deprive a white man or woman of freedom, or give a master power to beat and starve. Running away from a labor contract became a civil and not a criminal offense. The state couldn't be enlisted to pursue a runaway, nor would one state return another's fugitives. There was no longer any profit in chasing someone else's servant. And so, state by state, as imprisonment for debt vanished, so did the legal framework of indentured servitude, dismantled by people whose ancestors, but for the forced-labor system, would never have emigrated to America in the first place.

The indenture laws were still in force in Raleigh, North Carolina, in June of 1824, when the angry tailor James Selby offered a ten-dollar reward for his two runaway apprentices. He was so infuriated at the Johnson brothers, fatherless boys whom he'd taken in when their mother, who'd been scraping by doing weaving, at last remarried, that he'd mixed up their physical descriptions. It was Andrew who was of "a dark complexion . . . eyes . . . and habits," "a wild harum-scarum boy" with a budding gift for oratory and a frighteningly determined will. And it was Andrew that Selby was willing to settle for having back under his authority alone.

Instead, the Johnson brothers made their way to the town of Carthage, only seventy-five miles away. Here the young go-getter Andrew Jackson Johnson opened his own tailoring shop in a rented shack, and was soon doing so brisk a business that he feared word of it would get back to Selby. He moved on to

Laurens in South Carolina, where he cut and sewed and mended, and fell in love and was rejected.

A year after they'd left, the brothers drifted back to Raleigh, where a broke and hungry Andrew Johnson resigned himself to accepting whatever the law, and Selby, had in store. The embittered ex-boss could now savor the taste of revenge, served cold. He'd closed his shop and moved twenty miles from town. He had no place for young Johnson, yet as long as the boy remained in Raleigh he was under Selby's threat. At any time, the ex-master could put the law to Johnson for jumping his indenture. The jails were full of such people—small farmers and sharecroppers unable to pay their debts.

Johnson took his lesson from the unimprisoned freedmen, debtors, and runaways: The way to break the bonds of all indenture was to head west. With his brother Bill, their mother, and her feckless husband, Johnson rode and pulled a wheeled cart out to the Cumberland Valley in Tennessee. The family settled in the town of Greeneville, where Andrew set up in business in 1827 as A. Johnson, Tailor.

Here Johnson worked at his trade up until the time he entered Congress. He could spell a little and read simple words, but at his marriage to Eliza McCardle, a shoemaker's daughter, Johnson couldn't write. She tutored him, and through this and a hired "reader"—a man Johnson paid fifty cents a day to keep him informed of local and national events from newspapers while the tailor worked at his bench—Johnson developed the grandiloquent, sometimes overheated rhetorical style of the self-educated.

He became the town debater and was permitted to join the debating society at the local college. Here he was taken under the wing of Sam Milligan, a William and Mary graduate and teacher, who lent Johnson books and became his political and legal adviser. Johnson's expanded tailor shop, opened in 1831, became the town forum. Here it was argued who would run the town, the aristocrats or the democrats, property or people. It was clear from the start which side the vehement Johnson, who nursed a deprived child's hatred of privilege all his life, supported.

Andrew Johnson's indenture to the tailor Selby, and the long years he worked at the trade he'd learned in Selby's shop, was a wound that pained him all his life. His embrace of the virtues of simple people had a belligerence and defensiveness about it, a distrust of polish and finesse that stunted his own growth, and at times slipped over into truculence and demagoguery. At the same time, it gave him the visceral sense of right and wrong that Matthew Lyon had, and made him a man of profound physical and moral courage, and of unquestioned honesty. He had been impressed at a critical early age with the political dangers present in great inequities of wealth and power, and he made it his life's work to combat them.

Driven by his aggrieved energy, Johnson's local rise was rapid. An alderman at twenty, he went on to serve as Greeneville's three-term mayor. In 1833, a committed Jacksonian, Johnson took part in the calling of a Tennessee state convention which the following year abolished property qualifications for office and imprisonment for debt. He patterned himself after Andrew Jackson and took pride in the fact that as the Federalists had hated Jackson the Whigs now loathed Andrew Johnson. He appalled the propertied classes, and was loved for his enemies by working people.

Elected to the state legislature, he continued to work at his tailor's bench. Whigs and conservative Democrats sneered at his political pretensions, his humorlessness, his pedantic, sophomoric speeches. Yet they feared to oppose him openly because of his popular support. At the beginning of the age of campaign oratory, Johnson was a powerful stump speaker, a no-holds-barred scrapper with an appetite for invective and an instinctive connection with the mountain people of Tennessee. He ran for Congress and, after several tries, was elected. In the House of Representatives he became a Free-Soiler, an advocate of small-farmer homesteads that brought him closer to the congressmen of the North than of the South. He introduced the Homestead Bill in Congress. Gerrymandered out of office, he ran for governor of Tennessee and won in 1853. At the end of his second term, in 1857, a Democratic legislature elected him to the Senate.

As the Civil War approached, Johnson increasingly alienated himself from the South. He didn't hate slavery, but he detested aristocracy, which he believed grew out of it. For him, and the people he sprang from, the Union represented their only chance. "If the Union goes down," he maintained to the people of Tennessee, "we go down with it."

When, after Lincoln's election, South Carolina seceded, Johnson traveled throughout Tennessee, speaking in behalf of the Union, taking his stand as Jackson had in 1832 against South Carolina's nullification. Other Southern states were seceding, and the border states were crucial. Johnson was armed, and under threat of death. Secession speakers flooded the mountains; Tennessee was taken out of the Union; still Johnson stumped in favor of it. His mail was rifled, his name forged to false conspiratory letters. Unionist refugees fled East Tennessee for Ohio and Kentucky; thirteen thousand Andrew Johnson Democrats joined the Union army. Johnson was ordered to leave the state.

Back in Washington, his wife and children in Tennessee, Johnson found himself the only member of a seceding state to remain in the Senate chamber.

The war bound Lincoln and Johnson together as Unionists, sons of the Middle Border and representatives of a constituency descended from bound people. Johnson became Lincoln's counselor on how to hold the border states, his authority on all matters concerning Tennessee, a member of his Committee of Seven on the Conduct of the War. When in 1862 the city of Nashville was taken by Union forces, Johnson resigned his Senate seat and was installed as military governor. Charged by Lincoln with restoring Tennessee to the Union, Johnson levied taxes, controlled railroads, issued military proclamations, jailed secessionists, appointed officers, and ordered elections. Lincoln asked no questions.

Outside the city, guerrilla warfare swept the state. Over seven hundred engagements were fought in Tennessee, including some of the war's bloodiest pitched battles—Shiloh, Chickamauga, Chattanooga, Murfreesboro. Three times the city of Nashville was threatened with evacuation; for two months in the fall of 1862 Johnson was cut off, under siege. He threatened to shoot anyone who talked surrender. The Union troops fell back, but then rallied, and the Confederates were repulsed.

Johnson remained in Nashville until 1864; he defied the secessionists in their own country, without indulging in heroics or playing the martyr. His steadfastness was crucial in keeping the border states in the Union. From them came some three hundred thousand Union soldiers. His faith in the people had sustained him.

In 1864, Lincoln insisted that Johnson replace Hannibal Hamlin as Vice President on his election ticket. Johnson's body was "exhausted," his mind "tortured." On Inauguration Day, he was ill. On his way to the Capitol for his inaugural address in the Senate chamber, accompanied by Hamlin, he was given brandy by Hamlin's physician; the "medication" was unfortunate.

Obsessed with his humble origins, weary and sick and at least slightly drunk, Johnson made before the Senate, instead of a statesmanlike address, a stump speech, maudlin and vainglorious, identifying his rise with the strength and glory of the government. It appalled the senators and created an impression that Johnson was never able to overcome. Within six weeks, Richmond, the capital of the Confederacy, had fallen, Lincoln had been assassinated, and Johnson was President, without ever having been accepted as Vice President.

Johnson was handed unlimited responsibilities: the problem of reuniting the North and South, determining the legal status of the seceded states, deciding what to do with some four million freed slaves, and addressing a nation half of which was now conquered territory. He was also given severely circumscribed, and shrinking, authority. Congress, especially the Senate, alarmed at the expansion of presidential power during the war, was determined to retrieve its authority from Johnson.

The contrast between the two worked to Johnson's disadvantage. He simply did not possess Lincoln's genius for touching all humanity. His earliest experience as an apprentice and a fugitive had marked him, like someone out of Dickens. Even Dickens himself thought so—"a character of mark," the novelist wrote of Johnson after a visit to the White House, "with a remarkable face, indomitable courage and . . . watchfulness."

Like Lincoln, he opposed a punitive peace. It was the leadership of the South, not her ordinary people, who had led her astray. "Trust the Southern people," Lincoln had said, "to do the right thing." This Johnson set out to do. His origins were their origins, his faith in the Union their faith. Johnson proclaimed an amnesty. The seceding states complied with the President's demand, adopted the Thirteenth Amendment, repealed secession ordinances, and abolished war debts. The war had proved the Union indissoluble; it must be immediately restored, with the vote extended gradually to blacks, beginning with black soldiers.

To the abolitionists and the militant radical Republicans in Congress this was a moral and political affront. Among the Southern delegates now requesting admission to Congress were four Confederate generals, five colonels, six members of the Confederate cabinet, fifty-eight Confederate congressmen, and Alexander Stephens, Vice President of the Confederacy. To admit them would be an insult not only to Congress but to each of the Union dead. Also, based on the increase in representation of a population now including blacks, it would probably mean a Democratic majority in Congress. The South would have *gained* politically from the war. The power of the Republicans in Congress would be weakened still further—even congressmen who weren't zealots were sensitive to this. The South must be reconstructed. Purged. And Reconstruction was the business of Congress, not the President.

Johnson's plan for readmission of the Southern states was, said the radical Republican Senator Charles Sumner, "the greatest and most criminal error ever committed by any government."

Johnson, a lifelong Democrat, member of a split and weakened party, a man elected to Congress from a now-seceded state, was attempting to carry out Lincoln's plans, but without Lincoln's powers, against a Congress rebounding from Lincoln's assertion of them. Even some of Johnson's support—from among Copperheads, Northern Democrats favoring the South—was for the wrong reasons, and an embarrassment to him. During the war, Johnson had been reviled as a Southerner who had treasonably sided with the Union. Now he was castigated as a Unionist who was treasonably indulging the South.

The postwar conflict between President and Congress would have been unavoidable, even by a Lincoln. The man that Andrew

Johnson was, what life had made him, only intensified these differences. To Johnson, life was struggle, as it is to some degree for everyone; but for Johnson, the struggle was grim and desperate, against unrelenting enemies, with everything gained forfeit at any moment, and political differences turned into enduring enmities. The early hardship which should have united him with others' humanity instead set him apart.

As the Congress, with the Southern states excluded, passed the bills of Reconstruction—the Freedmen's Bill, the Civil Rights Bill, the Tenure of Office Act, the Bill Admitting Colorado and Nebraska—Johnson vetoed them as either unconstitutional or as intrusions by the Congress on presidential authority. He opposed the Fourteenth Amendment, which would immediately enfranchise all blacks while at the same time disfranchising enormous numbers of Southern whites. Whether the gradual enfranchisement advocated by Johnson might have served black people better in the long run is certainly worth considering in the light of the long years of poll tax and means and literacy tests that persisted in the South instead. It was Reconstruction, not war, that produced the politically solid South.

Johnson, digging in, became increasingly isolated. The press and some of his own cabinet turned against him. His veto of the Civil Rights Bill was overridden by Congress—the first override of a presidential veto in congressional history. In the South, relations between whites and blacks were worsening. In Memphis and in New Orleans, attacks were made on the black population, and scores of blacks were killed outright. As the number of radical Republicans in Congress grew, the radical position hardened. Acceptance of the Thirteenth Amendment was not enough for readmission. Neither was acceptance of the Fourteenth.

The climax came over the separation of powers. Johnson fired Edwin Stanton, his disloyal secretary of war. Stanton refused to go, citing the 1867 Tenure of Office Act, a Reconstruction measure giving Congress approval over the President's hiring and firing of his department heads. Ulysses S. Grant, whom Johnson had appointed secretary of war after firing Stanton, turned against Johnson when Congress would not approve.

Threatened with impeachment, Johnson remained blunt and tactless, referring to "military despotism controlling the country," blaming "the arbitrary power of Congress" and crying "treason." With his view of life as fierce struggle, he was unable to moderate his attack. He fought by throwing haymakers, even when jabs would have been more effective, more telling.

The radicals in Congress swung back just as wildly, implying that Johnson had conspired in Lincoln's assassination. The articles of impeachment however, when voted in 1867, boiled down to Johnson's firing of Stanton. In March of 1868, Johnson's impeachment trial, the oddly narrow conclusion to an unusually wide public life, began before a rump Senate, minus the scorned states of the South.

On a bill reduced to the single charge of violation of the Tenure of Office Act, Johnson escaped impeachment by one vote; the Senate barely missed the required two-thirds majority. It was, considering the odds, a victory, and Johnson accepted it as such. Later that year, Grant was elected to the presidency; the long transforming era that had begun with Andrew Jackson had ended. Andrew Johnson went home to Tennessee.

The poles of Andrew Johnson's life are as brackets to the American age of servitude. Beginning as an apprentice in an age of widest servitude, he rose to his country's highest office, and left it with involuntary servitude outlawed for everyone. His humble beginnings defined him; they gave him the instinctive connection with working people that was responsible for his rise, and engendered in him the resentment that set his limits. The whole history of American servitude lived in him. Like Lincoln, he seemed to grasp instinctively that the experience of bondage, black and white, which has caused America its greatest agonies can, honestly confronted, become the source of our greatest strength.

Back home in Tennessee, Andrew Johnson longed for vindication. He stood for senator and was defeated by a single vote. He ran for Congress and lost. In 1875, he was returned to the Senate, the only ex-President ever to serve in the upper house. In July of that year, he died of a stroke while visiting at Carter Station in Tennessee. For once, the epitaph on the gravestone caught the spirit of the man: "His faith in the people never wavered."

Voices

Section 1. Neither slavery nor involuntary servitude, except as a punishment for crime whereof the party shall have been duly convicted, shall exist within the United States or any place subject to their jurisdiction.

Section 2. Congress shall have power to enforce this article by appropriate legislation.

—The Thirteenth
Amendment, 1865

BIBLIOGRAPHY

There are a number of works which have served as the sources for and the measurement of the ideas in this book to such a degree that their influence can be felt upon every chapter. Rather than cite them repeatedly as they occur, I have chosen to list them as General Sources first, with the information about individual lives to follow.

I. GENERAL SOURCES

Bailyn, Bernard. *The Ideological Origins of the American Revolution.* Cambridge, Mass.: Belknap Press, 1967.
———. *Pamphlets of the American Revolution, 1750–1776.* Cambridge: Belknap Press, 1965.
Burke, Edmund. *The Works of the Right Honorable Edmund Burke,* Volumes 1–12. Boston: Little, Brown, 1904.
Herrick, Cheesman A. *White Servitude in Pennsylvania: Indentured and Redemption Labor in Colony and Commonwealth.* Freeport, N.Y.: Books for Libraries Press, 1926, 1970.
Jensen, Merrill. *Tracts of the American Revolution, 1763–1776.* Cambridge: Belknap Press, 1965.
Morgan, Edmund S. *American Slavery, American Freedom: The Ordeal of Colonial Virginia.* New York: W. W. Norton, 1975.

Morris, Richard B. *Government and Labor in Early America.* New York: Octagon Books, 1975.

Smith, Abbott Emerson. *Colonists in Bondage: White Servitude and Convict Labor in America, 1607–1776.* Gloucester, Mass.: Peter Smith, 1965.

II. INDIVIDUAL SOURCES

INTRODUCTION

Aldridge, Alfred Owen. *Man of Reason: The Life of Thomas Paine.* Philadelphia and New York: J. B. Lippincott, 1959.

Arendt, Hannah. *On Revolution.* New York: Viking Press, 1963.

De Tocqueville, Alexis. *Democracy in America.* New York: Random House, 1945.

Paine, Thomas. *The Selected Works of Tom Paine* and *Citizen Tom Paine,* by Howard Fast. New York: Modern Library, 1945.

Pryor, Mrs. Roger A. *The Mother of Washington and Her Times.* New York: Macmillan, 1903.

1. JAMES MADISON

Ballagh, James Curtis. *White Servitude in the Colony of Virginia: A Study of the System of Indentured Labor in the American Colonies.* Baltimore: Johns Hopkins Press, 1895.

Brant, Irving. *James Madison.* Vol. 1, *The Virginia Revolutionist.* Vol. 2, *The Nationalist.* Vol. 3, *The Father of the Constitution.* New York: Bobbs-Merrill, 1941–1950.

The Federalist. A collection of essays by Alexander Hamilton, John Jay, and James Madison interpreting the Constitution of the United States. Introduction by Goldwin Smith. New York: Colonial Press, 1901.

2. ALEXANDER HAMILTON

Beard, Charles A. *An Economic Interpretation of the Constitution of The United States.* New York: Macmillan, 1941.

The Federalist.

Flexner, James Thomas. *The Young Hamilton: A Biography.* Boston: Little, Brown, 1974.

3. THOMAS JEFFERSON

Brodie, Fawn M. *Thomas Jefferson: An Intimate History.* New York: W. W. Norton, 1974.

Defoe, Daniel. *The Fortunes and Misfortunes of the Famous Moll Flanders, &c.* New York: Modern Library, 1950.

Malone, Dumas. *Jefferson and His Time.* Vol. 1, *Jefferson the Virginian.* Vol. 2, *Jefferson and the Rights of Man.* Boston: Little, Brown, 1951.

4. SAMUEL ADAMS

Lewis, Paul. *The Grand Incendiary: A Biography of Samuel Adams.* New York: Dial Press, 1973.

Miller, John C. *Sam Adams, Pioneer in Propaganda.* Stanford: Stanford University Press, 1936.

5. BENJAMIN FRANKLIN

Franklin, Benjamin. *The Autobiography of Benjamin Franklin and Selections from His Other Writings.* New York: Random House, 1944, 1950.

————. *Papers of Benjamin Franklin,* Vol 1. New Haven: Yale University Press, 1959.

6. JOHN LAWSON

Carew, Bamfylde-Moore. *The Life and Adventures of Bamfylde-Moore Carew, Commonly Called the King of the Beggars.* Bath: J. Brown, 1802.

Johnson, Robert C. "The Transportation of Vagrant Children from London to Virginia," from *Early Stuart Studies.* Minneapolis: University of Minnesota Press, 1970.

Lauson, John. *The Felon's Account of His Transportation at Virginia in America.* Norton near Taunton, G. B.: J. Pile, 1754. Reprinted and edited by J. Stevens Cox, F.S.A. St. Peter Port, Guernsey, C.I.: Toucan Press, 1969.

7. JOHN HAMMOND

Hammond, John. *Leah and Rachel, or, The Two Fruitful Sisters Virginia and Mary-Land: Their Present Condition, Impartially Stated and Related.* London: "Printed by T. Mabb, and are to be sold by Nich. Bourn, neer the Royall Exchange," 1656.

McCormac, Eugene I. *White Servitude in Maryland, 1634–1820.* Baltimore: Johns Hopkins Press, 1904.

8. MARY MORRILL

Anderson, Florence Bennett. *A Grandfather for Benjamin Franklin.* Boston: Meador Publishing, 1940.

Franklin, Benjamin. *Letters to the Press, 1758–1775.* Collected and edited by Verner W. Crane. Chapel Hill: published for the Institute of Early American History and Culture at Williamsburg, Virginia, University of North Carolina Press, 1950.

Hinchman, Lydia S. *Early Settlers of Nantucket, Their Associates and Descendants.* Philadelphia: J. B. Lippincott, 1896.

Macy, William F. *The Story of Old Nantucket: A Brief History of the Island and Its People from Its Discovery down to the Present Day.* Boston: Houghton Mifflin, 1928.

Melville, Herman. *Moby-Dick; Or, The Whale.* Berkeley: University of California Press, 1979.

9. GEORGE ALSOP

Alsop, George. *A Character of the Province of Maryland.* Reprinted from the original edition of 1666. Freeport, N.Y.: Books for Libraries Press, 1966.

Bolton, Charles Knowles. *Portraits of the Founders: Portraits of Persons Born Abroad Who Came to the Colonies in North America Before the Year 1701.* Baltimore: Genealogical Publishing, 1976.

Dankers (Danckaerts), Jaspar, and Peter Sluyter. *Journal of a Voyage to New York and a Tour of Several of the American Colonies, 1679–80.* Brooklyn: Long Island Historical Society, 1867.

Lincoln, Abraham. *The Living Lincoln: The Man, His Times and the War He Fought, Reconstructed from His Own Writings.* Edited by Paul M. Angle and Earl Schenck Mieor. New Brunswick: Rutgers University Press, 1955.

10. THOMAS HELLIER

Defoe, Daniel. *The History and Remarkable Life of the Truly Honourable Col. Jacque, Commonly called Col. Jack.* London: Oxford University Press, 1965.

Hellier, Thomas. *The Vain Prodigal Life, and Tragical Penitent Death of Thomas Hellier Born at Whitchurch Near Lyme in Dorsetshire.* London: Sam. Crouch, 1680.

11. JENNEY VOSS

The German Princess Revived, or the London Jilt, Being a True Account of the Life and Death of Jenney Voss. London: George Croom, 1684.

12. ROBERT COLLINS

Records of the Suffolk County Court, 1671–1680, from Publications of the Colonial Society of Massachusetts, Vol. 39. Boston: The Society, 1933.

13. DAVID EVANS

Davies, Fareth Alban. "Y Parch. David Evans, Pencader—Ymfudwr Cynnar I Pennsylvania," *The National Library of Wales Journal,* Vol. XIV, No. 1, September 1965. Translation by Elvyn Jenkins of the University College of Wales, Aberystwyth.

Dexter, Franklin B., *Biographical Sketches of the Graduates of Yale College,* Vol. 1, October 1702–May 1745. New York: H. Holt and Company, 1885.

Evans, David. "Can Drwstan Gwynfan (aneglur) (A Song of Lament and Ill-Luck)." Written in manuscript, 1747. Translation by Elvyn Jenkins. Original is in the Library of the Rosenbach Museum, Philadelphia.

14. WILLIAM MORALEY

Eddis, William. *Letters from America.* Cambridge: Belknap Press, 1969.

Moraley, William. *The Infortunate: Or the Voyage and Adventures of William Moraley, of Moraley, in the County of Northumberland, Gent. From His Birth to the Present Time.* Newcastle: printed by J. White for the author, 1743. Used by permission of the William L. Clements Library, University of Michigan, Ann Arbor.

15. SALLY DAWSON AND SALLY BRANT

Craine, Elaine F. "The World of Elizabeth Drinker," *Pennsylvania Magazine of History and Biography,* Vol. CVII, January 1983.

Drinker, Elizabeth. *Extracts from the Journal of Elizabeth Drinker, from 1759 to 1807.* Edited by Henry D. Biddle. Philadelphia: J. B. Lippincott, 1889.

Mayor's Office, Philadelphia. *Record of Indentures of Individuals Bound Out as Apprentices, Servants, etc. Oct. 1771–Oct. 1773.* Baltimore: Genealogical Publishing, 1973.

Salinger, Sharon V. "Female Servants in Eighteenth Century Philadelphia," *Pennsylvania Magazine of History and Biography,* Vol. CVII, January 1983.

16. HENRY JUSTICE

Bibliotheque universelle, choisie, ancienne et moderne, contenant une tres curieuse collection de livres . . . comme aussi plusiers anciens manuscrits, recueillis . . . par feu Monsieur Henri Justice de Rufforth . . . lesquels seront vendus . . . le lundi 31 octobre 1763 & jours suivans a la Haye dans la maison de Nicholas van Daalen. The Hague, 1763.

The Gentleman's Magazine. Vol. VI, May. London: 1736

Virgil, *Works,* Vol. 1, edited by Henry Justice. Brussels: J. L. De Boubers, 1757. Translation by William Halsey, Classics Dept., University of California, Berkeley.

Kaminkow, Marion J. *Original Lists of Emigrants in Bondage from London to the American Colonies, 1719–1744*. Baltimore: Magna Carta Book Co., 1967.

17. HENRY PITMAN

Naipaul, V. S. *The Loss of El Dorado: A History*. New York: Knopf, 1969.

Pitman, Henry. *A Relation of the Great Sufferings and Strange Adventures of Henry Pitman, Chirurgeon to the Late Duke of Monmouth*. London: Andrew Sowle, 1689.

18. JAMES ANNESLEY

Annesley, James. *Memoirs of an Unfortunate Young Nobleman, Returned from Thirteen Years' Slavery in America: A Story Founded on Truth and Addressed Equally to the Head and Heart*. London: J. Freeman, 1763.

Lang, Andrew, ed. *The Annesley Case*. Edinburgh and London: William Hodge & Co., 1913.

19. PETER WILLIAMSON

Stevenson, Robert Louis. *Kidnapped*. New York: Scribner's, 1901.

Williamson, Peter. *The Life and Curious Adventures of Peter Williamson, Who Was Carried Off from Aberdeen and Sold for a Slave*. Aberdeen: printed for the booksellers, 1812.

20. DANIEL DULANY

Land, Aubrey C. *The Dulanys of Maryland*. Baltimore: Maryland Historical Society, 1955.

21. ALEXANDER STEWART

"Two Jacobite Convicts," from *The Maryland Historical Magazine,* Vol. 1, No. 4, December 1906.

22. GOTTLIEB MITTELBERGER

Dieffenderfer, Frank R. *The German Immigration into Pennsylvania Through the Port of Philadelphia, 1700 to 1775.* Part II, *The Redemptioners.* Lancaster: published by the author, 1900.

Geiser, Karl Frederick. *Redemptioners and Indentured Servants in the Colony and Commonwealth of Pennsylvania.* New Haven: Tuttle, Morehouse and Taylor, 1901.

Mittelberger, Gottlieb. *Journey to Pennsylvania.* Cambridge: Belknap Press, 1960.

23. ALEXANDER TURNBULL AND CARLO FORNI

Romans, Captain Bernard. *A Concise Natural History of East and West Florida.* New York: printed for the author, 1775.

Roselli, Bruno. *The Italians in Colonial Florida.* Jacksonville, Fla.: Drew Press, 1940.

24. MATTHEW THORNTON

Addresses at the Dedication of the Monument Erected to the Memory of Matthew Thornton at Merrimack, N.H., Sept. 29, 1892. Concord, N.H.: Republican Press Association, 1894.

Ford, Henry Jones. *The Scotch-Irish in America.* Hamden, Conn.: Archon Books, 1966.

Woodbury, Charles H. "Matthew Thornton," in *Proceedings of the New Hampshire Historical Society,* Vol. III, Concord, 1902.

25. JOHN HARROWER

Harrower, John. *The Journal of John Harrower, an Indentured Servant in the Colony of Virginia, 1773–1776.* Edited and with an introduction by Edward M. Riley. New York: Holt, Rinehart and Winston, 1963.

26. JOHN LAMB

Hofstadter, Richard. *America at 1750: A Social Portrait.* New York: Knopf, 1971.

Kaminkow, Jack and Marion. *A List of Emigrants from England to America, 1718–1759.* Transcribed from microfilms of the original records at the Guildhall, London. Baltimore: Magna Carta Book Co., 1981.

Leake, Isaac Q. *Memoir of the Life and Times of General John Lamb, an Officer of the Revolution.* Albany: Joel Munsell, 1857.

27, 32. MATTHEW LYON

Adams, Charles Thornton. *Matthew Lyon of New Hampshire, a Patriot of the American Revolution.* Philadelphia: Dando Printing and Publishing, 1903.

Campbell, Tom W. *Two Fighters and Two Fines: Sketches of the Lives of Matthew Lyon and Andrew Jackson.* Little Rock: Pioneer Publishing, 1941.

McLaughlin, J. Fairfax. *Matthew Lyon, the Hampden of Congress.* New York: Wynkoop, Hallenback, Crawford, 1900.

Smith, James Morton. *Freedom's Fetters: The Alien and Sedition Laws and American Civil Liberties.* Ithaca: Cornell University Press, 1956.

28, 30. CHARLES THOMSON

Harley, Lewis R. *The Life of Charles Thomson.* Philadelphia: George W. Jacobs, 1900.

Hendricks, J. Edwin, *Charles Thomson and the Making of a New Nation, 1729–1824.* Rutherford, N.Y.: Farleigh Dickinson University Press, 1979.

Lowrie, Sarah Dickson. "Lest We Forget: A Study of the Life and Services of the Patriot Charles Thomson." Printed address to the Athenaeum of Philadelphia, February 1953.

Thomson, Charles. "The Papers of Charles Thomson, Secretary of the Continental Congress," *Collections of the New York Historical Society,* Vol. 11, 1878.

29, 31. JOHN SULLIVAN

Peabody, Oliver W. B. *Life of John Sullivan, Major-General in the Army of the Revolution.* Boston: Little, Brown, 1844.

Scales, John. "Master John Sullivan of Somersworth and Berwick and his Family," *New Hampshire Historical Society Proceedings,* Vol. IV, Concord, 1903.

Whittemore, Charles P. *A General of the Revolution: John Sullivan of New Hampshire.* New York: Columbia University Press, 1961.

Wood, Gordon S. *The Creation of the American Republic, 1776–1787.* New York: W. W. Norton, 1969.

33. DANIEL KENT

Fearon, Henry Bradshaw. *Sketches of America: A Narrative of a Journey of 5,000 Miles through the Eastern and Western States.* London: Longman, Hurst, Reese, Orme and Brown, 1818.

Kent, Daniel. *Letters and Other Papers of Daniel Kent, Emigrant and Redemptioner*. Compiled by Ella K. Barnard. Baltimore, 1904. Used by permission of The Historical Society of Pennsylvania.

34. ANDREW JOHNSON

Schlesinger, Arthur M., Jr. *The Age of Jackson*. Boston: Little, Brown, 1953.

Winston, Robert W. *Andrew Johnson, Plebeian and Patriot*. New York: Henry Holt, 1928.

INDEX

Aberdeen, Earl of, 225
Abigail, ship, 92, 93
Academy of Philadelphia, 312
Act of 1717, 71
Adams, Abigail, 47
Adams, John, 34, 42, 47, 57, 207, 304, 322, 325, 327, 337, 338–339, 341
Adams, Samuel, 34, 55–59, 64, 276, 294
Aeneid (Virgil), 176, 324
Alien Act, 340
Alien and Sedition Acts, 54, 340, 341
Alison, Francis, 311–12
Allen, Ethan, 307
Alsop, George, 100–107
Altham, Arthur Annesley, Lord, 195–96
Altham, Lady, 195–96

American Crisis, The (Paine), 31
American Philosophical Society, 313
American Society for Promoting and Propagating Useful Knowledge, 313
André, John, 300
Andrews, Jedediah, 139
Anglesey, Richard, Earl of, 194–195
Anglican Society for the Propagation of the Gospel, 140
Annapolis Convention, 47
Annesley, Arthur, 195
Annesley, James, 194–207
Annesley, Richard, 196, 206–7
Arabella, ship, 128, 129, 130, 131, 132
Arendt, Hannah, 33

375

Arnold, Benedict, 299–300, 301
Articles of Confederation, 327,
    333
Austin, Thomas, 184
Autobiography (Franklin), 60, 349

Bacon, Francis, 328
Bacon, Sir Francis, 49, 274
Bacon, Jabez, 305–6
Bacon, Nathaniel, 73
Bacon's Rebellion, 73–74, 89,
    109, 266
Bailyn, Bernard, 82
Baltimore, Lord, 161, 232, 233,
    234, 236
Bank of the United States, 47
Barton, Mary, 165
Beard, Charles, 333
Bell, John, 216
Bennington, battle of, 307
Bernard, Francis, 244
Billey, servant, 41
Bill of Rights, 54, 80, 335, 339
Blacks, working conditions, 152–
    153
    see also Slaves
Blagdon, Captain, 127
Blair, David, 247
Bolingbroke, Henry St.
    John,Viscount, 262
Bonetta, ship, 148, 149
Bordley, Charles, 233
Boston *Evening Post,* 321
Boston Massacre, 57–58
Boston Tea Party, 58
Boucher, Jonathan, 31, 175
Bradbury, Eleanor, 165
Bradbury, Roger, 165
Brant, Sally, 166–68
Branthwait, William, 161
Broders, John, 205
Broders, William, 205
Brown, Joshua, 159
Browne, Margery. *See* Sullivan,
    Margery Browne

Buckingham, Earl of, 195
Burke, Edmund, 80, 186–87, 191,
    228, 277, 279, 297, 307, 329,
    336
Burnet, John, 224, 225
Burr, Aaron, 48

Callvert, Benedict, 246
Carew, Bamfylde-Moore, 91
*Character of the Province of
    Maryland, A* (Alsop), 102
Charles II, king of England, 194
Chattanooga, battle of, 359
Cherokee Nation, 342
Chickamauga, battle of, 359
Civil Rights Bill, 362
Cobbett, William, 339
Coffin, Tristram, 94-95
Coles, William, 159
College of New Jersey
    (Princeton), 40
Collins, Robert, 128-33
Colonel Jack (Defoe), 111
Colonies, penalties for crimes
    committed abroad, 51-52
Colonists in Bondage (Smith), 50
Colorado, statehood, 362
Committee of Safety, 277
Committees of Correspondence,
    58, 314
Common Council of London, 109
Constitutional Convention, 41, 42
Continental Congress, 41, 47, 278,
    296, 314, 315, 317, 318, 322,
    323, 325, 327, 332
Convicts, transportation of, 39–
    40, 50–52, 71, 109–11
Cook, Thomas, 174
Cooke, Ebenezer, 110
Copland, Mr., 224
Courant, 340
Crescent, ship, 86
Critical Review, 96
Culloden Moor, battle of, 241, 242

Cutter, overseer, 264, 265, 267, 268
Cygnet, H.M.S., 349

Daingerfield, William, 285–87, 292, 293
Dankers (Danckaerts), Jaspar, 103, 104
Dawson, Sally, 160–65
Deaf mute, instruction of, 287
Debts, servitude as punishment for, 51–52
Declaration of Independence, 53, 65, 278, 326
Declaratory Act (1766), 124
Defoe, Daniel, 50, 111
Democracy in America (Tocqueville), 34
Dickens, Charles, 360
Dickinson, John, 34, 258, 315
Dieffenderfer, Frank, 260
Drinker, Elizabeth, 163, 164, 166, 168
Drinker, Henry, 163
Drummond, taskmaster, 197–98, 200
Dublin, University of, 232
Dulany, Daniel, 231–39, 240
Dulany, Daniel, Jr., 237, 238–39
Dulany, Daniel, III, 239
Dulany, Thomas, 232
Dulany, Walter, 238, 239
Duncan, Sir William, 262, 263
Dunmore, Lord, 157

Eclogues (Virgil), 176
Eddis, William, 134
Eggleson, Thomas, 206
Enquiry into the Causes of the Alienation of the Delaware and Shawanese Indians from the British Interests, An (Thomson), 313
Escape, recovery of runaways after, 153

Eskridge, George, 31
Evans, David, 135–44
Evans, Owen, 162

Faneuil Hall, 57
Fearon, Henry Bradshaw, 81
Federalist, The, 46, 47
Felon's Account of His Transportation at Virginia in America, The (Lawson), 69–70
Fielding, Sir John, 51
Florida, land scheme, 262–69
Florida Packet, ship, 267
Folger, Peter, 96–97
Forni, Carlo, 261–69
Fort Duquesne, 218
Fort Montgomery, 298
Fort Ticonderoga, 307
Fort William and Mary, 322
Forward, Jonathan, 174, 235
Forward Frigate, ship, 296
Foulger, Abiah, 96
Foulger, John, 92, 93
Foulger, Mary Morrill, 92–98
Foulger, Peter, 92, 93, 94–96
Francis I, Holy Roman Emperor, 176
Franklin, Abiah, 98
Franklin, Benjamin, 51, 60–65, 96, 98, 142, 151, 312, 313, 325, 349
Frazer, Anthony, 288, 289, 290, 292
Freedman's Bill, 362
Freedmen, 80, 104
  and Bacon's Rebellion, 73–74
Freedom dues, 38
Freeman's Journal, 306
French, farmer, 333
French and Indian War, 32, 58, 212, 218, 259
Friends Public School, Philadelphia, 313

Gaines, Lucy, 288, 289, 290
Gallatin, Albert, 339
Galloway, Joseph, 34, 145
Gardner, John, 95
Gates, Horatio, 298–99
Gentleman's Magazine, The, 127
George I, king of England, 241, 242
George III, king of England, 52, 244
Georgics (Virgil), 176
Gildart, Richard, 241, 242, 245
Glasgow, University of, 311
Goddard, William, 208, 209
Grant, James, 263, 267, 268
Grant, Ulysses S., 362
Gray, Alexander, 223
Great Seal, 326
Green Mountain Boys, 307
Gregory, Miss, 196
Grenville, George, 262, 263
Grigerson, Alexander, 223
Griswold, Roger, 339
Grout, Dr., 276

Hamilton, Alexander, 43–48
Hamilton, James, 44–45, 46
Hamlin, Hannibal, 360
Hammond, John, 82–90, 162
Hancock, John, 59, 326
Hannah, Hugh, 306
Harrower, John, 281–93
Hawley, Joseph, 348, 349
Headrights, 38–39, 40, 110
Hearsy, William, 131–132
Help for Parents and Heads of Families, A (Evans), 141
Hemings, Sally, 49, 54
Henry, Patrick, 52, 144
Hicks, William, 248
Hobby, servant, 31
Holmes, Captain, 243, 245
Homestead Bill, 358
Hopkins, Stephen, 34, 119, 169
Horner, Robert, 243–45

Horsemanship (Newcastle), 171
Hughes, John, 276
Hunter, Robert, 249
Hutchinson, Thomas, 56, 58, 64

Ideological Origins of the American Revolution (Bailyn), 82
Impeachment of Andrew Johnson, 363
Indian Queen, ship, 223
Infortunate, The (Moraley), 149
Ingram, James, 223, 224
Iroquois Confederacy (Six Nations), 322, 323

Jackson, Andrew, 339, 341, 351, 358
Jamestown settlement, 83
Jamieson, John, 224
Jamieson, William, 224, 225
Jay, John, 325
Jefferson, Thomas, 34, 47, 49–54, 90, 316, 325, 340, 341
Jenkins, Elvyn, 135n
Jenny, ship, 127
Johnson, Andrew, 354–63
Johnson, Eliza McCardle, 357
Johnson, Samuel, 27, 52, 80
Johnson, William, 354, 357
Johnston, George, 222–23
Jonathan Forward and Company, 235
Jones, Samuel, 141, 142
Joseph II, Holy Roman Emperor, 176
Journey to Pennsylvania (Mittelberger), 249
Juno, ship, 267
Junto, 312, 313
Justice, Henry, 170–78, 235
Justice, William, 177

Kaunitz, Count Wenzel von, 176
Kent, Daniel, 347–53

Kent, Esther Hawley, 350
Kent, Richard, 349–50
Kent, William, 349
Kidnapped (Stevenson), 194
King, Alexander, 222
King's College, 45
King's Privy Council, 64
Knights, Thomas, 128, 129, 131

Lamb, Anthony, 296–97, 301
Lamb, John, 295–303
Land
  headrights, 38–39, 40
  settlement scheme, Florida, 262–269
Larimore, Captain, 115
Law and Gospel: Or, Man Wholly Ruined by the Law, and Recovered by the Gospel (Evans), 143–44
Lawson, John, 69–80, 196
Lawsuit, brought by ship's captain against indentured servant for nonperformance, 128–33
Leah and Rachel, or, the Two Fruitful Sisters, Virginia and Mary-Land: Their Present Condition, Impartially Stated and Related (Hammond), 82
Lecky, W. E. H., 277
Lee, Cornel, 245
Letters from a Farmer in Pennsylvania (Dickinson), 258
Lewis, Edmund, 154, 156
Ley, Peter, 222
Library Company of Philadelphia, 62, 142
Lidgett, lawyer, 133
Lincoln, Abraham, 356, 359, 360
Locke, John, 49, 231
London Magazine, The, 127
London Packet, brig, 29, 30
Long Island, battle of, 323

Lux, Darby, 173
Lyon, Chittendon, 343
Lyon, Matthew, 305–8, 338–43, 351

MacCardle, Eliza, 357
McIntire, farmer, 320
Macnemara, Thomas, 233
McWilliams, Peter, 226
Maddison, John, 37, 38–39, 40
Madison, James, 40–42, 47, 340
Madison, James, Sr., 40
Maria Theresa, empress of Austria, 176
Marriage, of servants, 164–65
Maryland Gazette, 120
Mason, George, 206, 340, 342
Mather, Cotton, 94
Mayflower, ship, 93
Mayhew, Jonathan, 140
Melville, Herman, 65, 96
Memoirs of an Unfortunate Young Nobleman, Returned from Thirteen Years' Slavery in America (Annesley), 196, 205
Menard, Russell R., 161
Mercer, James, 293
Millethopp, Nicholas, 165
Milligan, Sam, 357
Minister of Christ, The (Evans), 142
Mittelberger, Gottlieb, 249–59, 310
Moby-Dick (Melville), 96
Moll Flanders (Defoe), 50
Monroe, James, 340, 342
Montcalm, General, 218
Monticello, 53
Moody, Reverend, 320
Moraley, William, 146–58
Morgan, Edmund, 84, 85
Morrill, Mary, 92–98
Morris, Lewis, 175
Morris, Richard, 165

Morris, Robert, 114
Muhlenberg, Henry Melchior, 99
Mulatto children, 54
Murfreesboro, battle of, 359

Naipaul, V. S., 293
Nashville, siege of, 359
Nebraska, statehood, 362
New Hampshire Assembly, 318
New Hampshire Convention, 335
New Hampshire Provincial
    Congress, 277
New Smyrna, Florida, settlement,
    261–69
Newton, Sir Isaac, 49
New York, battle of, 301
New York Assembly, 302
New York *Independent Gazette,*
    344
North, Lord, 57, 64
Nuthall, John, 184–85

Ogle, Samuel, 235
On Revolution (Arendt), 33
Order of the Cincinnati, 302, 333
Orphan House, 63
Otis, James, 34, 280

Paine, Thomas, 30–31, 168
Paris, Treaty of, 262
Patapsco Merchant, ship, 173–
    174, 175
Peace Commission, 332
Pearson, Isaac, 149, 150, 154
Peel, Captain, 155–56
Peggy, ship, 247
Penn, William, 250, 312
Penne, George, 182
Pennsylvania, University of,
    62
Pennsylvania Assembly, 314
Pennsylvania Gazette, 62
Pennsylvania State Assembly
    House, 319
Peters, Hugh, 92, 93, 94

Philadelphia Library, 62, 142
Pitman, Henry, 181–92
Pitteri, Marco, 176
Planter, ship, 209–10
Plater, George, 232
Polk, James K., 351
Powell, John, 120
Pregnancy, of servants, 165, 166–
    167
Puritan Church, Salem, 92
Pusey, Caleb, 159
Putnam, Israel, 300

Quebec, battle of, 295–98
Quin, Thomas, 347

Ramsey, David, 175
Reade, Charles, 207
Reconstruction, 361, 362
Redding, Joseph, 206
Reed, James, 148
Reid, Robert, 222
Religious dissenters, as émigrés
    to colonies, 39
Rights of Colonies Examined, The
    (Hopkins), 119
Rights of Man, The (Paine), 31
*Rights of the Inhabitants of
    Maryland to the Benefit of
    English Laws, The* (Dulany),
    231, 234, 237, 238
Robinacracy, 262
Romans, Bernard, 267–68
Ross, Margaret, 223, 224
Royal Society, 62, 97
Runaways, 53, 76–77, 115–18
Rush, Benjamin, 326
Russell, Daniel, 296

Sadler, gang leader, 123–24
Salinger, Sharon V., 164, 168
Sandys, Sir Edwin, 83, 84
Saratoga, battle of, 307

Sedition Act, 340
Selby, James J., 354, 356–58
Septuagint, 328
Shays, Daniel, 334
Shays' Rebellion, 332
Sheffield, Mary, 195
Shelbourne, Earl of, 264
Shiloh, battle of, 359
Shirley, William, 217
Six Nations, 322, 323
Slaves
  and indentured servants, 76
  Jefferson's ambivalence about,
    53
Sluyter, Peter, 103, 104
Smith, Abbott E., 50, 71, 88
Smith, Joshua Hett, 299–300
Smith, Samuel, 241, 242
Snider, Jacob, 213
Snow Planter, ship, 282–85
Society of the Cincinnati, 302, 333
Sons of Liberty, 56, 296, 297
Sotweed Factor, The (Cooke),
  110
Soul-drivers, 255, 284
Sprague, Richard, 128, 129, 130,
  131, 132, 133
Stamp Act, 238, 276, 297, 314
Stanton, Edwin, 362, 363
Starbuck, Mary, 96
Stephens, Alexander, 361
Stevenson, Eleanor, 161
Stewart, Alexander, 241–47
Stockett, Thomas, 100, 103
Stone, William, 86, 87
Stuart, Charles Edward (Bonnie
  Prince Charlie), 242
Sullivan, Daniel, 331, 332
Sullivan, Ebenezer, 331
Sullivan, James, 331
Sullivan, John, 317–23, 330, 331–
  336
Sullivan, Margery Browne, 320–
  321, 331, 336
Sullivan, Mary, 331

*Summary View of the Rights of
  British America, A*
  (Jefferson), 52
Sumner, Charles, 361

Talleyrand, 46
Teddyuscung, Indian chief, 313
Temple, Sir Richard, 262
Tenants (sharecroppers), 84–85
Tenure of Office Act, 362, 363
Test Acts, 274
Thirteenth Amendment, 362, 364
Thomson, Charles, 310–15, 324,
  325–29
Thomson, John, 310–11
Thornton, Elizabeth, 275
Thornton, Hannah Jack, 276
Thornton, James, 275
Thornton, Matthew, 273–79
Thoroughgood, Thomas, 86, 87
Tocqueville, Alexis de, 34
Tonyn, Patrick, 268
Transportation, of convicts, 39–
  40, 50–52, 71, 109–11
Treaty of Paris, 262
Trenton, battle of, 323
Trinity College, Cambridge, 171
Turnbull, Alexander, 261–69
Tyrconnel, Earl of, 274
Tyrone, Earl of, 274

Uprisings
  Bacon's Rebellion, 73–74, 89,
    109, 266
  of indentured servants, 265–66
  in New Smyrna, Florida, 266–
    269
  Shays' Rebellion, 332

Van Buren, Martin, 351
Van Daalen, Nicholas, 170
Vane, Sir Harry, 92
Vernon, Edward, 205
Virgil, 176, 326
Virginia Company, 84, 109

Virginia House of Burgesses, 31, 73
Virginia House of Delegates, 41
Volney, Comte de, 54
Voss, Jenney, 121–26

Walpole, Horace, 52
Walpole, Robert, 262
Wanackmamak, Indian chief, 94
Wandering Heir (Reade), 207
Warren, John, 126
Washington, George, 31–32, 45, 157, 238, 296, 298, 328
Wentworth, John, 318, 322
West Indies, plantation economy, 43–44
Whatley, Thomas, 64

Whicker, John, 184
Whipping, 52
White Boys, 306
Williams, Mr., 111, 118, 119
Williamson, Cutbeard, 114, 116–117
Williamson, James, 222
Williamson, Peter, 209–27
Wilson, Hugh, 211
Wilson, Isabel, 222
Wreatback, William, 174

Yale College, 139
Yanche, Captain, 187, 189
Yorktown, battle of, 301
Young Princess, ship, 114